If you enjoy reading Hidden Madrid you may also want to purchase **HIDDEN MADRID II** by the same authors and **A History and Anecdotes of the Inns of Old Madrid** by P. Besas, both published by Ediciones La Librería and available at major book shops in Madrid, among them El Corte Inglés, FNAC, La Casa del Libro and in the publisher's own bookshop on the Calle Mayor 80.

Hidden Madrid

Madrid's Oddities and Curiosities

A Walking Guide

Mark and Peter Besas
Photos by Mark Besas

EDICIONES LA LIBRERÍA

1ª Edición: mayo 2007
2ª Edición: octubre 2008
3ª Edición: junio 2011

Visit our web page: *www.hiddenmadrid.com*

C/ Arenal, 21
28013 Madrid
Telf.: 91 541 71 70
Fax: 91 542 58 89
info@edicioneslalibreria.com

PORTADA: Héctor García
DIBUJO PORTADA: Ainhara Mora
MAQUETACIÓN: Héctor García y el equipo de diseño de Ediciones La Librería
IMPRESIÓN: Gráficas Rógar

ISBN: 978-84-96470-75-0
Depósito Legal: M-23563-2011
Impreso en España/*Printed in Spain*

Table of Contents

AREA 2: SANTA ANA

AREA 3: MAYOR

AREA 4: ROYAL PALACE

AREA 5: GRAN VÍA

AREA 6: CIBELES

AREA 7: RETIRO

TOROS

FRANCO

SILVER SCREEN MAGIC

ILLUSTRATIONS

SOL

ROYAL PALACE

GRAN VÍA

CIBELES

<u>RETIRO</u>

TOROS

FRANCO

SILVER SCREEN MAGIC

NOTE TO THE READER

In the course of the book, we have preferred to use the original Spanish names for places and persons rather than the Anglicized forms. Thus "Felipe II" instead of "Philip II", "Calle de Velázquez" rather than "Velasquez Street" and so on, since it is easier to find points mentioned with the Spanish names. As for our choice in spelling and terminology, we have opted for American rather than British usage, other than in direct quotes of English authors. The metric system has been used throughout, though we have included the Anglo-American equivalents on most occasions.

As in any guide, changes do occur in the city, especially in one evolving as fast as Madrid, but the information presented was as accurate as possible at the time we researched the book and it went to press.

Although we have included a map for each area pinpointing most of the sights mentioned, occasionally the subject described may fall within another map in another area. These are so noted in the text. A few of the places mentioned, due to their distance from the center, are not included in the maps.

The book is primarily geared to those unfamiliar with the city, its culture and its history. We trust, however, that even those who already know Madrid will discover facets of it that had escaped their notice in the past.

ACKNOWLEDGEMENTS

We are indebted to the following for their assistance in the preparation of this book: Toni Garrido and his radio show *Gran Vía,* who sparked the idea for this book and who introduced us to our publisher; José Antonio Pastor for reading through the Spanish version proofs of the book; Victoria Fontana for her useful comments on the MS; Antonio Castro for telling us about his night in a Franco era jail; Jane Walker for recounting her visits to the set of the filming of *Doctor Zhivago;* John von Bläuch and Gonzalo Tapia for touring Madrid with us in search of Masonic monuments and buildings; Iñaki Sarasola for the photos of the "lost" statues of the kings in Pamplona. Thanks go to Héctor García for designing the jacket and general look of the book and Pepa Eizaguirre for being the computer wrangler and being so patient in enduring our long absences during the researching and writing of this book.

We are especially indebted to all those who have preceded us in compiling books on Madrid, ranging from classic *cronistas de la Villa* such as Mesonero Romanos, Pedro de Répide, Federico Sainz de Robles and Juan Antonio Cabezas to modern writers who have penned works on the city, especially the *Guía del Madrid mágico* by Clara Tahoces, *Un Madrid insólito* by our good friend Jesús Callejo, *Curiosidades y anécdotas de Madrid* by María Isabel Gea, *Diccionario de Madrid* by Francisco Azorín, José Montero Alonso and José Montero Padilla, and José María de Mena's *Leyendas y misterios de Madrid* and *Historias notables de Madrid.* Finally, our heartfelt thanks to our publisher Miguel Tébar whose open-mindedness and understanding have made this project possible.

INTRODUCTION

As you wend your way through the city, you may come upon certain sights that arouse your curiosity and cause you to ask questions. Such, for example, as: Who exactly was the goddess Cibeles? What is the significance of the tiles in the old section of Madrid that read "Visita G"? Is there a story concealed behind the name of the street called "Calle de la Cabeza" (Head Street)? And why were a bear and a small fruit-bearing tree chosen to be on the coat-of-arms of Madrid? The answer to each of these questions conceals a curious tale.

Other stories lie buried within the streets, cafés and buildings around the city. Their significance, however, cannot be appreciated until you know the story behind each place. That's the case with the Anthropological Museum in which Dr. Velasco mummified his daughter, or with the site of the present Starbucks on the Calle de Alcalá, where once a dog called Paco hung out in the Café Fornos. Or the convents in the center of Madrid where you can buy home-made pastries from cloistered nuns handed to you through a wooden-turntable window that prevents the sisters from being seen.

All these curiosities are what we consider to be the hidden side of Madrid. Over the course of many years, we have delighted in telling these stories and amusing friends with them. We hope that our readers, too, will be entertained by this web of history, oddities, anecdotes and tales.

We have broken up the points of interest into manageable areas most of which lie in the heart of the city. There's no strict order of points to see, or specific route to follow. Ours will be a series of decidedly leisure strolls, a historical and anecdotal poking about, with plenty of time to stop for a *café con leche* or a *tapa* or do a bit of browsing along the way. You may, in fact, want to read some sections before sallying forth. It remains only for you to "discover" for yourself each of the "hidden" curiosities and even find some new ones on your own.

MARK & PETER BESAS
Madrid, April 2007

P.S. We'd be delighted to recieve your comments, observations or questions. Please contact us at our web page *www.hiddenmadrid.com* or our e-mail *info@hiddenmadrid.com*

TIO PEPE

Area 1: Sol

1. **Frascuelo's House** (Arenal 22). Bullfighter friend of Perro Paco.
2. **Aquarium de Madrid** (Maestro Vitoria 8). Crocodiles and snapping turtle.
3. **Casa Labra** (Tetuán 12). Where Socialist party was founded.
4. Former **Prast** confectioner's shop (Arenal 8). Ratoncito Pérez's house.
5. **La Mallorquina** (Puerta del Sol 2). Pastry shop and tea room.
6. **Casa de Cordero** (Mayor 1). House built by lottery winner.
7. Former **Gobernación** (Puerta del Sol 7). Clock tower.
8. **Kilometer 0** plaque. Starting point of national roads.
9. **Bear and Madroño Statue** (entry to Calle del Carmen). Emblems of Madrid.
10. **Mariblanca statue.** A replica.
11. Former **Hotel Paris** (Alcalá 2). Former cafés Montaña and Imperial.
12. **Real Academia de Bellas Artes de San Fernando** (Alcalá 13). Fallen Angel replica.
13. Former **Café Fornos** (Alcalá 21). Paco the Dog's haunt.
14. **Lhardy** restaurant and shop (San Jerónimo 8). Gourmet icon.
15. **Antigua Pastelería del Pozo** (Pozo 8). Ye olde pastry shoppe.
16. **Pasaje de Matheu**. Former "little Paris."
17. **Calle de Alvaro Gato**. Max Estrella's mirrors.
18. **Calle de las Huertas**. Street of the literati.

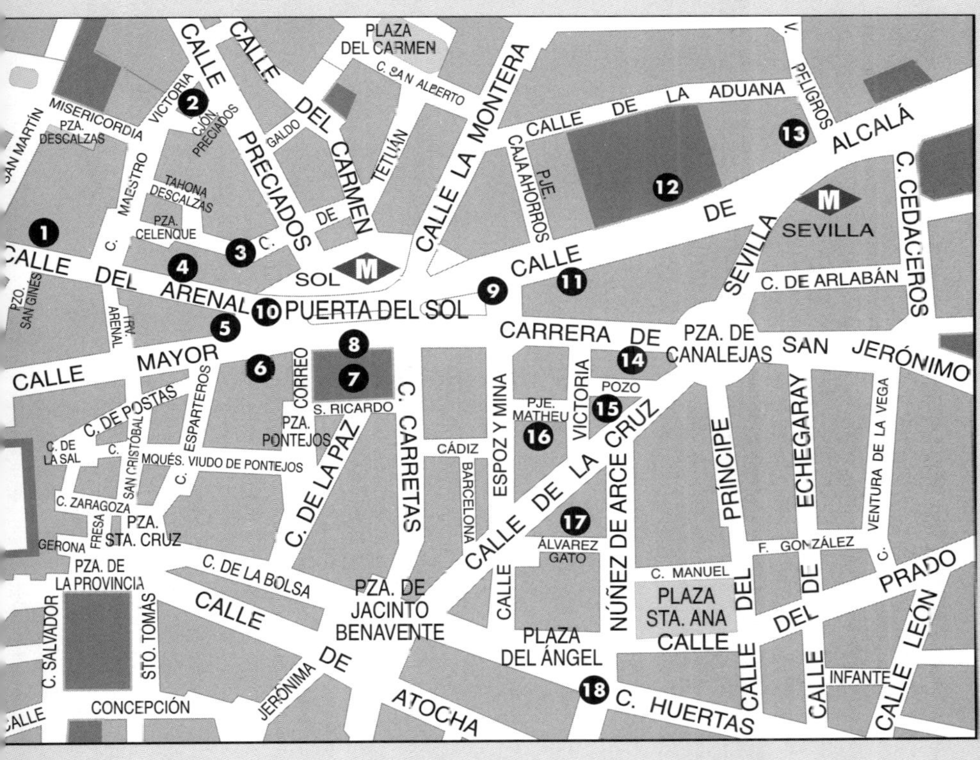
PLAZA DEL CARMEN
C. SAN ALBERTO
CALLE DE LA ADUANA
PELIGROS
ALCALÁ
CALLE PRECIADOS
CALLE DEL CARMEN
CALLE LA MONTERA
MISERICORDIA
VICTORIA
CJÓN. PRECIADOS
GALDO
TETUÁN
PZA. DESCALZAS
SAN MARTÍN
MAESTRO
TAHONA DESCALZAS
PZA. CELENQUE
C. DE
CAJA AHORROS
PJE.
CALLE DE ALCALÁ
SEVILLA
C. CEDACEROS
CALLE DEL ARENAL
SOL
PUERTA DEL SOL
C. DE ARLABÁN
PZO. SAN GINÉS
IRV. ARENAL
CARRERA DE SAN JERÓNIMO
PZA. DE CANALEJAS
CALLE MAYOR
CORREO
S. RICARDO
C. CARRETAS
POZO
PJE. MATHEU
ESPOZ Y MINA
VICTORIA
C. DE POSTAS
ESPARTEROS
PZA. PONTEJOS
C. DE LA SAL
SAN CRISTÓBAL
MQUÉS. VIUDO DE PONTEJOS
CÁDIZ
BARCELONA
CALLE DE LA CRUZ
NÚÑEZ DE ARCE
PRÍNCIPE
ECHEGARAY
VENTURA DE LA VEGA
C. ZARAGOZA
PZA. STA. CRUZ
FRESA
GERONA
C. DE LA PAZ
ÁLVAREZ GATO
F. GONZÁLEZ
PZA. DE LA PROVINCIA
C. DE LA BOLSA
C. MANUEL
PLAZA STA. ANA
CALLE DEL PRADO
CALLE
PZA. DE JACINTO BENAVENTE
PLAZA DEL ÁNGEL
C. SALVADOR
STO. TOMÁS
CALLE DE ATOCHA
JERÓNIMA
C. HUERTAS
CALLE DEL
CALLE DE
CALLE LEÓN
INFANTE
CONCEPCIÓN
1 2 3 4 5 6 7 8 9 10 11 12 13 14 15 16 17 18

TIO PEPE

Area 1 - SOL

Madrid's great crossroads

No matter which hotel or private house you are staying in, no matter what your reason for coming to Madrid, chances are that at some point or other you will be passing through Spain's most famous crossroads, the Puerta del Sol, the "Gate of the Sun."

The history of the Puerta del Sol is to a great extent the history of Madrid itself, for in it were enacted many of the events that shaped the city and often the rest of Spain. In the late 16th and 17th century, known as Spain's Golden Age, literary luminaries such as Lope de Vega, Miguel de Cervantes, Francisco de Quevedo, Tirso de Molina and Calderón de la Barca whiled away hours conversing and bandying the day's gossip on the steps of a former church/convent called San Felipe el Real which stood on the site now occupied by the building partly housing McDonald's (corner of Calle Mayor and Calle de los Esparteros). In the 19th and early 20th centuries, the Puerta del Sol was the hub and fountainhead of life in the capital. It was lined with a dozen cafés and hotels around which revolved the sparkling social, intellectual and political life of the city.

It was in the Puerta del Sol that the first public electric light in Spain shone in 1875, and there that the first electric streetcar started to ply service in 1897, and from there that the first line of Madrid's Metro (subway) began to run in 1919.

Ten streets feed into the Puerta del Sol. Even with traffic restrictions, and several of these streets now pedestrian walks, the square is still one of the busiest in the city, filled now more

The Puerta del Sol. Three oldtimers taking it easy as the equestrian statue of Carlos III rises behind them. *Author's photo.*

with people than with cars. Several buildings on the Puerta del Sol hold their store of hidden stories, some well-known and included in tourist guides, others unfamiliar even to most Madrileños.

Plenty of sun, but where's the Gate?

Where, then, does the name Puerta del Sol come from, when there is no "puerta" and no "sol"? One of the many theories that have been put forth harks back to 1520. This was a time of revolution, hunger and discontent in and around Madrid; a time when nobles in Toledo, Segovia, Ávila and a dozen other cities in Castile rebelled against the Flemish-born King Carlos V.

Carlos had appointed his own Flemish leaders to key governmental positions instead of Spaniards, and was accused of squandering funds as well as merely using Spain as a pawn

THREE REBELS

Three of the leaders of the ill-fated revolt of the Comuneros have streets named after them in Madrid: Juan Bravo, Juan de Padilla and Francisco Maldonado. All three streets run parallel and can be found in the Salamanca neighborhood. Shown in the painting by Antonio Gisbert, which can be seen in the Cortes, are the three rebel leaders shortly before their decapitation. Should you visit Segovia, one of the cities most prominent in the uprising, you'll see Juan Bravo honored with a huge statue in the Plaza de Medina del Campo (1921) as well as a major street named after him.

in his efforts to dominate Europe. Far too preoccupied with foreign involvements, the "foreign" king seemed to pay scant attention to the needs of the local populace. The rebels, or Comuneros, as they were called, became a dangerous threat to Madrid. Though the city was not yet the capital of Spain, it was fortified by a large wall and moat (some historians speculate that an entire castle existed at the time) to protect the royalists from attacks. It is said that one of its entrance gates was on the eastern side of the square, where the sun rises, and hence was called the Gate of the Sun. Others hypothesize that a painting or a relief of the sun was featured on the gate, and hence the reason why over the years the site came to be known as the Puerta del Sol.

However, speculations by local historians on the origins of the name are as plentiful as mushrooms after the rain. Some even conclude that the gate with the sun on it dated back to Moorish times, 500 years earlier. What is certain is that no mention of the Puerta del Sol can be found in any document prior to 1570. Meaning that a large dose of speculation if not downright invention has been employed in trying to unravel the derivation. However, the name of the square remains, as it has for nearly half a millennium.

The Devil hates French architects

Architecturally dominating the south side of the Puerta del Sol stands a large elegant building that has been one of Madrid's major landmarks since it was built in 1768. Originally intended for use as the main post office, it was commissioned by King Carlos III during the "Age of Enlightenment" and has also been used as the Ministry of the Interior, national police headquarters and, some even say, the haunt of the Devil.

The tale, perhaps a little "tall" by some standards but curious enough to include here, tells that among the official records pertaining to the construction of the building is one consisting of a list of all those involved in raising the edifice. Among these stands out a priest, Father López. Now although Spain was certainly a devout Catholic country, it was not customary to include a man of the cloth in the architect's list of those on his construction staff. So what was the good Father López's name doing midst those of assistants, surveyors, masons, stone-cutters, decorators and accountants? Admittedly priests are often called upon to bless a building after it is completed. But they do not normally appear on lists together with construction personnel.

Father López's help was enlisted for a very special reason. Local legend has it that when the masons and building crew began work on the project, the very Devil appeared before them early one morning and told them in no uncertain terms that the building they were laboring upon was cursed and belonged to the realms of Hell. Not only that: eternal Hellfire awaited anyone who continued to help in completing the doomed building. The reason, explained the Devil (this, after all, being the Age of Enlightenment, an explanation was called for), was that the architect chosen by King Carlos III was the *Frenchman*, Jacques Marquet, rather than the much-admired Spanish architect Ventura Rodríguez! The Devil warned the awestruck laborers that not only were their efforts a sign of impiety, but that they also amounted to a display of anti-patriotic behavior.

Intimidated by the anti-French Devil, the terrified masons refused to continue working lest the Evil Eye were cast upon them. There were those who even said that the Devil was in league with the Spanish architect. When Marquet heard of this contretemps, he decided that the only way to keep the Devil at bay was to contract a priest (Spanish, of course) to keep a constant vigil on the construction site. With crucifix readily at hand, he would banish any possible re-appearance of Satan and work on the building could proceed unhindered.

After that, the Evil One was never reported to have been seen again by the workers.

A night in the clink in the "bad old days"

In more recent times, during the Franco dictatorship, the aforementioned building was used as police headquarters. Its basement jail cells were often filled with recalcitrant demonstrators and political offenders, and many of today's senior Socialist Party and Communist leaders spent a night or two in detention there in the days when they battled gray-clad policemen in the streets and clandestinely pasted illegal protest posters on the walls of the city. It was also the place where nosy foreign reporters and indiscreet photographers and cameramen were hauled off to after being nabbed covering student and workers' demonstrations. Usually, after a dressing down and several warnings of possible expulsion from Spain, they were released.

Even today mention of the *sótanos* (basement) of the building among former leftwing activists evokes for them an era of harsh repression. Upon someone being arrested in a demonstration, or upon suspicion of possessing illegal propaganda, that person could be detained and held in jail for 72 hours without charges being filed.

A friend of ours, the film historian and critic Antonio Castro, recalled: "I spent several nights there on three or four occasions. It was called the DGS (Dirección General de Seguridad). They'd put me in a small, one-man barred cell, sometimes with a tiny window near the ceiling. They'd interrogate you at any time of the day or the night, the idea being to prevent you from sleeping properly. They'd try to pressure you, maybe by taking away your cigarettes, which for many people was really nerve-racking. Personally, I was never actually mistreated, but then I was only a small fish."

Castro recalled that on one occasion the late Spanish film director Juan Antonio Bardem, who belonged to the then-outlawed Communist Party, was arrested in the midst of his shooting the film *Calle Mayor* (1956) and hauled off to the sótanos. He was subsequently released and his film, one of the first of the "new Spanish cinema", became an icon for the neo-realistic wave of filmmaking that would revolutionize Spanish movies.

Other "celebrities" subjected to a night of interrogation in the Puerta del Sol clink were José María Ruíz Gallardón, father of the present mayor of Madrid; Juan Barranco, who went on to become mayor of Madrid in the post-Franco period, and who was thrown into a cell with his wife just as he was on his honeymoon in 1973; Ramón Tamames, a well-known economist, as well as the former head of the Communist Labor Union, Marcelino Camacho, to mention just a few.

Nowadays, the building which the Devil could not prevent from being built houses the Presidency of the autonomous government of the Community of Madrid. Throughout most of its existence, the building has been referred to locally as "Gobernación" (Government House). It is not open to the public but is frequently used for celebrations and gala occasions held by the local authorities.

The clock that couldn't keep time

In the early and mid-19th century the matter of knowing what time of the day or night it was tended to be limited to those relatively affluent persons who could afford to carry their own timepiece on them. Others had to rely on public clocks, on the chiming of church bells, or by looking at clocks in the dozen or so cafés around the Puerta del Sol. Indeed, having a proper, accurate public clock in the Puerta del Sol was of the essence for knowing when the time was ripe for the diligence to set off for some distant city, when it was time to head home for dinner and whether or not one was late for an appointment or for work.

And therein lies our story. As far back as the 18th century there had been a large clock on the façade of a church located on the eastern side of the square, the Church of Buen Suceso. Engravings dating back to 1773 already show the clock,

although at that time it only had the hour hand. Problems with the clock arose from the very beginning. It was not a very accurate clock and prompted endless complaints from all and sundry. Constant editorials appeared in the press clamoring for a new, more reliable, clock to be installed. Finally in 1848 a new mechanism for the clock was commissioned, and special gas lights were installed inside so the dial would be visible at night.

But the same old problems persisted. The clock could not be relied upon to keep accurate time. One newspaper reported: "Some gadabouts went to see the lighting up of the dial on the clock of Buen Suceso, but neither saw the light nor heard the strokes of the hour."

When the Church of Buen Suceso was torn down in 1854 its problematic clock was kept and set aside, for the intention was to install it in the upper part of the façade of Gobernación on the Puerta del Sol. However, after much discussion, a new

Clock in the Church of Buen Suceso, 18th C.
For many years this was the only clock in the Puerta del Sol. It constantly failed to keep the right time. Even after being repaired it still remained unreliable.
19th century engraving by Esteban Boix.

Façade of Gobernación 1858. City Hall commissioned a new clock to be placed in Gobernación, this one with three dials. Unfortunately, it didn't work very well either. *Author's archive.*

clock, made by Tomás de Miguel, was installed instead. In fact there was considerable confusion at the time whether it was the old Buen Suceso clock or a new one that was installed.

Thus the journal *La Esperanza*, in its April 26, 1855 edition, wrote: "According to one newspaper, work on installing the old Buen Suceso clock in the front of Government House is due to start today…" And 12 days later: "Work is to begin on building a small tower which will accommodate the clock that was in the Buen Suceso". Finally, five days later, the same paper announced: "The clock that is to be installed in Government House is not the one that was in the Church of Buen Suceso, but a new one that has been built for the purpose."

This new clock, featuring three dials, was more elaborate and showy than its predecessor in the church. The expectation, of course, was that it would work faultlessly. At last passers-by would be able to know the correct time of day and be able to tell if they were on time for an appointment or a romantic tryst. Alas, chronometric precision remained beyond its grasp. Its efficiency can be gathered from another press report of the time:

"If the new clock in the Puerta del Sol continued to work as it has thus far, it will not displease anyone, since the hours it shows on its three dials are completely different, so that everyone can choose the time that best suits him."

The Puerta del Sol itself was being radically rebuilt at that time; the shabby dilapidated buildings on the north side were being torn down and replaced by the semi-elliptical sweep of the elegant new ones that still grace the square. Taking advantage of this overhauling, the tower which housed the clock was modified and a large ball that was to drop at the stroke of 12, known as the *bola eléctrica* (electric ball) was added.

However, the clock still refused to keep time accurately. Sometimes it stopped altogether. Wags thus came up with the following epigram:

"Este reló tan fatal	"Why does this terrible clock
Que hay en la Puerta del Sol",	In the Puerta del Sol
Dijo a un turco un español,	Always work so poorly?"
"¿Porqué anda siempre tan mal?"	A Spaniard asked a Turk.
El turco, con desparpajo,	The Turk, like an old hand,
Contestó cual perro viejo:	Pertly replied,
"Este reló es el espejo	"This clock is the reflection
Del Gobierno que hay debajo."	Of the government beneath it."

It was in 1863 that the respected horologer José Rodríguez Conejero, better known as "Losada", after the county in León he was born in, visited Spain, staying at the Hotel Paris, which had been built on the site of the former Church of Buen Suceso. Losada was a master clockmaker who had earlier made high-precision instruments for the Spanish Navy and who in 1856 had been appointed the Navy's official watchmaker and

Façade of Gobernación 1868.
After countless complaints from frustrated Madrileños, the master horologist José Rodríguez de Losada constructed a new clock and donated it to the city. A new tower for it was built and finally in 1866 the clock was successfully inaugurated. *Museo Municipal, photo by Laurent.*

chronometrist. He had received various prestigious medals from the Spanish government, but now lived in London where he had set up shop and taken on British nationality.

In fact, the back room of his establishment at 105 Regent Street had become a meeting point for liberal-minded Spanish politicians in exile. In 1862, at the world's fair held in London's Crystal Palace, he prided himself on being the official watchmaker for the Spanish royal family and of the Armed Forces of Spain.

During his sojourn in Madrid, as day after day Losada peered out of his hotel window overlooking the square, he was appalled at seeing the malfunctioning clock perched in the tower of Government House. Surely there was something that could be done to rectify this shameful shortcoming. As a man of action, he took steps to remedy the situation. After meetings with the proper authorities, it was agreed that he would construct a completely new clock that would be worthy of the main square in the capital of Spain. He was not only prepared to build it, but proudly announced that he would donate it to the people of Madrid. As it turned out, it took three years to build the hand-crafted timepiece in London.

Finally, on November 19, 1866, Losada's new clock was inaugurated with full pomp in the presence of Queen Isabel II, a truly historic event. Now, at long last, the Puerta del Sol would have a reliable clock to tell Madrileños the correct hour. The clock worked perfectly and continued to tell time accurately with only minor flaws. In 1928 one of the weights came loose and plummeted through the roof into somebody's office. And during the Spanish Civil War one of its dials was damaged by a shell. But barring such mishaps, and more recent mechanical problems, Losada's clock has been keeping accurate time from the day it was installed to the present.

As for Losada, the master clockmaker died in London in 1870, aged 72. The Spanish poet José Zorrilla, who when in London would drop in on the *tertulias* (periodic chat sessions) on Regent Street, wrote:

Losada es un gran mecánico
Que alcanzó inmenso renombre,
Y, no obstante, vale el hombre
Más que su reputación.
Aunque seco, cejijunto
Y algo brusco en sus modales,
Leal entre los leales,
Tiene de oro el corazón.

Losada is a great mechanic
Who became immensely famous,
Yet, the man's worth
Is greater than his reputation.
Although he is dry,
And his eyebrows meet.
Sometimes brusk in his manners,
He is loyal to the end
And has a heart of gold.

A mouth full of grapes for New Year's

The clock in Government House takes on special significance once a year when the golden ball starts to descend just before the first stroke of midnight of December 31st, marking the end of the old year and heralding in the new. Large

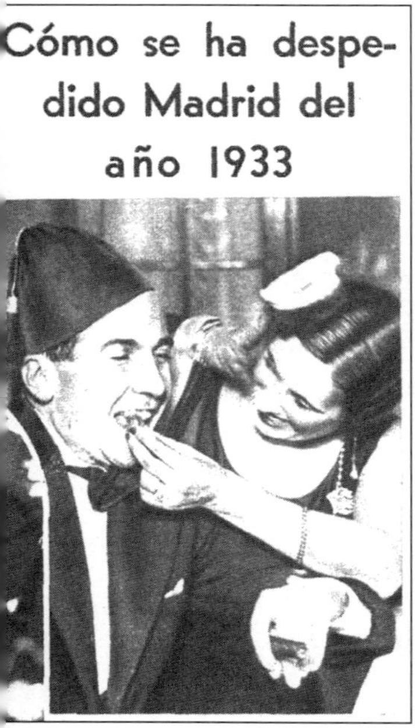

New Year's 1933. Curious clipping from the magazine *Estampa* showing a couple swallowing the traditional grapes. Estampa, *January 6, 1934.*

crowds of merrymakers then assemble on the Puerta del Sol to celebrate the occasion, the way they do in Times Square or Trafalgar Square, well supplied with bottles of Spanish bubbly, firecrackers and a bag of twelve grapes. Twelve grapes? Well, yes, because there's a tradition that dates back to 1909.

In that year, there happened to be an oversupply of grapes during the autumn harvest. So, to celebrate the arrival of the New Year, a large supply of them was handed out free to the crowds in the Puerta del Sol. At some point that night, someone had the notion, or challenged a friend, to try to swallow one grape at each stroke of the clock. The challenge was accepted and soon crowds of people were following suit. These grapes, of course, were not seedless, and it's not recorded how many succeeded in the feat nor if anyone choked to death. In any case, ever since, all over Spain, indeed wherever Spaniards may gather, whether at home, in a restaurant, in the Puerta del Sol or even in a foreign land, the New Year's celebration will invariably include the grape ceremony: one grape swallowed with each stroke of the clock at midnight. This tradition has become as much a part of New Year's Eve as noisemakers and firecrackers and a round of friendly kisses to all those accompanying you. Those who want to "cheat" can now buy specially-prepared canned grapes in supermarkets that contain exactly twelve skinless and pitless grapes meant for the occasion.

In 1996 revellers trying to swallow the 12 grapes at midnight had an especially hard time of it. The reason was that due to an error in the clock mechanism, upon sounding the twelve successive strokes, rather than doing so in the expected 36 seconds, the clock did it in 17 seconds, which made it even more difficult to swallow the grapes in the allotted time. The malfunction was promptly corrected.

The Puerta del Sol on the 2nd of May. Angry Madrileños attack the occupying French troops stationed in the Puerta del Sol only to be massacred by a squadron of mounted French Mameluke troops. *Author's archive.*

Dos de Mayo: When pitchforks and knives challenged Napoleon

As you walk on the sidewalk in front of Government House, you'll be treading ground that for Spaniards is hallowed. Here blood was shed when a handful of sparsely-armed Madrileños confronted Napoleon's crack cavalry.

Of the many dramatic events that the Puerta del Sol has witnessed —from the entry of monarchs to the proclamation of the Republic in 1931, to modern anti-war rallies and peace marches and gay rights demonstrations— the most famous was the bloody uprising of Spaniards against the occupying Napoleonic troops on May 1 and May 2, 1808.

Battle at the Gates of Monteleón. This oil painting shows the bloody battle waged on May 2nd when several hundred Spaniards seized the arms depot of Monteleón. It was here that the Spanish heroes Daoiz and Velarde died. *Artist: Manuel Castellano, 1862.*

The revolt was brought on by a complex series of historical events. Napoleon had dispatched a military force under Marshal Murat (his brother-in-law), ostensibly to bolster the rule of King Carlos IV and his minister, Manuel Godoy. In fact, however, Napoleon's purpose was to seize power in Spain in view of a rising threat from England, which was at war with France at that time.

The anti-French feelings caused by the occupation and the virtual house-arrest of the king and part of his family, who were being held in Bayonne, France, reached a head on the night of May 1, 1808 when a large group of Spaniards saw two carriages leaving the Royal Palace with the king's youngest son, Francisco de Paula, and suspected that the remaining members of the royal family were being whisked away by the French. Disturbances broke out in front of the Palace and the

French opened fire. Ten Spaniards lay dead or wounded on the cobblestones. The following day, May 2, these skirmishes turned into a full-scale revolt as Madrileños, armed with sticks, poles, knives and a few guns, streamed into the Puerta del Sol and attacked the French soldiers that were stationed there. Both French and Spanish troops (since both nations were nominally allies) were ordered to put down the disturbances. When a squadron of Mameluke troops from Egypt, in the service of France, was ordered to gallop in to put down the revolt in the square, they were attacked by the mob, but they were no match for the crack French cavalry, and many civilians were massacred. The fighting then moved to another part of town where a contingent of Spanish troops, disobeying orders, joined the rebellion. The rebels, led by the Spanish officers Daoiz and Velarde, seized an arms depot called the Parque de Monteleón in the site now known as the Plaza del Dos de Mayo (see Area 5 map, Pg. 207) and a confrontation against the French ensued. However, even with the newly-seized weapons, the rebels were easily overwhelmed when the Gallic forces brought out heavy artillery. After fierce Spanish resistance, the French troops finally overcame the Spaniards. Daoiz and Velarde perished in the battle, and were subsequently honored as national heroes.

The street fighting in Madrid on May 2, 1808 left some 200 Spaniards dead, perhaps the same number wounded, and 300 taken prisoner in the fighting, who were shot during the night. These summary executions of May 3, 1808 were carried out in an area called the Montaña del Príncipe Pío. This hillock later became the site of a barracks and is now a park, containing the Egyptian Temple of Debod. According to one recent British source, the French occupiers' losses were 31 dead and 114 wounded, while some Spanish history books put the French casualties at 2,000 with about the same number of Spaniards. What is known is that eighteen wagons were loaded with the bloody corpses of the Spanish victims and carted off to mass graves.

The insurrection became the subject of Goya's two famous canvases, one depicting the uprising in the Puerta del Sol as the

Spaniards struggled against the mounted Mameluke troops, and the second showing the execution of a group of patriots on May 3. Both canvases can be seen in the Prado Museum.

Though the uprising in Madrid was easily quelled by Murat, it was the spark that touched off revolts around all of Spain and induced Spanish statesmen to appeal to England to dispatch an expeditionary force to oust the Napoleonic usurpers from the Peninsula. The resulting conflict, known to us as the Peninsular War, and in Spain as the Guerra de la Independencia (War of Independence), was to drag on for five long devastating years. It pitted a combined Anglo-Portuguese-Spanish force commanded by the Duke of Wellington against Napoleon's "Grand Armée". At the end, the French were driven back across the Pyrenees, but not before the whole country was laid waste and innumerable atrocities committed. Poignant testimony to the cruelty and mayhem accompanying that conflict was once again captured by Goya in his series of drawings, the Caprichos, on display in the Prado.

Monument to Daoiz and Velarde. In the center of the Plaza de Dos de Mayo (where the Monteleón depot formerly stood) rises the monument honoring these two patriots. The swords shown in the photo have long since been stolen by vandals. *Author's archive.*

No fewer than seven monuments have been built in Madrid to commemorate Daoiz and Velarde. Perhaps the most impressive is the one standing on the Plaza de la Lealtad (Loyalty Square) (see Area 2 map, Pg. 85) in front of the Ritz Hotel. An obelisk originally marking the burial place of the two patriots now commemorates all those who fell during the insurrection. The monument is also Spain's tomb of the Unknown Soldier, in remembrance of those who have died in the service of their country in past wars.

More directly evocative of the May uprising is the monument in memory of the resistance-fighters erected at the very place of one of the key confrontations, the site of the former Parque de Monteleón depot, now the Plaza del Dos de Mayo. The monument incorporates the sparse remains of the entry gate to the depot, which was seized and defended by the Spaniards. Daoiz and Velarde, sculpted by Antonio Solá, are dressed in the garb of Indibil and Mandonio, two Iberian chieftains who defended their independence from Carthaginian and Roman invaders. Originally, they brandished two magnificent swords in their hands; but these have been stolen by vandals and have not yet been replaced. The surrounding streets bear the names of the Spanish officers who died in the battle: Daoiz, Velarde, Goicoechea and Ruíz.

In the Puerta del Sol itself a large plaque on the façade of Government House recalls the heroic deeds. It reads: "To the Heroes of May 2, 1808. They here fought the first battle against Napoleon's troops".

(Another more recent plaque commemorates the people of Madrid who helped the victims of the March 11, 2004 terrorist attack that killed 191 persons.)

The Florida Cemetery. Within this hidden-away cemetery rest the remains of 43 Spanish patriots who were executed by the French. A reproduction on tile of Goya's famous painting commemorates their sacrifice. *Author's photo.*

In addition, a little-known curiosity associated with the May 2nd fighting is a small cemetery, the Cementerio de la Florida, where 37 of Napoleon's victims are buried in a common grave. Unfortunately, the cemetery is closed throughout the entire year and is only opened on May 2nd, when a ceremony is held to celebrate the dead. However, if you visit the place, there's a large gate which allows you to peer in and see the pillar at the far end commemorating the victims, as well as a reproduction in ceramic of Goya's painting *Los Fusilamientos del 3 de Mayo* with an inscription honoring the dead patriots. The cemetery is a bit tricky to find. It is a short distance behind the chapel of San Antonio de la Florida, up and over the railroad tracks, on the corner of the Calle de Francisco y Jacinto Alcántara and Paseo del Rey. As you cross the railroad tracks, you'll see a huge monument to Goya made by Vaquero Turcios consisting of four monoliths spelling out his name. In the back of each are quotations of Goya's comments on art.

Kilometer zero

Stand on the Meridian in Greenwich, or step on the intersection where Utah, Colorado, Arizona and New Mexico meet. Something comparable in Madrid can be done in the Puerta Sol, where you can step on "Kilometer Zero" located in front of Government House.

Madrid has been the political center of the country since the rule of King Felipe II in the 16th century when that monarch decided to make it the capital of Spain. Previous to that time, the royal court tended to travel about from one city to another, and might reside in Toledo or Valladolid or Burgos or Barcelona. Felipe, who spent much of his life in San Lorenzo de El Escorial in the famous monastery-palace he had built there outside Madrid, wanted a new capital that would be in the center of the Iberian Peninsula, more or less equidistant to all seaports in the country. This would make travel to the different points of the kingdom easier and enable him to exert better control of the different areas.

Kilometer "0" Plaque. Shown is the map of Spain with the six national highways radiating from the center. *Author's photo.*

In the reign of King Felipe V, in the 18th century, six main highroads leading out of Madrid were established, with stone road markers showing the distance from each marker to the capital. The "zero" or starting point was determined as being at the Puerta del Sol. Originally, of course, the road distances were measured in leagues, so if there had been a plaque at the time of Felipe V it might have read "League Zero".

Later, under King Carlos III, these roads were assigned Roman numerals, from I to VI, preceded by the letter "N" (for "national"). They are still referred to as such at the present time and are toll-free, though toll speedways may run parallel to them at some stretches.

It wasn't until 1950 that an actual plaque was placed on the sidewalk in front of Government House to pinpoint the exact spot from which all kilometric distances on Spanish national highways are measured. Thus, if you see a road marker or a sign saying “345 kilometers”, it is 345 kilometers to the plaque.

In addition to being the starting point of the six major roads leading out of the capital, Kilometer Zero also marked the geographical center of Madrid. However, by 1978 it was determined that the actual geographical center of the city had moved to behind the Prado Museum. The center now is estimated to be at the intersection of the Calles Goya and Serrano, though no plaque marks the spot. On a larger scale, the geographical center of the whole Peninsula has been calculated as lying in a place called the Cerro de los Angeles, about 10 kilometers (six miles) south of Madrid.

The Puerta del Sol is also the central point for the numbering of all houses in the streets of the city. Thus, in any given street, you’ll notice that the house numbers rise as they move further away from the Puerta del Sol.

TÍO PEPE LIVES ON

On the roof of what was formerly the Hotel Paris, in the Puerta del Sol, you can still see the large “Tío Pepe” sign (the name of a sherry wine), a leftover from the days when the square was filled with billboards and advertising panels. These were subsequently outlawed by the municipal authorities, but the “Tío Pepe” sign was excepted, being considered tantamount to a national landmark, rather like the huge silhouetted bulls on some of Spain’s roads, which originally were billboards advertising Veterano brandy. It reads: “Tío Pepe. Sol de Andalucía embotellado. González Byass.” (Uncle Joe. The Sun of Andalucía bottled up. González Byass, distiller.) The sign is slated to remain there even though the building has recently been sold to new owners.

Searching for the Mariblanca statue

On the west side of the Puerta del Sol, near the entrance to what is now a pedestrian walk, the Calle del Arenal, stands the statue of the Mariblanca. You may catch a glimpse of a statue of a woman which topped a fountain known as the Mariblanca. The statue holds more secrets than at first meets the eye. Because this is only a replica. The story of the original is shrouded in a web of confusion, contradictions and... mystery in terms of its identity, its sculptor, and its final resting place.

You can see what the original fountain looked like on the pretty street-sign tiles scattered around the corner buildings of Sol. In its day, the huge octagonal structure rose five meters (15 feet) high and featured 30 water spouts, among them some in the form of bronze masks surrounded by coats-of-arms of the city. In the upper part of the fountain were basins from which water spurted from the breasts of eight harpies. Crowning the large fountain rose the Mariblanca statue, with a child to her side and dolphins at her feet.

The Mariblancas: the fake and the real. On the left is the Mariblanca statue that stands in the Puerta del Sol, which is a replica. The original, on the right, can be found in a place of honor in the City Hall. *Author's photo.*

Mariblanca on Recoletos. This photo taken in the 70's shows where the Mariblanca once stood. Now only the columns and fountain remain. *Author's archive.*

It was around the Mariblanca that political plots were hatched, gossip bandied and secret trysts arranged. Water-carriers milled about the fountain, vied for positions, and filled their casks; the water was then dispensed to thirsty Madrileños for a small fee. Buckets of water were even carried up to private apartments, for a consideration, of course.

In 1838 the fountain was moved from the Puerta del Sol to the Plaza de las Descalzas Reales. After that, the fountain itself was destroyed in 1892 and the Mariblanca statue ignominiously deposited in a municipal storehouse, seeing as it was not considered to be of any great artistic value. Later, in 1914, it resurfaced for a while in the Retiro Park. In 1962, the peripatetic statue was transferred to the Municipal Museum.

Then, in 1969, a stretch of the Paseo de Recoletos, just north of the Plaza de la Cibeles (see Area 6 map, Pg. 235) was landscaped and beautified by building a long decorative strip of water lined by Grecian columns. In a special temple-like

Second replica of the Mariblanca. This replica can be found in the Museo de la Ciudad. *Author's photo.*

structure, the long-maligned Mariblanca statue was pulled out of storage and installed there, opposite house number 7-9, in a place of honor. Even though the statue's artistic value may have been doubtful, its historical significance was beyond question.

There she remained for a few years, until vandals started to damage her. Deemed too important a relic to be left to the hazards of modern city life, the authorities returned the statue to Madrid's Municipal Museum on Fuencarral 78, where it stood neglected for a great many years on the landing of a staircase, which visitors hurried past. The statue, however, is no longer there. In our search, we discovered that there is an impressive, full-sized copy of it in the Museo de la Ciudad (Museum of the City of Madrid) on the Calle del Príncipe de Vergara 140. But questions still remained: Where is the original? Was it destroyed or is it again moldering in some dank municipal vault? Who did the statue represent and who sculpted it? No one we consulted seemed to know.

Sources disagree on the identity of who the statue represented, some saying it was the goddess Diana and others claiming it was Venus while a third group avers the figure is an allegory of Faith. As for the identity of the artist who sculpted her, some say that it was a certain Rutilio Gassi while others aver that it was sculpted by an Italian called Turqui.

However, our tale ends on a happy note, for in the course of researching this book we managed to track down the peripatetic lady. We discovered that on March 26, 1985 Enrique Tierno Galván, the greatly-respected intellectual and then-mayor of Madrid, had the Mariblanca moved to what was the the Ayuntamiento (City Hall) on the Plaza de la Villa 5 (see Area 3 map, Pg. 117A), and there she has remained, now proudly standing in a well-lit niche in the Vestíbulo de Honor (Foyer of Honor), a fitting site after her 169-year odyssey from the time she was removed from her emplacement on the Puerta del Sol.

As for her identity, a plaque near the statue merely states that the Mariblanca dates back to 1625 when she was "acquired" by the Florentine sculptor Florentino Ludovico Turqui to top the fountain which stood in front of the Church of Buen Suceso in the Puerta del Sol, which was known as the Fountain of Faith, since the figure topping it, the "Mariblanca", was an allegory of Faith. You can see the statue and some of the sumptuous rooms in the former City Hall as part of a guided tour of the building.

As a curiosity we might mention that the original statue was never properly restored, hence the two replicas, that in Sol and the one in the Museum of the City of Madrid, maintain the same defects, among them the missing arm of the child beside her.

The bear and the madroño tree

What is a statue of a bear climbing up a small tree doing on the Puerta del Sol near the entrance to the Calle de Alcalá? Is it a tribute to some popular children's tale or a cuddly nod to a local legend? Not at all! The bear and the madroño tree, a motif you'll constantly run across in the city, is part of the capital's official coat-of-arms and the symbol of Madrid, like the she-wolf is of Rome or the bear of Berlin.

Like most heraldic symbols, the origins of Madrid's coat-of-arms are somewhat nebulous. The city's first emblem, prior to 1200 AD, depicted a flintstone partially submerged in water, with two pieces of steel striking it on either side, and sparks flying off. This was garlanded by a ribbon with the Latin inscription, *Sic gloria labore* (Thus is the glory of labor) and the word *paratur* (be prepared) beneath which ran the line, *Fui sobre agua edificada. Mis muros de fuego son. Esta es mi insignia y blasón.* (I was built on water. My walls are of fire. This is my insignia and shield.)

The three Spanish sentences refer to the fact that Madrid was originally built on top of subterranean springs; that the defensive walls were made of flint, causing sparks to fly off when struck by metal-tipped arrows, and that this was its coat-of arms.

Should you pass by the Plaza de Puerta Cerrada, down from the Plaza Mayor (see Area 3 map, Pg. 117A) you can see a street mural that covers the whole side of one building which depicts the elements of the above-described shield, with a shower of sparks flying off the flintstone.

In 1202, Alfonso VIII bequeathed special privileges upon the inhabitants of Madrid and specified certain legal jurisdictions. Around that time the coat-of-arms was changed, since we know that in the battle of Navas de Tolosa against the Moors in 1212 a pennant used by the soldiers from Madrid depicted an escutcheon showing a bear walking on a silver field, with the constellation of the Little Dipper on the bear's back, with the North Star pointing towards the tail.

Madroños in Madrid. Almost forgotten in the bustle of the city, several madroños have been planted by City Hall along the Calle Mayor. The ones pictured here, on the corner of Calle del Bonetillo, are marked with a plaque. *Author's photo.*

Why a bear? Most historians believe that it was chosen because bears were found in abundance around Madrid at a time when the area was covered with forests. Indeed, some aver that in fact it was a she-bear, commonly associated with fertility. Apparently in the city archives of the "Casa de la Panadería", located in the Plaza Mayor, manuscripts confirm that the bear in question was a female.

As for the stars on the animal's back, clearly there is a link between the Little Dipper constellation, Ursa Minor, literally "small bear", and the use of the bear as a symbol in the coat-of-arms. Some local historians argue that the seven stars may

Madrid's coats-of-arms.
New

1. Street waste basket
2. Street bench
3. Plaza Mayor wall
4. Street flower/tree pot
5. Public lighting
6. Fireman's water outlet
7. Anti-parking pole

Old
8. Gate of Retiro Park
9. Street plaque
10. Water fountain

instead represent seven astronomy schools that supposedly existed in Madrid in the 10th century, when the city was still under Moorish rule. Another version suggests that the stars represent the sky of Madrid, renowned for its clarity and purity.

Moreover, from the time Madrid was awarded its charter of privileges, a dispute arose between Church and State about who would have jurisdiction over the lumber supply and hunting grounds as well as the grazing land. The controversy raged for 20 years until finally a compromise was reached, whereby the Church was allotted the grazing land and the Crown the wood and hunting grounds. Though each of the parties involved drew its own coat-of-arms, they were then consolidated into one design. The bear, previously shown roaming in the fields, was now depicted with its hind legs solidly on the ground, symbolizing the Church's dominion of the fields, and its forward paws poised on a tree, in representation of the State's claim to lumber and hunting. The bear and tree were enclosed in a blue orle, symbolizing celestial blue, spangled with seven stars representing the Little Dipper, each star containing eight points, as though to suggest its glitter.

However, the term "tree" in this case needs some explaining. Though the tree is usually thought of as being a madroño, in strict botanical terms it is not a tree, but rather a heath. Its scientific name is *Arbutus unedo*, sometimes called a strawberry tree in English, and bears red edible berries. Yet it decidedly is not a tree native to the area of Madrid.

So why was it chosen to be included on the seal? It seems probable that at the time the coat-of-arms was designed, this tree was meant to represent a generic, non-specified tree whose sole purpose was to pictorially symbolize the conciliation between Church and State. Some sources suggest that it may very well have been a type of oak tree such as were very abundant in the area. Moreover, it is argued that at some later time an artist added touches of red color to make the tree look more attractive, although it is anyone's guess exactly what kind of fruit these marks were intended to represent, if any.

However, we do have a clue that may shed some light on the subject. At one point, centuries later, a devastating plague hit Madrid in the early 1500's just as Carlos V was visiting the

MADROÑO LIQUEUR

There is a tavern called "El Madroño" on the Plaza de Puerta Cerrada 7 (see Area 3 map, Pg. 117 A) where on the wall, behind the counter, you'll find an extensive explanation, including various painted tiles, tracing the evolution of Madrid's coats-of-arms. While you're there, order their home-made madroño liqueur, quite a delicacy, or buy an entire bottle. If only Carlos V had been able to get his hands on this!

Also, should you be interested in seeing an actual madroño tree, head down the Calle Mayor past the Plaza Mayor (see Area 3 map.) Most of the trees planted on both sides of this street are madroños. The ones on the corner of Calle de Milaneses are clearly marked as such with a plaque. More madroños can be found in the Retiro Park on the corner of the Paseo del Duque de Fernán Núñez and the Paseo de Uruguay, next to the Rose Garden (see Area 7 map, Pg. 259).

city. The king became very ill with a malarial fever and it seemed no remedy could be found. However, the townsfolk had discovered that by boiling the leaves of the madroño, a concoction was made that cured the fevers. The king was persuaded to try this home remedy and eventually recovered. Not only did the madroño brew save the life of the monarch, but it also was believed to have cured many of the townspeople, and in appreciation of this, future coats-of-arms more clearly identified the life-saving tree as a madroño.

Despite the various theories put forth, no one is exactly sure how or why a "madroño" tree was chosen. What is certain is that in the course of the centuries, although there have been various changes to Madrid's coat-of-arms, all of them have featured the bear and the madroño.

In 1554, the Parliament of the Castilian city of Valladolid granted Madrid permission to add the royal crown on its coat-of-arms, therewith officially raising it to the status of a "villa". Strange as it may seem, Madrid at the time, far from being the capital of Spain, was a relatively unimportant small town. Hence this new status was considered of great importance, and the royal crown was immediately incorporated in its coat-of-arms. However, exactly where in the shield the crown was to be placed was not specified. So the crown was placed over the madroño, since it was the easiest spot to add this new feature without having to redesign the whole shield.

Later, in the 17th century, the crown began to appear over the crest of the coat-of-arms, for no apparent reason other than aesthetic considerations.

Then in 1842 two new additions were made to the coat-of-arms. The first was to add the Civic Wreath which had been awarded to Madrid 20 years earlier for having fought so fiercely and heroically in the Peninsular War. The second addition was somewhat stranger. It was a dragon.

A dragon? How did that get in there? It would seem that many years earlier, in 1569, a city gate called the Puerta Cerrada featured a carving of a dragon over its entrance. Some historians claimed that this mythical creature was a sure sign that Madrid had been founded originally by the Greeks, since the same kind of dragon at times appeared in banners and coins used by them. This entire notion has been held up to ridicule and in fact one of the best and most trustworthy chroniclers of Madrid, Mesonero Romanos, states that the carving on the gate was not of a dragon at all, but rather a meek-looking serpent. Nevertheless, the scaled dragon, with ears of a dog, wings of a bat, tail of a snake and talons of an eagle was incorporated into the city shield and has remained there along with the Civic Wreath for over a hundred years.

Fortunately, in 1967 City Hall changed the coat-of-arms back to the former one showing a green madroño with red berries in a field of silver with a black bear leaning on it, framed in blue, with seven silver stars, topped by a large crown. Only a few minor modifications have been made in the past decades, such as changes in the contours of the shield or the number of points on each star.

As you walk around town, you'll see the coat-of-arms on sewer lids, police cars, disposal baskets, entrances to tunnels, benches, on all public transportation and on all municipal facilities. In a few places, however, you can still find the pre-1967 coat-of-arms with the dragon and the wreath. Look for these on the old blue street plaques on the corners of buildings, in the entrance gates to the Retiro Park, on old public water fountains, and metal lids on utility accesses.

As for the bear and madroño statue in the Puerta del Sol, in 1987 a spray painter called Juan Carlos Argüello went about the city putting his alias, "Muelle" ("spring" as in a mattress), on walls, buildings and monuments all over town. The police unsuccessfully attempted to catch the culprit until he tried to put his graffiti on the Bear and Madroño statue. It was the last straw and the police nabbed him. He was fined 2,500 pesetas, (approximately the equivalent of $20), not an exorbitant amount considering that he then went on to become something of a pop icon, even registering his "tag" in the trademark office and on one occasion taking City Hall to court for using his logo without first getting permission.

The jackpot that bankrupted a government

Santiago Alonso Cordero. This man won a combination of State lotteries so large, that the Spanish Treasury could not pay him. He is dressed in the typical "Maragato" style. *Museo Romántico, Madrid, painting by Esquivel.*

Imagine if you were lucky enough to simultaneously win every major government lottery in the country. However as you went to collect your winnings, perhaps imagining all the possible luxuries and caprices you'd indulge in, you suddenly were told that the State Treasury wasn't going to pay you, not because your tickets had the wrong numbers on them, or because you were collecting your money too late, but because the amount involved was so huge that State coffers couldn't meet the payment.

Well, that's exactly what happened back in the 19th century. Thanks to this dilemma, one of the best-known buildings in the city, the Casa de Cordero on the Puerta del Sol, was built. Today you can tell any taxi driver in London to take you to Big Ben, or in Paris to the Eiffel Tower and he won't hesitate for a moment to conduct you to these famous landmarks. The Casa de Cordero was in that category in the mid-19th century. For it was the very first large apartment house built in the city, completed in 1845 at a time when the Puerta del Sol was still largely ringed by dilapidated old houses. Most of these were torn down when the present semi-oval buildings on the north side of the square were constructed starting 1858. However, the Casa de Cordero has survived, though it would be a rare Madrileño today who would be able to identify it.

The building in question was also known as the House of the Maragato, since it was owned by a man who formerly was a simple villager from the northwestern region near Astorga whose inhabitants were famous for being muleteers, known as Maragatos. Santiago Alonso Cordero hailed from there. One year extraordinary good fortune came unexpectedly to Señor Cordero. Like so many Spaniards then as now, Cordero played the national Christmas lottery, where jackpot winners can wind up with millions. In those days, by betting a variety of combinations simultaneously, the prizes could be staggering, though virtually no one ever hit on the whole winning combination. But… you guessed it… Cordero did hit multiple combinations! The amount owed him was so huge that the Treasury Department, often strapped for cash in those turbulent years under Queen Isabel II, couldn't effect payment. So instead it was decided that, in lieu of payment, or most of it at least, the government would give Cordero a huge plot formerly occupied by the Convent of San Felipe el Real. This church had recently been torn down and appropriated by the State. It was situated in one of the prime, most expensive locations in the city – smack on the Puerta del Sol.

Cordero accepted the offer and built the largest apartment house complex in Madrid, consisting of six new buildings in one block which were joined together and given a common façade overlooking the Calle Mayor and the Puerta del Sol. Seven interior courtyards provided light and air to the comfortable suites, some of them very large. On the ground floor were shops, storage rooms as well as an establishment for baths, with marble decorations. The staircase leading up to the main floor was lavishly decorated with marble of different colors as also was the floor. The whole complex contained 100 luxurious apartments and understandably was the talk of the town, being one of the most prestigious and elegant houses in the city. In fact, when the Puerta del Sol was rebuilt ten years later, the architectural style used sought to emulate the most distinguished building on the square, the Casa de Cordero.

The suddenly-wealthy Cordero was not only a property-owner, but even managed to become a Member of Parliament in days when influence-pulling and venality were rather more blatant than today. In fact, Cordero created a considerable stir in Madrid when he attended sessions of Parliament attired in the regional costume of the county he represented, while other members wore fashionable Parisian-style suits.

A rather less romantic version avers that Cordero was already very wealthy and politically in league with the radical minister Juan Álvarez Mendizábal. The lottery story may have been floated to cover the large sum of laundered money needed to buy the plot at auction.

Whatever the source of financing, architects of the time considered the Casa de Cordero to be the best building that had been constructed in Madrid in many a year. The building, moreover, was well-known in those days for another reason, especially among foreign travellers. For in it was housed the best-known and most elegant of the *casas de huéspedes* (boarding houses) in the capital, referred to by most people as "La Vizcaína", since it was run by a woman from Vizcaya (Biscay) province.

One traveller of that time, a 28-year-old English clergyman, William George Clark, who called his book on Spain *Gazpacho*, stopped off at the Vizcaína in 1849 and wrote:

"After my luggage had undergone a polite pro formâ examination, I proceeded in quest of La Vizcaína, who occupies the third floor of the Casa Cordero, an enormous house in the very centre of the town. I was received at the door by the lady herself, a beaming, bustling housewife, still so fat and fair that I should have pronounced her forty. I have since learnt that – to use the language of mediaeval romance – she has numbered sixty winters. May she double the reckoning, for the benefit of travellers yet unborn! A delicious warm bath washed away the memory of fatigue, and prepared me for the olla (the daily stew) promised at five o'clock precisely. The company at the 'round table' – so a table d'hôte is termed in Spain – some twenty persons, formed a little quadruple alliance, for it contained representatives of each of the four powers, and of none other. In this case, the French had it all their own way. They carried on a clamorous discussion on the politics of Europe; and if any slow-spoken Englishman or Spaniard ventured upon a deprecatory 'mais', he was immediately borne down by a dashing reckless Polish-lancer-like charge of

Arches in the Casa de Cordero. (Left) Now filled with slot machines, this used to be the interior courtyard of the luxurious "Casa de Cordero". *Author's photo.*

Cordero´s Coat-of-Arms. (Right) On the corner of Calle de Esparteros and Calle Mayor, right above McDonald's, remains the coat-of-arms (marked with an arrow) of Alonso Cordero, the man who constructed the building. *Author's photo.*

assertions and inferences, so rapid that you had no time to comprehend, much less reply to them.

"After dinner, sundry silver or pseudo-silver dishes, with handles to them, filled with glowing charcoal, were placed on the table, whereat every one lighted his cigar. A lull ensued, and the discussion ended, as usual, in smoke."

The Casa de Cordero still stands at Calle Mayor 1, although its former splendor has long since faded. On the ground floor and inside the building you will find an amusement arcade called Sol Park. Enter the arcade, and midst the crowds of people playing the slot machines, cast your eyes up and you'll see the remains of the graceful stone arches that formerly ringed the patio, which was one of the inner courtyards where well-heeled travellers arrived to lodge in Madrid's best boarding house.

To the right, in the hallway before entering Sol Park, you can walk up the old staircase leading to the upper stories of the building, where you'll still find the old beams and iron banisters from the mid-19th century.

Even though the architectural significance of the old Casa de Cordero has been long since forgotten, a few mementoes from earlier years still linger on, such as the date of its construction, 1846, over the main entrance, as well as a plaque reminding us that this was formerly the site of the

Monastery of San Felipe el Real. In addition, you can still see Cordero's large, ornate coat-of-arms that shows a spinning wheel in the center and a bear on either side on the corner of the Calle de los Esparteros and the Calle Mayor, above the present-day McDonald's.

The Hotel Paris, R.I.P.

Wedged in the corner between the Calle de Alcalá and the Carrera de San Jerónimo on the Puerta del Sol still stands the building that until May 2006 housed one of the oldest hostelries in the city, the Hotel Paris. Opened in 1864, it was in those days known as the Grand Hôtel de Paris and remained the most elegant and expensive hotel in Madrid until 1910 when the Hotel Ritz finally eclipsed it. Until then, the Hotel Paris was the last word in elegance; its prices were high, some travelers said "outrageous", but it provided all the comfort and conveniences of the best Parisian hotels and played host to countless celebrities.

Façade of Hotel Paris
May 31, 2006: the last day the once luxurious Hotel Paris remained open to the public.
Author's photo.

A room with French windows commanding a view overlooking the Puerta del Sol with its fascinating sight of the constant hustle and bustle on the square - street vendors, water-carriers, newspaper hawkers, mules, horses, fine ladies, elegant soldiers and gypsies — sent some travelers into ecstatic descriptions.

Among the great attractions of the old Hotel Paris was its mezzanine dining room which prided itself on its fine French cooking. No oil. No garlic. A welcome respite for foreigners from standard Spanish fare. The traveller paid one standard price for room and board no matter how much or how little he or she ate. House wine was served ad libitum.

The same year that the Hotel Paris opened, the whole of the ground floor of the building was converted into one of the city's most famous cafés, called the Café Imperial, which held about 500 people. It had entrance doors on the two side streets and in the Puerta del Sol itself and was a favorite hang-out for a whole cross-section of Madrid society, ranging from politicians to journalists, tourists, loafers, swindlers, hawkers, domino-players and just about anyone who wanted to while away a few hours people-watching, writing or reading the newspaper, of which ten were published each day in Madrid. The clientele lingered until the wee hours of the morning, a tradition that is still upheld in modern Madrid, especially on weekends when there are traffic jams in the center of town at 3 a.m. Later, the café's name was changed to the Café de la Montaña, referring neither to the American state of that name, nor to the mountains outside Madrid, but to the northern Spanish region of Santander, known as "La Montaña".

Valle-Inclán: The one-armed troubadour

In the first years of the 20th century, the Puerta del Sol was the hub of café life in the capital as well as the site of the city's best hotels. At one point, seven huge cafés vied for attention in the square, plus as many on Alcalá, each with its particular politically-oriented clientele, each the site of different tertulias, or gatherings, to discuss literature, politics, medicine, bullfighting or any other special interest of those participating. It was largely in these cafés that the political, social and intellectual life of the city was thrashed out.

On the Alcalá side of Sol you'll see a plaque attached to the wall that informs you in Spanish, "Here stood the Café de la Montaña, site of tertulias, animated by Ramón del Valle-Inclán."

Valle-Inclán belonged to that group of Spanish writers known as the "Generation of '98". He was one of the most respected and linguistically innovative of that group and his plays are considered to be forerunners of the Theatre of the Absurd. He was a great iconoclast, bohemian, poet, dramatist as well as a scintillating conversationalist and unabashed spinner of tales and was universally known as "Don Ramón".

Don Ramón, born in a small Galician village in 1866, came to Madrid in 1896 to try his luck in the literary whirligig of the capital, which ipso facto revolved around the cafés and

IN SPAIN, IT'S "DON" NOT "MISTER"

Originally the use of "Don" in front of a Christian name was reserved for the nobility; later it came to be used when addressing important gentlemen. In Cervantes' *Don Quixote* the use of "Don" before his name is used sarcastically. "Don" was used with the person's Christian name as a term of respect, thus "Don Ramón", "Don Jorge", "Don Pedro". By the 19th century "Don" was commonly placed before the Christian name of any educated or "higher class" person (Doña for ladies), and until very recently the correct formal address to use when writing someone a letter was "Sr. D. So-and-so..." (Señor Don...), though that custom, like so many others in Spain, as also the use of "Mr." and "Ms" in English, has gone the way of the manual typewriter.

newspaper offices near the Puerta del Sol. Soon he started publishing newspaper articles, stories, translations and poetry. Valle-Inclán had early begun to affect extravagant dress. He cultivated a flowing beard, let his hair grow long and haughtily swaggered about the streets of the city with spats and cane.

Don Ramón's strange appearance was further heightened due to the loss of his left arm. It was in the smoky Café de la Montaña that some of the poet's more outspoken friends would ask him how he came to lose the arm. The writer's face would become stern, he'd take a sip of cognac and as his audience hung on every word, he would solemnly expatiate:

"There was a time when I was living in a large palace in Galicia. One day my trusted old servant, Rubén, came into my study, his face mournful and apprehensive.

"'Sir, there are no victuals left to throw into the stew.'

"To which I answered, 'What? And the hundreds of *reales* which I gave you yesterday to buy provisions? And the legs of pork that were hanging in the larder?'

"'All is gone, sir!'

"For a while I remained pensive, and finally I made a radical decision and told Rubén to bring me a large cleaver from the kitchen. The puzzled servant quickly obeyed and came running back with the blade. I then stoically held out my left arm and told the servant, 'Take a good chunk out of this!' Rubén, who like a good servant of old never contradicted his master, took a mighty swing with the cleaver and in one fell swoop severed my arm at the shoulder. I then told him, 'This house shall never be wanting food. Throw *that* into the stew!'"

Don Ramón would then take another sip of his cognac, while those at his table either gasped or raised their eyebrows. However others at the back of the huge café snickered, for they had already heard this story and many others, since Don Ramón delighted in making up far-fetched new yarns each time he was pressed to give an explanation. These ranged from tales that his arm was eaten by a lion, that he hung it in a church as an ex-voto or that it was lost in a battle with the fierce Mexican bandit Quirico.

The true story harks back to the Café de la Montaña in July of 1899. The writer was taking part in an argument regarding a proposed duel between two of his friends. One of these was a Portuguese artist, Leal de la Cámara, the other an Andalusian youth. The quarrel had continued from the previous evening and concerned the relative bravery of Portuguese and Spaniards. Valle-Inclán pontificated upon the subject of dueling while others of the group listened respectfully. Enter a certain Manuel Bueno, writer in his own right, who tried to cut into the conversation.

Ramón del Valle-Inclán. Spanish author and playwright known for his *esperpentos* (a precursor to the Theatre of the Absurd.) Notice that his left arm is missing. How exactly he lost it was cause for much debate in the Madrid cafés near the Puerta del Sol. *Fototeca del Patrimonio Histórico.*

"Don't tire yourself out, Valle; the duel can't take place anyway, because Leal de la Cámara is still under age."

"What do you mean to say by that, majadero?" the poet replied haughtily, using an expletive that was very strong in those days.

Bueno took a step back, and started to brandish his cane. Valle-Inclán instinctively grabbed a water flask and struck out at his adversary. Bueno's cane came down with full force upon Don Ramón's left wrist, which he had raised over his face to defend himself, hitting it just where he wore a cuff-link, which became encrusted in his flesh due to the blow. Although the wound didn't seem to be serious, his friends convinced him to go to a nearby first aid station, where the wrist was bandaged. Unfortunately, the wound became infected and within a few days gangrene set in. When Don Ramón finally went to a doctor, he was told that the arm would have to be amputated.

But let us return to the Calle de Alcalá. Next to the Café de la Montaña plaque, you'll also see a second plaque. It tells us that the very same café was called the Café Colón in the play *Luces de Bohemia (Bohemian Lights)* in what is locally known as

Plaque on the Calle de Alvarez Gato. (Left) Every April 23rd Valle-Inclán admirers retrace the steps taken by the blind poet Max Estrella in *Luces de Bohemia*. This street is one of the high points of the tour. *Author's photo.*

Mirrors on the Calle de Alvarez Gato. (Right) It is here that the blind poet in Valle-Inclán's play paradoxically encounters a series of deformed mirrors. The original mirrors were full length. *Author's photo.*

the "Night of Max Estrella". Indeed, as you wander around this section of town you will come across other plaques referring to Max Estrella. What is more, each year on April 23 about a hundred admirers of the play "do" what is known as the Max Estrella circuit, which includes nearby sites associated with Spain's greatest Golden Age writers and poets in and around the Plaza de Santa Ana and the Calle de las Huertas (see Area 2 map Pg. 85).

Who, then, was Max Estrella? You won't find him in any encyclopedia or book of biographies, since he never existed except in fiction. Max Estrella was the name of the blind poet in the aforementioned play, written by Don Ramón, and originally published in 1920.

This *esperpento*, a word Valle-Inclán coined to describe his theatre of the absurd, is probably the most popular and highly-regarded of his writings today. It is a broadside against all of contemporary Spanish society of the time. The central figure is the impoverished Max Estrella, whose perambulations we follow through the course of one long, excruciating night as he makes the rounds of the Puerta del Sol taverns, a newspaper office, bookshops, cafés, the Ministry of the Interior, a jail and various narrow alleys. In his wanderings he encounters a cross-section of Madrid society including a corrupt minister, an editor, policemen, prostitutes, impecunious writers and even the poet Rubén Darío.

Since *Luces de Bohemia* was first published, Max Estrella's all-night via crucis has become a metaphor for many down and out anti-Establishment students and intellectuals. The play has been often produced and was also made into a film. Though the circumstances of Madrid life in the 1920's under the dictatorship of General Primo de Rivera were totally different from those of today, Max's odyssey and Don Ramón's incisive, skeptical and anti-bourgeois prose have remained popular with literati who refuse to accept the status quo. The spectacle of the blind poet stumbling through the Madrid night, inveighing against society in a vernacular which brilliantly mixed local slang and erudite language, with its allusions to Romantic ideals and cynical observations of reality, continues to cast a spell over readers, making Max Estrella one of the most beloved fictional characters created in modern Spanish literature.

Almost all of the places Max visits during his nocturnal quest are now gone, though a very few still survive. Among these are copies of the two curved deforming mirrors mentioned in the play on the outside of a bar called Las Bravas in the squalid little Calle de Álvarez Gato, off the Plaza de Santa Ana. Two other replicas, which were smashed by vandals in 1993, are preserved inside the bar. The originals are long since gone. (Las Bravas is actually part of a chain and its name refers to the hot sauce served on the typical dish of *patatas bravas* — "brave" or "fierce" potatoes in the sense of them being spicy.)

As for Valle-Inclán, a smallish rather expressionless statue of him standing in an erect position was placed in 1973 on the Paseo de Recoletos, (opposite street number 19); another, a bust of his head, can be seen in the street named after him in the outlying Carabanchel neighborhood.

Unfortunately, all of the old cafés on the Puerta del Sol have gone the way of the donkey-cart. About the only place still somewhat reminiscent of those days is the Mallorquina pastry shop, founded in 1894, on the corner of Calle Mayor, which is still popular with Madrileños with a sweet tooth for confectionery or wanting to while away a half hour sipping a coffee in its upstairs "tea room". Specialties here are the *napolitanas de crema* (a cream-filled pastry) and *trufas* (chocolate balls).

Paco, the dog. One of the best-known and loved personalities of Madrid in the 1880's was not a Madrileño, but rather an ugly mutt known as Paco. Everyone adored Paco and it was common practice to let him prance into select restaurants, plays, *zarzuelas* and bullfights. *Author's archive.*

Paco, the dog

There is another "personage" who haunted the cafés of the Puerta del Sol and the Calle de Alcalá in the late 19th century. His name was Paco, and he was a roving pooch.

It was on a day in October of 1879 that a stray dog somehow managed to trot into one of the most elegant restaurants in the city, the Café Fornos, located on the corner of the Calles Alcalá and Virgen de los Peligros, a block from the Puerta del Sol.

The dog sniffed about from table to table, almost as though he were the owner of the café, doubtless expecting some generous diner to slip him a scrap from his plate. Paco must have had a sharp eye for benefactors, for he went right up to a table at which sat the Marqués de Bogaraya. Perhaps because of the dog's frisky manner, the nobleman, amused by the mutt, threw him a bone. As it happened to be the day of the festivities of San Francisco de Asís, the marquis dubbed the dog Francisco, which in colloquial Spanish became "Paco".

Paco's physical attributes were not exceptional: he was medium-sized and had a smooth black fur with white spots. Every now and then he would be known to chase an errant flea with his teeth.

The marquis's generosity was not lost upon the dog, and as the nobleman ate regularly in Fornos, so Paco too would drop in at dinner time and be assured of at least a morsel from the table and a good many pats on the head. His friendship with his benefactor increased. Meanwhile others took a fancy to him as well, and within a short while he was practically a fixture in this most popular of all Madrid cafés. Even the waiters began to like him.

Since Fornos never shut down, Paco started to stay there overnight, for it was certainly cozier curling up under a divan than sleeping in some cold doorway. Soon his presence became known to all of Madrid. He had no trouble being admitted to places barred to other dogs. In fact, no doors were closed to Paco, and he nonchalantly trotted into theatres, circuses, bullrings, gardens and went just about everywhere his influential benefactor did. No doorman, usher or guard ever denied the privileged pooch entrance, or booted him out once on the premises. Waltzes and gallops were written in his honor, and his likeness splashed over the covers of sheet music. There were pictures of him in the windows of every music shop of note. Confectioners' shops had their windows filled with hundreds of sugary models of the dog about whom all Madrid was talking. A positive Pacomania seized the capital and every day the newspapers featured the latest bit of Paco news, recounting the latest anecdotes and peregrinations of the dog. A newspaper called El Perro Paco professed to give the opinions of the popular pooch on every subject, especially politics, thus making him the mouthpiece of all manner of squibs against the government.

In addition, Paco was an honored guest in the carriages of the two legendary bullfighters of the time, *Frascuelo* and *Lagartijo*. The morning after the corrida, the papers would announce Paco's presence at the arena, just as they might the king's. Paco was known to sit outside *Frascuelo's* house on the Calle del Arenal 22 (a plaque now shows where the torero lived) on the day of the bullfight to accompany him on his way to the Plaza de Toros, in those days located just beyond the Puerta de Alcalá.

Paco might have continued his carefree, libertine perambulations to ripe old dogdom had he not been the unfortunate victim of a novillero, a tyro bullfighter. One day in May 1882, a second-rate bullfight was held in the Plaza de Toros which Paco had condescended to attend. The young bullfighter was making a mess of his bull. The spectators were indignant and Paco finally jumped into the arena and ran up to bark at close range at the matador. The novillero, furious at the uncooperative bull and especially at the nagging dog, in a fit of pique, directed his sword at Paco and ran him through with one thrust.

The spectators were aghast. Incensed that their illustrious pet had been injured, they would have lynched the bungler right then and there, if he hadn't been escorted out by the police and saved from the angry Madrileños' wrath.

Paco was taken up by the owner of a tavern on the Calle de Alcalá, but despite the best medical treatment he died a few days later. His death occasioned a veritable day of mourning in Madrid. Women cried. Newspapers commented upon the tragedy at great length in sentimental phrases, and the subject of Paco's death even filtered into the chambers of the Parliament, the Atheneum, the learned academies and the Royal Palace. But it was perhaps at the Café Fornos where he was mourned more greatly than anywhere else.

Some sources claim that Paco was then taken to a taxidermist to be preserved and affectionately displayed in a small taurine museum which existed in those days on the Calle de Alcalá. When the museum shut down in 1889, Paco was buried in an unmarked grave somewhere in the Retiro park.

On the site of where the Café Fornos was located, you can still visit a café, although it is somewhat different... It is a Starbucks. Perhaps among the crowds drinking caramel macchiato or a banana mocca frappuccino, you may feel a strange presence brushing past your leg. Don't be alarmed, it may just be the spirit of Paco searching for a scrap of food, even if it's only a piece of vanilla chocolate muffin.

Casa Labra and the Socialist conspiracy

There are precious few bars and establishments left in Madrid that date back to the 19th century and that have remained more or less as they were. A few have taken on the names of former famous establishments, such as the Fontana de Oro, now an Irish pub, near Sol, on the Calle de la Victoria 2.

However, one old tavern does still ply its trade. It is the

Casa Labra. Tavern next to the Puerta del Sol where the Spanish Socialist Party was first clandestinely founded. The arrow on the left of the photo points to the plaque commemo-rating the occasion. *Author's photo.*

Casa Labra, on the Calle de Tetuán 12, which was founded in 1860. It was in this building on May 2, 1879 that a group of men met clandestinely for lunch on the second floor to set in motion what was then considered to be a political conspiracy, at a time when capitalist exploitation of the working masses had triggered increasingly militant reactions. The meeting was the result of earlier conversations held in local cafés, such as the Café Brillante and the Café Lisboa on the Puerta del Sol, both now defunct, in which spokesmen for the working classes had urged setting up an organization to defend workers' rights.

Gathered in the upstairs room of the house were 16 printshop workers, four doctors, a scientist, two jewelers, a shoemaker and a marblecutter. After speeches were made underlining the social injustices of the time, a radical program of change for the working classes was proposed. This included the right to strike, political freedom, shortening of working hours, banning children under the age of nine from working, setting up free schools and other improvements in the lot of the laboring masses. Pablo Iglesias, aged 28, president of the typesetters association, who was in touch with Paul Lafargue, Karl Marx's son-in-law, was elected to be the first president of what would henceforth be known as the Spanish Socialist Workers Party (PSOE). Iglesias remained president of the new

A GRAB BAG OF ANIMAL SPECIMENS

As you jostle past the shopping crowds and bustling stores near the calle de Preciados, you can easily miss a local curiosity on the Calle de Maestro Victoria 8. It is a pet shop which doubles as an aquarium and terrarium. Called the Aquarium de Madrid it was first opened in 1958 by Manuel Serrano Sánchez and is still run by the founder's son Dionisio.

Below the pet shop, which sells the usual assortment of animals, you can for a couple of Euros visit two downstairs fioors displaying a small collection of animals. Scattered about, some built into the walls, are several dozen tanks containing such curiosities as black piranhas, a small shark, scorpions, a python, lizards, boas, a chameleon and chipmunks. One of the most spectacular specimens is a huge meter-long alligator-snapping-turtle, indigenous to North America, often referred to as a "dinosaur turtle" due to its prehistoriclike appearance (top photo).

At one point the shop owned two crocodiles, one from the Nile and the other a black one from Cameroon, who did not see eye to eye and attacked each other in the shop. The result was the Cameroon specimen's entire snout being bitten off. When the Nile crocodile became too large, it was donated to the Madrid zoo, but the snoutless one is still on display (bottom photo).

Though Crocodile Dundee never visited the Aquarium, according to the present owner on one occasion Salvador Dalí used a live turtle's shell to paint a design on, and this was then displayed in the shop for two days, drawing large crowds. As had been stipulated by the artist, the turtle was later set free in the sea.

party until his death in 1925. The party that he secretly founded after the meeting, and which became legal in 1881, is the one currently in power in Spain at the writing of this book (April 2011).

In its day, Casa Labra was probably just one of hundreds of nondescript *botillerías* (grog shops). However today, as one of the few survivors, and thanks to it being just off the Puerta del Sol, it is a popular haunt to "wet one's whistle" and have a *tapa*. The specialty here is pieces of fried *bacalao* (codfish) known as *soldaditos de Pavía*, so named because their color is reminiscent of a uniform that was worn by the Spanish army division that won the Battle of Pavía in 1525.

You order drinks at the regular counter, but food must be ordered and paid for separately at a smaller section on the right side of the bar. Casa Labra's decoration is still the original, the clock on the wall, the wooden counter, the painted ceiling and the sayings on the walls, such as that to the left of the entrance which reads "*El que bien bebe; hace lo que debe*". (He who drinks well; does what he should.) Although Labra's bar tends to be overcrowded throughout the day, it is nonetheless worth a visit. The small restaurant on the side, with a separate entrance, serves the standard dishes at somewhat inflated prices. A plaque on the outside of the building reminds us that this is where the Spanish Socialist Party was founded.

The Spanish Tooth Fairy: El Ratoncito Pérez

Spaniards have their own version of the Tooth Fairy, only in this case rather than a fairy it's a friendly mouse by the name of Pérez, commonly known as El Ratoncito Pérez. When a child's tooth falls out he or she is told to place it under the pillow, and by the next morning the mouse will have taken the tooth and, in appreciation, in return leave a coin. Every Spanish moppet knows all about that.

Portrait of Alfonso XIII and his mother. When the future king lost one of his teeth, Queen María Cristina, asked Father Luis Coloma to write a story. This resulted in the literary creation of the Ratoncito Pérez. *Author's archive.*

What neither the kids nor even most of their parents know is that the beloved fictional mouse was described as living at a specific place: the basement of a confectioner's shop called "Carlos Prast".

Imagine our surprise when one day, while walking near the Puerta del Sol, with the hubbub of noisy traffic all around us and crowds of people passing by, we caught sight of an official plaque at Calle del Arenal 8 marking the exact spot where the little mouse Pérez actually was supposed to have lived and the place, now an arcade, where the confectioner's shop used to be. We couldn't resist entering to see if there were any remaining traces of the shop or the mouse. Lo and behold, we did actually find a mouse! No, it wasn't a street rodent. It was a metal figure of the Ratoncito Pérez wearing a straw hat and glasses perched on the small ledge of a lamppost inside the arcade. Along with the statuette there was a plaque commemorating the fictional character and the author who created him.

The story of how Spain's Tooth Fairy came into being dates back to the decade after the death of King Alfonso XII in 1886. At that time his widow, María Cristina, ruled as Queen Regent in lieu of her son, the future King Alfonso XIII, who wouldn't be crowned until aged 16, in 1902.

During his infancy, the future king suffered from delicate health and was much pampered and fussed over by the queen. When Alfonso was eight, one of his milk teeth fell out which greatly upset the child who was easily frightened and was even wary of having his hair cut. In order to put a fanciful spin to the boy's "tragedy", María Cristina asked a well-known novelist, Father Luis Coloma, to write a short story about the fallen out tooth.

Coloma, a Jesuit priest from Jerez de la Frontera (Cádiz), was not only a distinguished writer and the author of such Spanish classics as *Pequeñeces* and *Jeromín* but also a teacher. Among his pupils was the philosopher José Ortega y Gasset, best-known to Anglo readers for *The Revolt of the Masses*.

The Jesuit priest thus dutifully sat down and penned the story that would engender a new character in Spanish folklore and literature: El Ratóncito Pérez. In the tale, the main character, a boy called King Buby I (the nickname that the queen affectionately called Alfonso) loses a tooth. Before going to sleep, the boy places his tooth and a letter he has written to the mouse under his pillow. That night the mouse pays him a visit and Buby makes a new friend.

Pérez is described as wearing a straw hat, golden spectacles, linen shoes and sports a red bag on his back. Buby asks the mouse if he can join him on his errand to pick up his next tooth. The mouse agrees and sticks the tip of his tail into the boy's nostril, causing Buby to sneeze. Upon sneezing, the boy magically turns into a mouse himself and the two of them scuttle along to Pérez's house where he must pick up a gift for another boy who has also lost a tooth. They then proceed to Calle del Arenal 8 and enter the aforementioned "Carlos Prast" shop. There, behind a huge mound of Swiss cheese, is where Pérez has made his home. His house consists of a large empty Huntley biscuits box, a British brand that little Alfonso was particularly fond of. The mouse then introduces Buby to his family, and, while his wife knits beside a fire made of grape stems, they have a nice cup of tea and listen to a harp duo played by the mouse's two daughters.

Former Prast confectioner's shop. It was in this shop, behind a huge mound of Swiss cheese, that the mouse Pérez and his family supposedly lived. The store has long since been closed, but the building still remains. *Author's archive.*

Homage to the Ratón Pérez. In the arcade on Calle del Arenal 8, the memory of the Ratoncito Pérez lives on. Several posters and even a small statue have been placed there illustrating the history of the character. *Author's photo.*

Soon thereafter Buby and Pérez continue their mission to visit the other child who has lost a tooth. Off they go, scurrying through the streets until they reach the Calle de Jacometrezo (near Plaza del Callao), a somewhat bedraggled part of town in those days. There they visit a small boy, Gilito, who is sleeping on a straw bed, tended by his mother. The family is so poor they lack bread to eat and even a proper blanket to cover themselves with during the cold night. Buby is so shocked by what he sees that although the mouse places a golden coin under the child's pillow to help them in their poverty, the memory of what he has seen remains indelible. Once home, Buby practically forgets about the gift that Pérez has given him for his tooth — a medal with the Golden Fleece on it – and, on the verge of tears, asks his mother why such injustice exists in the world. She explains: "You are the older brother, for you will be king... and God has given you everything so that you can care, as best as possible, for your smaller brothers so that they may never lack anything."

Therewith ends the 13-page short story, in which Coloma not only creates the character of Ratoncito Pérez, but also teaches the future king a moral lesson.

In the small arcade in the Calle del Arenal, where the little metal statue of Pérez stands, you will also find several plaques commemorating the mouse as well as posters giving biographical details on the author, facts about the king and illustrations from books of the fictional rodent.

One flight up the staircase at the rear of the arcade will take you to the Casa-Museo del Ratón Pérez, a small shop that sells items relating to the mouse and a room featuring a dolls' house arranged like the home of the mouse, a mail box where children can post their fallen teeth to Mr. Pérez, copies of the book, Huntley biscuit boxes and the like. Admission to the latter room costs one Euro.

Lhardy: A gastronomical time-capsule

L'Hardi, Lardy, Lardi...? Since it was founded in 1839, no one ever seems to get the spelling of one of Madrid's oldest restaurants correct. It matters not, for in its over 160 years of existence on the Carrera de San Jerónimo 8, Lhardy has played host to just about every important personality in the capital, first as a French pastry shop and then as one of the most elegant and exclusive restaurants in the city. Its venerable downstairs shop, oozing old-world charm, is still a popular place to buy pastries, but even more so to serve yourself a cup of hot consommé in the winter months. To do so has been a local tradition in Lhardy since the close of the 19th century, and is intended to restore your spirits, in the original sense of the French *restaurer* from which the word "restaurant" is derived. You sip the nourishing broth standing up near the ornate old dispenser, which gives you plenty of time to observe the décor and the people coming in to buy pastries. Some head to a small round glass cabinet, where they open little compartments and help themselves to the different hors d'oeuvres. Best in our opinion are the *croquetas* (fritters). The large mirror hanging over a console at the far end of the room has reflected generation after generation of everyone who has ever been anyone in Madrid.

Lhardy restaurant and delicatessen. One of the few shops that still maintains practically the same décor as when it opened in the 19th century. *Author's photo.*

Interior of Lhardy. In the back, beside the mirror, is the silver dispenser that has been serving hot consommé for many generations. *Author's photo.*

At the entrance, to the right of the shop, going up a flight of stairs from the street, you'll come to several quaint dining rooms in which celebrities ranging from Alexandre Dumas to King Alfonso XII have feasted. The most famous of these rooms is the Salón Japonés (Japanese Room). Built during the craze for all things Oriental at the end of the 19th century, around the time when Gilbert & Sullivan's *Mikado* opened in London, the Salón Japonés remains a favorite venue for celebrities and the haute monde.

In 1880, the entire storefront of Lhardy was redone. Rather than giving it a "modern" look, the decorator Rafael Guerrero opted for maintaining the more homely look of the past by adding wooden mahogany panels brought all the way from Cuba.

The restaurant's founder, a Frenchman of Swiss origin, Émile Huguenin, learned pastry-making in Besançon and then went to work in Paris as a cook. Thereafter he found a job in Bordeaux, where he met many Spanish political exiles. Supposedly it was the French writer Prosper Mérimée (author of *Carmen* and a great Hispanophile) who suggested to Huguenin to try his luck in Madrid and introduce the delicacies of French pastry to Spanish palates, where such Gallic refinements were unknown. He took the suggestion to heart and called his pastry shop, later also a restaurant, Lhardy, probably in imitation of a prestigious Parisian restaurant on the Boulevard des Italiens called the Café Hardy. When Huguenin died in 1887, his son Agustín took on the name Lhardy as his own family name. He ran the establishment until 1918, when it passed to his son-in-law, Adolfo Temes; it is now managed by a direct descendent of his, Agustin Temes Lhardy.

Of the many anecdotes concerning Lhardy, many revolving around the innumerable banquets held by locally-

YE OLDE PASTRY SHOPPE

Hidden on the Calle del Pozo 8, in a small side street off the Calle de la Victoria, you'll see Madrid's oldest pastry shop, called the Antigua Pastelería del Pozo.

Originally, when it was founded in 1830, it was known simply as the Horno de la Calle del Pozo. Its wooden-paneled exterior reflects the flavor of the decorations inside. Its speciality are pastries made of *hojaldre* (flaky puff pastry) which have been popular with its clients for over 170 years.

famous writers, politicians, financiers, bullfighters and sundry celebrities, there is one that has a charm to it reminiscent of an O. Henry story:

The year is 1933, and the Yuletide season is in full swing, when a minor swindler and con artist by the name of Antonio Bernardini, who is doing "time" in Madrid's Modelo Prison, comes up with a scheme worthy of his counterfeiting talents. He takes a sheet of paper and writes a letter to Lhardy's restaurant. In the letter he requests that two sumptuous five-course meals be sent to the prisoner Bernardini, number 873, fifth gallery of the Modelo Prison, on Christmas Eve. "Don't send any wines, since these are prohibited in the prison," he adds in the last paragraph, "but do include several of your best Havana cigars." He then forges the signature of the famous banker Juan March at the bottom of the letter.

Lhardy's, not suspecting a forgery, and eager to serve their imagined wealthy patron, dispatches a Lucullian meal to the prison on Christmas Eve which includes a sole meunière, a roast veal, chicken à la king, delicious Yuletide pastries, assorted nuts and a few of their special, expensive Havana cigars.

The meal was devoured with great jubilation by Bernardini and his cellmate, probably the best meals they ever had in their delinquent lives.

A few days later, Juan March was flabbergasted to receive a huge bill for the meals he had supposedly ordered for the jailbird. Indignant, he refused payment. The authorities soon tracked down the culprit, who was thereupon thrown into solitary confinement for a long spell. But what a meal he had devoured! What a cigar he had smoked! How he had savored the scrumptious dishes, otherwise reserved only to rich swells!

Pasaje de Matheu: vestiges of "Little Paris"

Hidden away just behind the Puerta del Sol, squeezed between the Calle de Espoz y Mina and the Calle de la Victoria, you'll come to a small, one-block passageway called the Pasaje de Matheu, a good bet if you're looking for atmospheric outdoor restaurants serving paella, sangría and other Spanish staples beloved of locals and tourists alike. The Pasaje until recently was reminiscent of the Spain of several decades ago, when the smell of frying oil and the acrid odor of cheap wine were the hallmarks of budget restaurants around the country. But in the past few years the Pasaje has been spruced up and made more attractive.

When the weather gets hot, the restaurant owners span awnings over the passageway, and after a heavy mid-day meal and a bottle of inexpensive red wine or a pitcher of sangría, diners can shuffle off to their nearby hotels for the time-honored siesta until the sun stands lower on the horizon and the temperatures start to drop.

The Pasaje de Matheu was originally the site of the Convent of Nuestra Señora de la Victoria. When this building was torn down, the plot was purchased by one Manuel Matheu in 1843. Those were the years in the 19th century when arcades were the rage all over Europe. Madrid never had the likes of London's Burlington Arcade or the elegant galleries of Paris,

Pasaje de Matheu. It is here where for the first time, in the 1850's, two cafés began to put tables outside their locales, hoping to attract the public by imitating the fashionable galleries in Paris. *Author's photo.*

but several small ones did make their appearance in the Spanish capital, most of them now gone or reduced to little better than dark alleyways.

The Matheu was originally a covered arcade with impressive arched entrances that had sumptuous statues, allegories of Commerce and Elegance. It was covered by an metal and glass roof and housed a three-story department store called the Bazar de la Villa y Corte, long since torn down. Interestingly, the word galería, like the French galleries, still has connotations of a large department store, such as the Parisian Galleries Lafayette and the defunct Spanish Galerías Preciados, formerly the prime competitor to the now ubiquitous El Corte Inglés.

In the 1870's, the Pasaje de Matheu became the site of the first two Madrid cafés which placed tables outdoors. Not surprisingly, their competitive owners were two Frenchmen, but they happened to be of radically opposing political views. One had escaped from Paris during the suppression of the Commune, which radicals had set up to govern France follow-

Street plaques on Pasaje de Matheu. *Author's photo.*

ing its defeat in the Franco-Prussian War (1870-1871) and had sought refuge in Madrid. He opened a café-restaurant in the Pasaje de Matheu and called his establishment the Café de France. Across the way, another Frenchman, of a monarchist, conservative stripe, also opened a café-restaurant which he called the Café de Paris. Each tended to attract expatriate Frenchmen in accordance

A ROMAN SIESTA IN MADRID

Curiously, the origin of the word siesta, thought of as being so typically Spanish, actually harks back to ancient Roman times; it refers to the "sixth hour" or *sexta hora*. This, in the Roman daily timetable of 12 daytime and 12 nighttime hours, corresponded roughly to our lunchtime, (11:15 a.m. – 12:00 in winter, and 10:44 a.m. – 12:00 in summer). The ninth hour of the day, *nona*, from which our "noon" was derived, is actually a misnomer since it originally came after noon, anywhere from 1:29 to 3:46 p.m.

In the sixth century, Saint Benedict (photo on left), strongly feeling that only when the day was properly ordered would the monks in his monastery be able to perform the tasks required to serve God, he even instructed them to build clocks to count the hours in order to guide them in their duties. Benedict adapted the Roman timetable and set up a rule whereby at certain hours the monks would be required to work, to pray or to stop for meals and rest. All these were part of the daily routine. Among the time divisions, the *sexta* corresponded to midday and was the hour in Benedictine monasteries set aside for rest, many times including a small snooze, in other words for a siesta.

with their political sympathies. Both placed tables and chairs on the sidewalk in Parisian style, a practice which heretofore had been frowned upon by Madrileños. It is not recorded that the rivalry between the two ever degenerated into fisticuffs, but the two opposing café owners did manage to make the short street into a "little Paris" almost a century before the fashion for outdoor cafés was finally introduced to the city.

Though all traces of its "French" past are now gone, the Pasaje de Matheu is filled with outdoor tables where you can still dig into a moderately-priced meal or *tapas* indoors or *al fresco*.

Area 2: Santa Ana

1. **Café Central** (Plaza del Angel 10). Jazz hangout.
2. **Former Hotel Victoria** (Plaza de Santa Ana 14). Former bullfighters' hotel.
3. **Villa Rosa night club** (Plaza de Santa Ana 15).
4. **Plaza de Santa Ana**
5. **Viña P restaurant** (Plaza de Santa Ana 3). Bullfighting ambiance.
6. **Cervecería Alemana** (Plaza de Santa Ana 6). Hemingway hangout.
7. **Las Cuevas de Sésamo** (Príncipe 7). Cave-like underground bar.
8. **Convento de San Ildefonso de las Trinitarias** (Lope de Vega 18). Cervantes' burial place.
9. **Plaque to Cervantes's house** (Cervantes 2).
10. **Futbolín.** Bar La Galería (Prado 13).
11. **Futbolín.** Bar has no name (Ventura de la Vega 21).
12. **Plaque to first film screening in Madrid** (San Jerónimo 34).
13. **Statue of Cervantes** (Plaza de las Cortes). Hans Christian Andersen's oasis.
14. **Congreso de Diputados** (San Jerónimo). Bronze lions.
15. **Carillon** (Plaza de las Cortes 8). Dancing Goyesca figures.
16. **Palace Hotel** (Plaza de las Cortes 7).
17. **Plaque to Paula Martí** (Marqués de Cubas 15). Stenographer.
18. **Plaza de la Lealtad.** Monument to the Unkown Soldier.
19. **Taberna del Avapiés** (Lavapiés 5 corner with Cabeza). Inquisition's Ecclesiastical Prison.
20. **Calle de la Cabeza.** Street with a story.
21. **Plaque to Juan de la Costas' print shop** (Atocha 87). Don Quixote 1st edition.
22. **Plaque to Juan de la Costa's print shop** (San Eugenio 7). *Don Quixote* 2nd part.
23. **Futbolín.** La Gramola (Corner of Manuel Fernández y González and Echegaray).

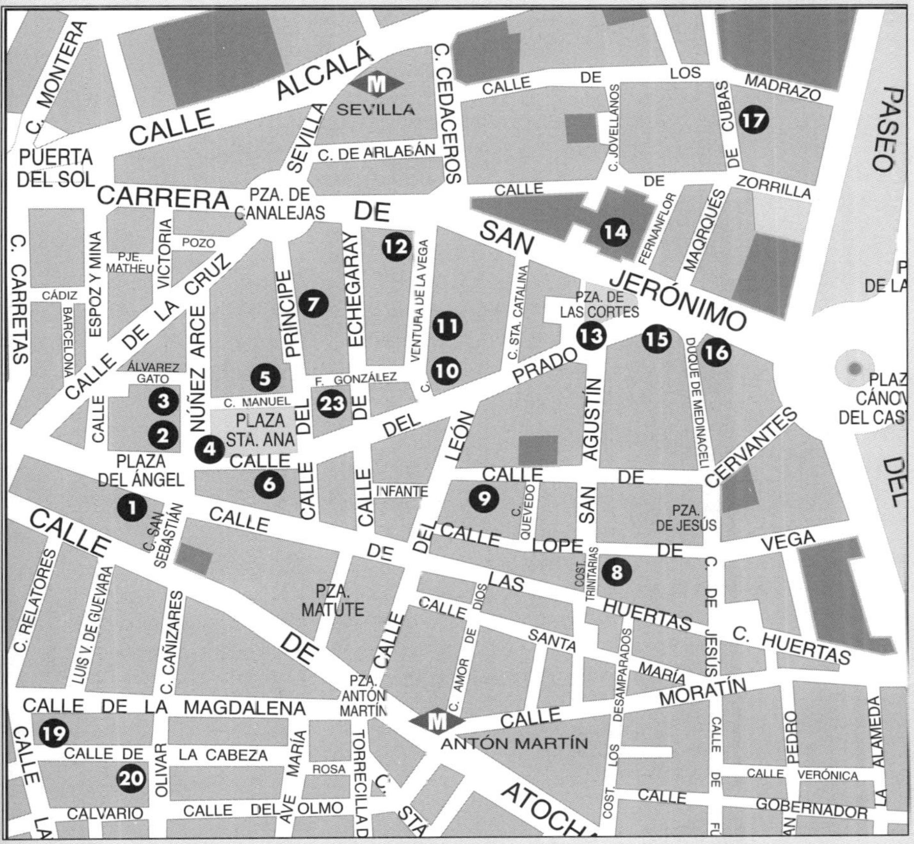
C. MONTERA
PUERTA DEL SOL
CALLE ALCALÁ
SEVILLA
C. SEVILLA
C. CEDACEROS
C. DE ARLABÁN
CARRERA DE SAN JERÓNIMO
PZA. DE CANALEJAS
CALLE DE LOS MADRAZO
C. JOVELLANOS
CALLE DE ZORRILLA
DE CUBAS
FERNANFLOR
MARQUÉS
PASEO
C. CARRETAS
ESPOZ Y MINA
PJE. MATHEU
VICTORIA
POZO
CÁDIZ
BARCELONA
CALLE DE LA CRUZ
ÁLVAREZ GATO
NÚÑEZ ARCE
PRÍNCIPE
ECHEGARAY
VENTURA DE LA VEGA
C. STA. CATALINA
PZA. DE LAS CORTES
PRADO
DUQUE DE MEDINACELI
PLAZA CÁNOVAS DEL CASTILLO
C. MANUEL F. GONZÁLEZ
PLAZA STA. ANA
CALLE DEL PRADO
CALLE DEL LEÓN
AGUSTÍN
PLAZA DEL ÁNGEL
CALLE
CALLE INFANTE
CALLE DE CERVANTES
C. QUEVEDO
SAN
PZA. DE JESÚS
CALLE LOPE DE VEGA
C. SAN SEBASTIÁN
CALLE DE ATOCHA
C. RELATORES
LUIS V. DE GUEVARA
C. CAÑIZARES
PZA. MATUTE
CALLE DE LAS HUERTAS
COST. TRINITARIAS
DIOS
C. AMOR DE
SANTA MARÍA
DESAMPARADOS
C. DE JESÚS
C. HUERTAS
MORATÍN
CALLE DE LA MAGDALENA
PZA. ANTÓN MARTÍN
ANTÓN MARTÍN
CALLE DE LA CABEZA
OLIVAR
MARÍA
ROSA
TORRECILLA
CALVARIO
CALLE DEL OLMO
AVE
COST. LOS
CALLE
PEDRO
ALAMEDA
CALLE VERÓNICA
GOBERNADOR
DEL
1 2 3 4 5 6 7 8 9 10 11 12 13 14 15 16 17 19 20 23

Area 2 - SANTA ANA

Santa Ana: the liveliest little square

Over the past half century, the small Plaza de Santa Ana has become one of the most animated squares in town. The many bars and taverns and outdoor cafés found on it are usually brimming over with locals and tourists alike, turning it into something akin to what the Puerta del Sol used to be in the old days.

However the Plaza de Santa Ana was already an important hub in the early 19th century, for it was the site of the Teatro del Príncipe, one of the leading theatres of the city, which is now known as the Teatro Español. To the right of the theatre stood one of the most famous cafés of the time, the Café del Príncipe, better known by its nickname of El Parnasillo (Little Parnassus), a favorite hang-out for poets, writers, actors and revolutionaries.

The Plaza de Santa Ana, like many squares in the city, was non-existent in 1800. Its creation and that of other plazas was largely due to the destruction of old convents and monasteries. This task was first undertaken by Napoleon's liberal-minded brother, Joseph, who ruled Spain for five years from 1808-1812, and who created, among other squares, the Plaza de Santa Ana, the Plaza del Rey, the Plaza de la Cebada, the Plaza de Isabel II and the Plaza de Oriente. In fact, Joseph had so many religious institutions torn down in Madrid in order to make public squares that he came to be nicknamed *El rey plazuelas* (The King of the Small Squares). Further breathing space in the cluttered narrow streets of old Madrid was provided thanks to a radical

The Plaza de Santa Ana. A few empty tables linger on the Plaza de Santa Ana as the last days of autumn descend on the city. *Author's photo.*

financier and Prime Minister of a Masonic/Jewish stripe, Juan Álvarez Mendizábal, who in 1835 seized Church property for the cash-strapped government, auctioned it off and thus raised badly-needed money for the crown.

Within six months 17 convents and monasteries in the center of the city were turned into rubble. Once again, some of the resultant space became squares in present-day downtown Madrid, the largest of which is the Plaza de Tirso de Molina.

The Plaza de Santa Ana only a few decades ago was a homely, local sort of square, with tamped earth ground where children played in the sand and strips of greenery welcomed strollers. More recently it was a place where artisans set up stands to sell their handicrafts. Since then it has been overhauled several times, first to build an underground public parking lot, then to "modernize" it. The result has been the present rather ugly, impersonal asphalt quadrangle. The old comfortable wooden benches have been replaced by what appear to be cinderblocks, and instead of the greenery we now have cement. Fortunately, the surrounding hubbub and lively outdoor bars help to make you forget the outrages perpetrated by City Hall. Happily, at least the stately monument to the Golden Age writer, Calderón de la Barca, placed there in 1880, still survives on its original site. And a new one, rather less imposing, of Federico García Lorca, was added in 1998 for the centenary of the poet's birth.

Besides the Teatro Español, and the door-to-door bars on the Plaza de Santa Ana, the old Cervecería Alemana (one of Hemingway's favorite hang-outs) and the striking Villa Rosa night club with its hand-painted tiles on its façade, the square was until recently home to the Hotel Victoria, built between 1917 and 1923, partly to house a department store called Simeón and partly as a hotel. For decades after, the fairly modest hostelry was a favorite with budget-minded tourists and became a hangout for bullfighters and their managers. It was where the legendary bullfighter *Manolete* used to stay when he was fighting in Madrid. But the hotel was sold and after extensive alterations, re-opened in 2006 as the Hotel Me Madrid Reina Victoria.

Carmen, bulls and the former Hotel Victoria

It was on the site of the aforementioned Hotel Victoria that the Counts of Montijo y Teba built a huge mansion in 1810 which was famed throughout much of the 19th century due to the sumptuous balls and parties held there. Two of the countess' pretty daughters, Francisca (better known as "Paca") and Eugenia, were the center of attention. All the leading luminaries of the time as well as the diplomatic corps and illustrious foreign visitors attended these gala fiestas, which became the high points of the Madrid social calendar.

One of those joining the fun was the French writer Prosper Mérimée who visited Madrid on numerous occasions and became very chummy with the Countess of Teba, whose mother was Scots. This well-educated and charming lady fascinated her French visitor with countless tales of local life in Spain, splashed with plenty of romantic color. The result of what Mérimée heard eventually was turned to good use many years later when he penned what may be the best-known "Spanish" story of the time, *Carmen*, later set to music by Georges Bizet in the opera of the same name.

One of the daughters, the pretty Eugenia de Montijo, later married a distinguished Frenchman, who subsequently took on the title of Napoleon III. In France she is better known as the Empress Eugénie. Her elder sister, Paca, didn't do badly either, for she married the Duke of Alba.

The Montijo palace, in sharp decline in the late 19th century when it became a commercial building, finally was torn down after the First World War. However, a huge neighboring building on the adjacent Plaza del Angel, known as the Teba Palace, also constructed by them, is still standing. It occupies the whole block between the Plaza del Angel and the Calle de Atocha, and predates the former Montijo mansion. It, too, has a memorable history. In the late 18th century it was the site of a famous café and *fonda* (hostelry) remembered today thanks to a play by Fernández de Moratín, *La Comedia Nueva o el Café*, (The New Comedy or The Café) and was a favorite gathering place for *literati* and liberals.

In the autumn of 2010 the former Teba Palace was converted into a modern four-star hotel. A few doors down on Plaza del Angel 10 you'll come to one of the city's best places to hear live jazz, the Café Central.

Those seeking a bullfight atmosphere can head to a bar and restaurant, the Viña P. on the north side of the Plaza de Santa Ana 3, founded by the father of the present owner, a great bullfight *aficionado*. For decades, this bar has been a favorite hangout for bullfighters and flamenco singers, and often enough, after a successful *corrida*, a group of the matador's entourage will gather here for typical drinks and dinner. Among the notables have been the guitarist Paco de Lucía, the flamenco fusion group Ketama, and one of the best contemporary bullfighters, *El Juli*.

A half block away, on the Calle del Príncipe 7, a curious hangout you might want to look in on is the Cuevas de Sésamo (The Sesame Caves). This cellarlike haunt, with sayings painted on the walls, where the typical drink is *sangría*, has been going strong since it opened in the 1960's.

Royal *tapas* with sand

To talk about Madrid and not mention "*tapas*" would be a sacrilege. You will find that in almost any bar, *tasca, mesón* or tavern, when ordering an alcoholic drink, the bartender will, at no extra charge, place an appetizer on a small plate next to the drink. These *tapas* range from olives to potato chips, to a wedge of *tortilla española*, (potato omelet), to *jamón serrano* (cured ham), *chorizo* (cured sausage), *salchichón* (salami), cheese, potato salad, anchovies, sardines or even a small dish of *paella*.

Locals will sometimes skip dinner altogether and instead make the rounds of various bars consuming a variety of *tapas* and *raciones*. This is called *ir de tapas* or *tapear* (*tapa*-hopping), which involves the eating of the free side dishes as well as dipping into *raciones* (a full serving of a dish), which you *do* have to pay for. A word of caution: although *"ir de tapas"* and ordering *raciones* is great fun, making the rounds of the bars can run up quite a tab and wind up costing more than a sit-down dinner, especially in the tourist areas such as the Plaza Mayor or the Plaza de Santa Ana.

Alfonso X "the Wise". This Spanish king created the *tapa* when he made it mandatory to serve a small piece of food at no extra cost whenever any alcoholic beverage was ordered. No wonder he was called "the wise"! *Author's photo.*

Every Madrileño and foreigner has his or her own favorite *tapa* bars around the city and just about any travel guide will provide a list of the author's favorites. There are even special *tapa* guides published, just as there are guides for pubs in London, or bistros in Paris.

You'll find that most Spaniards love *tapas*, but few seem to be aware where the custom of serving them came from or why the tidbits are called *tapas*. As in so many derivations, fact is intertwined with legend. But the following is the most widely-accepted story:

In the 13th century, during the reign of Alfonso X, known as "The Wise" — and you'll shortly see why — the king came down with an illness. His doctor advised him to drink sips of wine accompanied by small bits of food between meals. The treatment went well and the king soon recovered. Alfonso realized that the advice was excellent and that he shouldn't be the only one to heed the doctor's recommendation. So he passed a law that required all taverns in Castile to serve gratis a small portion of food with the wine that they sold. It was a most sensible law, especially considering that at the time Spain was agricultural, and it was normal for most workers to take a mid-day break from work in the fields to have a drink. Being poor, they tended to abstain from food and only order a beverage. Hence they would often return to the fields under the influence of the wine. The new law attempted to allay this problem, since having a small snack would prevent them from drinking on an empty stomach. Which is why from that time on to the present, food is always served when alcoholic beverages are dispensed.

Teetotalers ordering a soft drink will find that no *tapa* will be forthcoming; but should they take heart and decide to switch to wine or beer, the bartender will promptly place a tidbit on the counter in front of them. Without even knowing it, he is still being faithful to the spirit of the former law promulgated by the king over 700 years ago!

As for the term *tapa*, it apparently dates back to a trip taken by King Alfonso XIII in the early 20th century. The king was travelling to Cádiz with his entourage and stopped to rest and have a drink at a beach tavern called El Ventorillo del Chato (which still exists today.) Alfonso ordered a glass of sherry, but just as he was about to take a sip, a strong gust of wind swept in a cloud of sand from the beach. The waiter, quick to react, placed a slice of cured ham over the king's glass. Alfonso, not understanding, asked the waiter what he was doing. The waiter explained that the ham was a "*tapa*", which literally means "cover", so that the wine would not be affected by the sand. The king was amused by the idea, ate the ham and finished off the wine, soon ordering another sherry and asking that he again wanted it with a *tapa*, just like the first. Soon the king's entourage also ordered glasses of wine accompanied by those curious "*tapas*". And so the term was coined.

We confess that we've always wondered what that first slice of ham with sand on it tasted like.

Futbolín: From war therapy to national pastime

Although nowadays they are increasingly rare, you can still find some bars in Madrid featuring games called *futbolines* (Fuzball or Foosball in the U.S.) This is a tabletop game simulating a soccer match. On the elongated boxlike table are

Futbolín. The owner of the bar "La Galería" (left) defends his position at the table defeating new rivals in a typical *futbolín* game. *Author's photo.*

eight metal rods that skewer little wooden figures of soccer players, whose movements are controlled by handles at one end of the rods that extend beyond the sides of the table. By turning or spinning the handles you can make the figures "kick" a miniature ball placed on the table. As in soccer, the object is to score goals by driving the ball into one of the goalholes located at either end of the table.

The figures are usually painted with the colors of the Real Madrid and the Atlético de Madrid, the rival teams in the capital. In other cities around Spain the figures will be painted to represent their own local teams. The game is usually played by four persons, two on each team, with each player handling two rows of rods; one controls the defence and goalie positions, and the other the center field and offence. At present, the cost of playing a game is one Euro, placed in a slot on the side of the table, which allows you to kick around from seven to nine balls

Alejandro Campos Ramírez. The inventor of *futbolín*, who came up with the idea for a game based on soccer in order to entertain wounded children during the Spanish Civil War. *Author's archive.*

(if none has been stolen or lost). Once you score a goal, the ball drops into a receptacle inside the table, not to emerge again until a new Euro is inserted into the slot. The game is quite easy to play and is a favorite pastime in bars around the country, and there are championships held both at national and even international levels to determine which players are best at it.

Although many have played the game, few are aware of who invented the game or that there was a specific reason for inventing it. Some claim it originated in Germany in the 1920's; others aver that variations of *futbolín* already existed in different countries at other times. However, here is how and why it was invented in Spain.

The story dates back to the Spanish Civil War (1936-1939). Alejandro Campos Ramírez, nicknamed *Finisterre* for the region in northwestern Galicia he came from, was a liberal poet who was living in Madrid in 1936. In November of that year, when he was only 17 years old, Madrid was bombed by General Franco's forces, who were encamped just outside the capital. Alejandro was caught in and almost died under the rubble of a building that had been hit. After being hospitalized in Madrid, he was transferred to an infirmary near Barcelona that cared for wounded children and the elderly. Most of the patients were on the road to recovery and often the largest problem was alleviating their boredom, especially among the youngsters.

When Campos's health improved, he was given the task of giving classes to the wounded; but the younger kids were more interested in soccer than in reading books. Even though some of the children were seriously incapacitated from wounds and would never be able to play soccer again, they continued to talk passionately about the sport.

It was at this point that Campos decided he wanted to do something for the children in the hospital. *Finisterre* was something of a handyman and had already invented a mechanical page-turner for one of the nurses who played the piano to entertain the wounded. Enlisting the help of a carpenter friend, Campos set about designing and then constructing the first *futbolín*. When completed, it was a virtual work of art, made with the finest wood. The game was an immediate success with the children who could now once again play soccer, albeit vicariously.

Finisterre patented his invention in Barcelona, but after the war was over he had to flee Spain, having been on the losing Republican side. He emigrated to Paris and then moved to Latin America. There, in Guatemala in 1952, he perfected his *futbolín* invention, using interfitting rods made of Swedish steel and a table constructed with the best mahogany wood. But just when sales of his game were increasing, he once again was forced to emigrate on account of his political ideas. He tried to sell the game in the U.S. but encountered difficulties when he found he had to cope with the Mafia, who had complete control of all arcade games. Meanwhile, his invention was being pirated in Mexico and he was unable to collect any royalties. Finally, *Finisterre* threw in the towel and gave up trying to commercialize or make money from his game. He spent the following years writing and publishing poetry, which was his true passion.

Imagine, then, his surprise when he returned to Spain in the 1960's and saw that his invention, originally created to help the wounded children in a hospital during the Civil War, had become a popular national pastime and could be found in practically any bar, restaurant, lounge or hotel in Madrid!

Sr. Alejandro Campos passed away, aged 88, in early 2007. He had been president of the León Felipe Foundation, was a member of the Royal Academy of Galicia, as well as of many other prestigious academic and cultural organizations.

Internationally, there are hundreds of *futbolín* tournaments and championships, some with huge cash prizes. There was even a film made in 1986 called *Long Shot Kids* in which two foosball enthusiasts, one played by Leif Garrett, wishing to become professional soccer players in Europe, develop a plan to raise enough money to finance their trip to Europe. Their plan is to work up the ladder through local foosball tournaments to the grand $50,000 world championships. The film is as cheesy as it sounds, but is a lot of fun.

Should you want to try your hand at the game in the Santa Ana neighborhood, head to the bar La Galería on the Calle del Prado 13, La Gramola on the corner of Calle de Manuel Fernández y González and Calle de Echegaray (the foosball table is downstairs) or a nameless bar at Ventura de la Vega 21, which has a foosball table at the back, all open only at night. Other places where you can play foosball are La Leyenda, on San Bernardino 8 and Marx Madera, a bar on Calle de la Madera 9, more famous for its Communist paraphernalia than foosball. (See Area 5 map, Pg. 207, for the latter two).

When Houses of Malice hoodwinked the king

When you walk around the old neighborhoods of Madrid, especially near the Plaza de Santa Ana or the Plaza Mayor or Calle de las Huertas or Cervantes, you'll see small tiles with blue lettering placed on the corners of streets or over doorways, which are unrelated to the official street signs. One of these tiles might read, for example, "Visita G Manzana 309" or "Visita G Piso 3."

The explanation of their meaning involves a slice of archaic local history dating back to the time when the entire city was broken up into numbered blocks. But first we must go back to the 16th century when Felipe II was king of Spain and had made Madrid the capital. Upon the court moving from the huge monastery of El Escorial to Madrid, the king

Model of Houses of Malice. In this model from the Museo de la Ciudad, you can see how Madrileños attempted to outwit the Quartering Ordinance. From the outside it appears that the house has only one floor (left) But in fact, from the back, it can be seen that there are two floors (right). *Author's photos.*

found that the city lacked adequate housing for all the thousands of civil servants, foreign ambassadors, guards, priests, caretakers, functionaries and secretaries that constituted the court. Consequently, in order to provide living space for all those in his service, he promulgated a law obliging property-owners in the new capital to set aside living quarters for the use of the crown. The law specified that anyone who owned a house with more than one floor in it had to set aside the upper stories to accommodate members of the royal entourage. This law was known as the *regalía de aposento*, or Quartering Ordinance.

To get around this bothersome imposition, many Madrileños thus started building houses of only one story. However others, in the best tradition of the Spanish picaresque, sought ways to avoid the invasive law. Thus began the existence of what were nicknamed the *casas a la malicia* (houses of malice). Which is to say, the townspeople constructed homes so it became difficult to perceive, looking from the street, exactly how many floors they contained. One of the tricks was to jumble the windows. Sometimes garrets were added and additional floors wedged between the regular ones which technically couldn't be considered as floors. Another common ploy was to build a sunken lower floor under the entrance level which could not be seen from the street. Thus, for appearance's sake, the building *looked* like it had only a ground floor, but in fact was a two-story building. Hence, the owners *seemed* to comply with the law, but in fact avoided the royal decree It is estimated that at that time there were over 1,000 such houses. A good model of one is on display in the Museum of the City of Madrid on the Calle del Príncipe de Vergara 140. If you want to see an example with jumbled windows, there is one on the Calle del Toro and another on the Calle del Conde. (See Area 3 map, Pg. 117 A.)

In the 18th century, efforts were made by the government to identify households, not so much for the purpose of billeting members of the court, but for collecting property taxes. However, the problem was that Madrid streets were still not signposted with official names or any sort of consistent or logical system of numbering houses.

Until the mid 18th century, a letter to a resident of Madrid would be addressed in the following manner:

Sr. D. Rodrigo Pérez
Street behind San José Church
Next to Hernández Brothers bakery
Capital

Admittedly, the leading streets had been referred to by their names for many years, such as Alcalá, Caballero de Gracia, Montera or Arenal, and thus there was less confusion concerning these; but many others were merely identified by a popular name given to them because of some anecdote or legend associated with them. Thus, the Calle del Reloj was so named because it had a sundial on one of the buildings. And the Calle de la Sal was called that because there were shops on it selling salt. But none of these were official names registered by the municipality.

To make matters worse, there were multiple streets with the same name. Or you might find that the same street had two different names, since names were given arbitrarily. In addition, even to this day, there are 31 official designations in the nomenclature of thoroughfares, such as *callejón, travesía, plazuela, ronda, paseo, pasadizo, corredera, cava, costanilla, glorieta, escalinata, postigo, cañada, vereda* and so on.

Hence, in 1740 the government embarked on a new

effort to enforce the Regalia inspections and tightened the screws on those who were not paying their taxes. For 11 years tax collectors struggled and stumbled through the numberless and nameless labyrinth of streets and houses attempting to collect from tax evaders. Finally in 1751 someone came up with a "brilliant" new idea, what he imagined to be an invention of the wheel for tax purposes. To allay the reigning confusion and make sense out of this impossible skein of nomenclature, it was decided that every city block would be assigned a number. Tiles were placed on the corner of each building that read *Visita G Manzana...* followed by the number of the block. *Visita G* stands for *Visita General de la Regalía de Aposento* (Quartering Ordinance) and *Manzana* means city block.

Houses of Malice on Calle del Conde. This house on the Calle del Conde is an obvious example of how windows were jumbled and placed at different heights making it impossible to know how many floors the building actually had. *Author's photo.*

The tax collectors could now identify each block and then number the doorways consecutively around its four sides. Sounds simple, but it wasn't. Problems arose when one particular house had more than one entrance. Matters were further complicated when a house in the middle of a street was torn down, which could then create two distinct blocks. Additional trouble occurred when building reforms were undertaken and old doorways walled up, new doorways opened or houses were joined together. This meant adding additional tiles to the new doorways. These would read *Visita G Piso* followed by a number. So now you might have a block number, an unnumbered old doorway and a new doorway that had a tile over it. The system turned out to be utterly confusing to all concerned. Moreover, people still identified a house by saying it was the one "next to the tailor shop" or "behind the church".

After 80 years of struggling with this maddeningly

Visita G tiles. Here's an example of how confusing the old "Visita G" system for numbering streets, blocks and doorways was. Shown is a single entrance to a building on Calle de los Latoneros 1 (near the Plaza Mayor) which corresponds to four houses or "CASAS": 1, 2, 14 and 15. How can there be four houses in one building? Where are houses 3 – 13? *Author's photo.*

inefficient system, the Marqués Viudo de Pontejos, mayor of Madrid, finally came up with a sensible new system of identification. From then on, every street would be identified with an official name and a plaque would be placed on every single corner building with the name of the street. With the help of Ramón de Mesonero Romanos, one of the most influential 19th century chroniclers of Madrid, the mayor changed and reformed over 240 streets giving them the names of important historical figures and events. He also numbered the doorways in such a way that they would begin on each street on the end closest to the Puerta del Sol; even numbers on the right and odd numbers on the left.

However, in the old part of town you can still see the former tile plaques reading *Visita G* in many of the streets; they are the vestiges of a system that must have driven many a tax collector and hundreds of visitors looking for a given house to near distraction. Look for the *Visita G* signs, for example, on the Calle Lope de Vega, Calle de Cervantes and Calle de las Huertas and on all the side streets off the Plaza Mayor. Once you start looking for the tiles, you'll notice them throughout the old part of town.

Does Don Quixote live here?

On Calle de Cervantes 2, almost on the corner of Calle del León, not only will you see two of the *Visita G* tiles mentioned earlier, but you'll also see why this particular street is named after the great Spanish writer. Because it was here that stood the house where the author of *El ingenioso hidalgo Don*

Quijote de la Mancha, more familiarly known simply as *Don Quixote*, breathed his last breath. An ornate plaque commemorates the spot. In fact, there's a curious story associated with the building.

Back in the reign of King Fernando VII (early 19th century), the original building where Cervantes lived and died was put up for public auction and bought by a businessman, Luis Franco, who, ignoring its historical significance, planned to tear it down and replace it by one that would provide higher income.

When demolition began, word leaked out to the aforementioned Mesonero Romanos. Don Ramón, as he was respectfully called, was not only an accomplished writer, but also an active defender of Madrid's traditions and legacies. In addition he was an alderman in the city government. Thus, upon hearing that the house where Cervantes had lived was being torn down, he personally sought an interview with the king to inform him of the terrible cultural outrage that was being contemplated. Fernando VII agreed with Don Ramón and allowed him to buy the house in the name of the crown and convert it into "some sort of literary establishment." But Luis Franco refused to sell, and replied as follows:

"I'll have none of that. The house is mine and only I will make the decision of what happens to it. What does this Fernando VII think? I know why he wants the house, but I'm not going to sell it. Does His Highness imagine that I'm not aware of the fact that Don Quixote de la Mancha lived here? I read his book every day and I have the pleasure of owning his house."

Mesonero Romanos. Fondly remembered by Madrileños as a chronicler of the city, Ramón de Mesonero Romanos was also a historian of local customs and a talented mannerist writer. *Museo Municipal de Madrid.*

Site of Cervantes' former house. (Left) Plaque marking where Cervantes lived out the latter part of his life and where he died. **Plaque on the Convent of the Trinitarias.** (Right) The plaque commemorates the final resting place of Miguel de Cervantes. However, the exact burial spot has been forgotten over the years. *Author's photos.*

Poor Don Ramón was left speechless and at the end was unable to prevent the demolition of the building. Several years later, after a new house had gone up, Mesonero returned to the owner asking permission to at least put up a commemorative plaque stating that Miguel de Cervantes had once lived there. Luis Franco replied, "A plaque? For Cervantes? I don't even know who that man is!"

However, in 1834 a plaque was nonetheless put up, which in English translation says:

"Here lived and died
Miguel de Cervantes Saavedra
Whose genius is admired worldwide.
Died in MDCXVI"

Shortly thereafter the name of the street was changed from the Calle de Francos to the Calle de Cervantes.

The exact resting place of the earthly remains of Cervantes is today unknown. When the writer died, he was interred in the Convent of San Ildefonso de las Trinitarias, on the Calle de Lope de Vega 18, only a stone's throw away from the Calle de Cervantes. Over the years, the location of the tomb of the writer's remains has been lost and nowadays it is only known that the bones rest somewhere within the four walls of the convent, which is still inhabited by cloistered nuns.

Hans Christian Andersen's literary oasis

A few blocks down from the Plaza de Santa Ana, proceeding along the Calle del Prado and past the Madrid Atheneum (Ateneo), you'll come to the Plaza de las Cortes or Parliament Square, famed for several quite unrelated reasons. Here stands the Congreso de Diputados, previously known as the Palacio de las Cortes Españolas, Spain's Congress building. Across the street from it is a regreattable and ugly cement square that in 2010 usurped the quanit garden with trees and flowers that used to exist. There stands a relatively modest monument, the first of several placed around the capital, in homage to Miguel de Cervantes.

Cervantes' statue. Upon discovering this statue of Cervantes, Hans Christian Andersen, who had been disappointed in the city, was suddenly "filled with joy and thanksgiving" as he was reminded of the writer's immortal works. *Author's photo.*

Ironically, the monument's presence is due to the efforts of the much-maligned Joseph Bonaparte who in 1810, during the five years he reluctantly sat on the Spanish throne in Madrid, decreed that a monument to Spain's most famous writer should be erected. However the statue was not completed and unveiled until 1833.

Hans Christian Andersen, who came to Madrid in 1862, was one of many visitors not particularly impressed by the city, other than by the Prado Museum. But Madrid's shortcomings were atoned for in his eyes when he saw the statue to Cervantes.

"The Plaza de las Cortes," he wrote, "is a very insignificant square, only an irregular extension of the street in front of the building where the legislature meet, the Palacio de los Diputados, and has nothing

Juan de la Cuesta print shop plaque. At this spot, on the Calle de San Eugenio 7, stood the former print shop where the second part of Don Quixote was first printed. *Author's photo.*

worth the observation of a stranger except a monument, which stands there – the statue of a man in an old-fashioned, military Spanish dress, with a stiff ruff, and a sword. The whole monument is wanting in grandeur; one is inclined to pass it carelessly, supposing that it has been erected in memory of some military commander who has no particular claim to our admiration. But when we heard the name, we arrested our steps and gazed at it with the deepest interest; for in that figure which we saw before us we beheld a king in the glorious intellectual world, one whose works are immortal, whose name is honored in every part of the earth where literature flourishes. While in the full vigor of manhood, he bore the chains of a slave; in battle, he offered to his fatherland, Spain, his left arm: his contemporaries left him to suffer from want; they treated him with scandalous indifference; they could neither comprehend him, nor appreciate him. Now, however, a monument stands in memory of him.

"…No one knows where his grave is: who of all his contemporaries would have inquired about it? On no tombstone is his name carved, but it is engraved in the hearts of the people. Spain is proud of it; Europe speaks with admiration and honor of Cervantes."

Lovers of the Knight of the Sorrowful Countenance can visit several other nearby sites related to the publication of the first issue of *Don Quixote*. On the Calle de Atocha 87, you'll come to a building with an ornate metal plaque marking the place where the first edition of the first part of the book was printed by Juan de la Cuesta in 1605 (the *editio princeps* came out the year before). The building now houses the Sociedad Cervantina. Across the street from the Calle de Atocha, on the Calle de San Eugenio 7, you'll see another plaque marking the spot where Juan de la Cuesta printed the second part of the Spanish classic in 1615. No other book, other than the Bible, has been translated into so many languages or been published in so many editions.

The lions nobody liked

Spain's Parliament, or Congress, was built on the site of an old convent, the Espiritu Santo, which burned down in 1823. The cornerstone of the Congress building was laid by Queen Isabel II in 1843, and its interior contains a splendidly plush semi-circular auditorium where each of the democratically-elected parties sit, argue, propose laws, inveigh against each other, scheme, disagree and do all the things that lawmakers all over the world are prone to do.

At either side of the ceremonial entrance to the building, opened only when the king visits it, you'll see two bronze lions, as harmless as those in front of the New York Public Library or those in Trafalgar Square. Though closely associated now with that august Spanish building, the presence of the two feline sentinels of law and order were an afterthought.

The need for a proper congressional chamber had been on the government's agenda for years before work on it finally began. But progress on the building proceeded far slower than expected. In fact, at the time of its inauguration, in 1850, the building was not completed yet, but parliamentarians, eager to take possession of the elegant new chamber, started holding sessions there, while the proverbial paint was still drying on the walls.

First Lions in the Palacio de las Cortes. These were the first plaster lions placed in front of the Congress building in 1853. Notice how tame they look and how they do not have a ball under their paws. *Historia de la Villa y Corte de Madrid*

The architect responsible for the new Cortes apparently had not included any decorative touch to distinguish the entrance to the building. Two ornate lampposts were placed there, perhaps with the idea of some sort of symbolic message involving "illumination" intended.

However, the lampposts were considered quite inadequate and unworthy of the noble position they occupied. So the parliamentarians sought the assistance of the sculptor Ponciano Ponzano, whose star at that time was quickly rising in Spain. Ponzano set to work on the task of finding appropriate additions to the new Congress building to give it a greater sense of majesty. Inspiring himself on an already-existing building in Zaragoza fronted by two figures of giants, he proposed instead decorating the Congress entrance with two impressive-looking, long-maned seated lions.

The proposal was accepted by the government; Ponzano sculpted two models, cast them and made two plaster molds of the lions finishing them off with a coat of bronze paint. These were placed on either side of the entrance to the building in 1851 on the extended pedestal, behind the two lampposts. Not surprisingly, within a year the not very resistant plaster lions started to show the effects of the elements, with discernible chips and scratches. Hence the parliamentarians and press clamored for the lions to be properly cast in bronze. However, Ponzano, now at the height of his fame as the most popular sculptor in Madrid and having been elected a member of the Royal Academy of Fine Arts of San Fernando, and, in addition being disgruntled about previous payments from the government, presented the politicos with a budget so high that it was considered quite unacceptable, not to say outrageous.

Lions in the Monforte Gardens. These stone lions which were to replace the first plaster ones in front of Congress wound up at the entrance of the Marquis of San Juan's gardens in Valencia, where they still remain. *El Palacio de las Cortes. I.E.M.*

Hence the contract to sculpt two new lions in stone was awarded to José Bellver, the artist who had done the spectacular statue of the Fallen Angel now standing in the Retiro Park. Bellver, after laboring for a year, presented his two stone lions to the government, but they were considered unimpressive and not worthy of being placed in front of Congress. Instead, they were sold and wound up in Valencia, in the Garden of Monforte, a property owned by the Marquis of San Juan.

What then to do with this congressional dilemma? It was at this point decided to seek the help of the Army who might be able to offer a solution

Lion at the Palacio de las Cortes. It was a long and treacherous struggle before two lions finally were placed in front of Congress. They were cast out of melted-down cannon captured in a war in Morocco. *Author's photo.*

which would fulfill the aims of patriotism together with the practical problems involved. Could Ponzano's two original plaster lions be cast in bronze in an artillery factory in Sevilla? A general was approached and obligingly said he would study the problem. Preceding Queen Isabel II on a trip to Sevilla, he met with the head of a foundry and was assured that the proposal would carefully be studied to see if the Sevilla facility was capable of handling the job of casting the lions in bronze.

Further complications, political bickering and changes in government put the project on hold for another two years. It was even suggested that the lions be cast in a foundry in Paris. At this point, the queen personally intervened exclaiming: "It would be shameful for Spain to have a work meant to adorn the Spanish Parliament cast in a foreign country!" She then unequivocally gave the order for the lions to be cast in Sevilla, no matter what the cost.

On an earlier occasion, a number of bronze cannon captured during a war with Morocco (1859-1860) at the Battle of Wad-Rass, along with the key to one of the gates of the city of Tetuán, had been shipped by the commanding general,

Lion replicas in Sevilla. The exact replicas of the lions found in front of Congress can be found in the vestibule in Sevilla's Capitanía General. They originally were in the Fábrica de Artillería, but in November 2009, they were restored and moved. *Author's archive.*

O'Donnell, to the city of Sevilla as a trophy commemorating the Spanish victory. Upon receiving the gift, the Sevilla authorities were contemplating making it into a monument in memory of the heroic deeds of the Spanish army. Instead, it was now decided that these cannon would be melted down for the purpose of making the two lions. Although the felines would not be directly commemorating the Army, they were seen to be noble adjuncts to a building dedicated to the Spanish nation.

The work casting the lions thus proceeded. But again there were problems, this time technical ones concerning the alloys of bronze used. Never before in Spain had statues been cast in a foundry used for making military ordnance. After numerous laboratory tests, the compositions of copper and tin to make the bronze lions were determined. Meanwhile, the sculptor, Ponzano, had reached an agreement with the government and had re-sculpted the statues, placing one of each lion's paws on a sphere. In his presence, the lions were cast.

The completed lions, one weighing 2,219 kilograms (4,882 pounds) and the other 2,668 kilograms (5,870 pounds) were finally shown to the press in Sevilla in 1865, and were enthusiastically praised for their artistic and technical perfection. Plaster replicas of the two lions are presently on display in Sevilla's Capitanía General. In addition to the obvious difference that one lion is looking to the left and the other to the right, the lions' tails have different positions. Another difference, less obvious, is that one of the lions has his "private parts" exposed, while the second has them hidden.

However, when the lions were shipped to Madrid,

politicians once again started quarreling among themselves about the statues. Some averred that using statues made from the spoils of an unpopular imperialistic war with Morocco ran contrary to their pacifistic and political convictions. They decried the idea of enshrining what they considered to be ill-gotten trophies of war by using them to flank the entrance to an august chamber representing democratic ideals. The political in-fighting was so fierce that at one point there was even talk of selling the lions, as had been done with Bellver's ones.

It took seven years more to reach an agreement on the fate of the lions. Finally, thanks to the good offices of Federico Madrazo, the scion of a long line of distinguished painters, and the Marqués de Cubas, a parliamentarian and later mayor of Madrid, the politicians at long last reached an agreement. The felines were finally positioned in their two places of honor in 1872, twenty-two years after they had originally been commissioned. There they have proudly remained ever since.

Although well over a hundred years have elapsed, the commentary they elicited in a Madrid newspaper on the day after they were placed in front of the Cortes is still as apposite now as it was then: "The bronze lions are finally placed in front of the Congress. And what mouths they have! One might imagine them to be parliamentarians!"

Democracy under gunpoint

Those well past the age of puberty may recall an attempted overthrow of the Spanish government in February 1981 by a Civil Guard lieutenant-colonel named Antonio Tejero. The attempted coup, six years after Franco's death, started around 6 p.m. on February 23. News of it leaked out when several independent radio stations announced that inside the Cortes an officer of the Civil Guard and several under his command had pulled out their guns and, after firing several warning shots inside the august chamber, held the members of the government convening there at gunpoint.

For the rest of that evening the news seeping out was confused. There had been a military uprising in Valencia, with

Tejero's coup in Congress. Colonel Antonio Tejero holds members of Congress at gunpoint in an attempt to overthrow the democratic government. *Author's archive.*

tanks on the streets. The installations of State-run Spanish Television on the outskirts of Madrid had been seized by a military column. No official communiqués were issued. Rumors circulated throughout the country, contradicting each other or asserting that wild speculations were true. Had the democratically-elected government been overthrown and Spain jettisoned back to another military dictatorship?

All of Spain held its breath and kept its ears glued to their radios, the only source of information on what was happening, since TV continued grinding its scheduled programs without saying a word about the events unfolding. Different armed groups formed circles outside the Cortes building – Civil Guards, police, military units – but that evening it was still unclear where their loyalties lay, who was supporting the attempted coup and who was against it.

The lobby and bar of the nearby Palace Hotel, cater-cornered with the Cortes, filled with journalists, politicians, and gawkers who milled about the hotel swapping the latest intelligence. Meanwhile, the radio stations, expecting at any moment to be closed down by the insurgents, kept on repeating assurances that they were still broadcasting freely and unhampered.

Finally, at 1:20 a.m. King Juan Carlos made an appearance on television in which he assured Spaniards that he supported the democracy. Meanwhile, Tejero and his cohorts were still holding the parliamentarians prisoners inside the building. The culprits, whose actions had been seconded in some other parts of Spain, especially in Valencia, didn't give themselves up until the morning when, bleary-eyed, they were conducted to police wagons. The ringleaders of the uprising were subsequently put on trial and convicted of their crimes. Tejero was sentenced to 30 years in jail, but after serving only 15 of these was released on parole.

For those who lived through that episode, walking past the Cortes is always bound to evoke the memory of events of that tension-filled night when democracy was put on the line and the threat of a new dictatorship loomed over the country.

On December 6th, the Day of the Constitution, crowds of people take the opportunity of visiting the Congreso de Diputados which is then open to the general public. Many seem not to be aware that, in fact, the building can be visited most Saturday mornings between 10:30 and 12:30 when every half hour free guided tours of the interior are provided by the authorities. Among the curiosities seen on the conducted tour of the salons is a copy of Spain's first constitution, issued in Cádiz in 1812, an astronomical clock built in 1857 which shows the movements of the earth in relation to the moon and the sun and the time in 20 different countries around the world, and the democratic constitution signed by King Juan Carlos in 1978 which is now the legal cornerstone of modern Spain.

Of greatest interest to most visitors is the so-called Hemicycle where the Spanish lower house holds its legislative sessions. The guide will even point out some of the remaining bullet holes produced when Lieutenant-Colonel AntonioTejero held the government at gunpoint during the failed attempt at a

coup. At that time, several blasts were fired from a machine-gun into the air, causing close to 30 impacts in the ornate painted ceiling, now recognizable as small white chips. Many appear above and to the side of the painting of a green-clad woman, an allegory of Reform. Those interested in watching the sessions of the Cortes from the public gallery can apply for a pass on Fridays between 6-8 p.m. at the back entry gate on the Calle de Zorrilla. Only about 20 passes are issued for each sitting.

The Hotel Palace and the Carillon

The Palace Hotel has been an icon on the Madrid scene since its inauguration in 1912, having been built by French interests in only 16 months. For a few years, starting in 1922, its owners even bought out a property across the street, on the Calle del Duque de Medinaceli, where they built an elegant three-story complex which was the talk of the day. It was called the Ice and Automobile Palace and featured a huge ice skating rink, an automobile showroom, a shopping arcade, a Louis XIV-style ballroom, a restaurant and an English-style smoking lounge.

The venture proved to be a total flop and the whole was taken over in 1928 by the State and converted into a Center for Historical Studies. Although the lavish glamor of the old Ice Palace is gone, an inkling of its opulence can be seen in the public salons of the Hotel Palace itself.

The Palace bar for decades was a favorite hangout for journalists and celebrities and expatriates. During the Civil War, like all hotels in the city, the Palace was converted into a hospital. After the war it reverted to its former glory, and has been renovated, sold and resold multiple times. The present bar/lounge is new, but retains much of the charm and comfort of the original one, while the hotel's public rooms, especially the magnificent rotunda, are a delightful place to while away a few hours, have a cocktail or a coffee, and relax to the sound of soothing live classical music, usually played on a piano, harp or guitar.

Carillon. This charming carillon often goes unnoticed since its figures only come out and its bells chime at noon and at 8:00 p.m. *Author's photo.*

When you come out of the Palace Hotel, you might just happen to hear the tinkle tinkle and tintinnabulation of little bells. Should you hear these, it doesn't mean you've had too many cocktails at the Palace bar, but rather that you have emerged from the hotel lobby at noon or 8 p.m. and are on the corner of the Calle del Duque de Medinaceli. At those hours, you'll see that the tinkling comes from the chimes of a carillon, consisting of 18 bells. Located on a balcony of the corner building, a group of figures emerge, known as "*figuras goyescas*" (since they remind you of the personages in Goya's paintings) who for a few minutes enact a mechanical pantomime. The six figures, designed by the well-known Spanish cartoonist Antonio Mingote, represent Goya, the Duchess of Alba, King Carlos III, the bullfighter Pedro Romero (a *matador* from Ronda, near Sevilla, who lived from 1754-1839 and who was inmortalized in Goya's paintings), a *manola* (a Madrilenian working class woman) and a toy dog with a ribbon.

During the Yuletide season, between December 20th and January 7th, the figures also emerge at 7 p.m. and 9 p.m. The chimes were inaugurated by Pilar de Borbón (King Juan Carlos's sister) on December 20, 1993 and continue to be a favorite with young and old alike.

HEAD STREET
(Calle de la Cabeza)

Legend has it that in a house located on this street once lived a priest whose wealth and possessions were coveted by his Portuguese servant. One night, the servant murdered the unsuspecting priest, cut off his head, seized the gold and valuables that his victim had in the house, and fled to Lisbon. When the priest's body was discovered, the murder became the talk of the town. But since the servant had escaped, in the course of time the crime and its perpetrator came to be forgotten. However, the servant, some years later, now in the guise of a prosperous gentleman, returned to Madrid.

One morning, as he was walking through the Rastro (then the site of a market and the city's main slaughterhouse), not far from where the crime had been committed, he took a fancy to buy a ram's head for his dinner (a common dish, still served in many Spanish villages). After doing so, he placed the head under his cape and started on his way home. However, a watchman happened to notice drops of blood dripping on the sidewalk which came from under the man's cape. He approached him and demanded to know what he had under the cape. "A ram's head I just bought in the market," he replied. Suspicious, the watchman asked to see it.

But as the former servant opened the cape he saw to his astonishment and horror that it was the head of the priest he had murdered. The watchman immediately collared the culprit and led him off to jail. At the ensuing trial, he was found guilty and sentenced to be hanged in the Plaza Mayor. When the execution had been carried out, the priest's head turned back into that of a ram.

Area 3: Mayor (detail)

1. **Bocadillos de Calamares**, Bar Casa Rúa (Ciudad Rodrigo 3).
2. Restaurant **Las Cuevas de Luis Candelas** (Cuchilleros 1). Food and Candelas memorabilia.
3. **Escalerilla de Piedra** (a.k.a. Arco de Cuchilleros).
4. **Púlpito**, preacher's corner.
5. **Sobrinos de Botín** restaurant (Cuchilleros 17). Hemingway hangout.
6. **Casa de la Panadería**, tourist office.
7. **Bar Andaluz La Torre de Oro** (Plaza Mayor 26). Bullfighting memorabilia.
8. **Equestrian statue of Felipe III** (center of square). Bird-swallowing statue.
9. **Moore's Pub** (Felipe III, 4). Inquisition dungeon.
10. **Bocadillos de Calamares**, Bars La Campana & La Ideal (both on Botoneras).
11. **Site of El Cuclillo**, (on Calle Imperial exact location unknown). Candelas' hangout.
12. Former site of **Cárcel de la Corte** (Plaza de la Provincia 1).
13. **Posada del Peine** (Postas 17). Former posada and flop house.

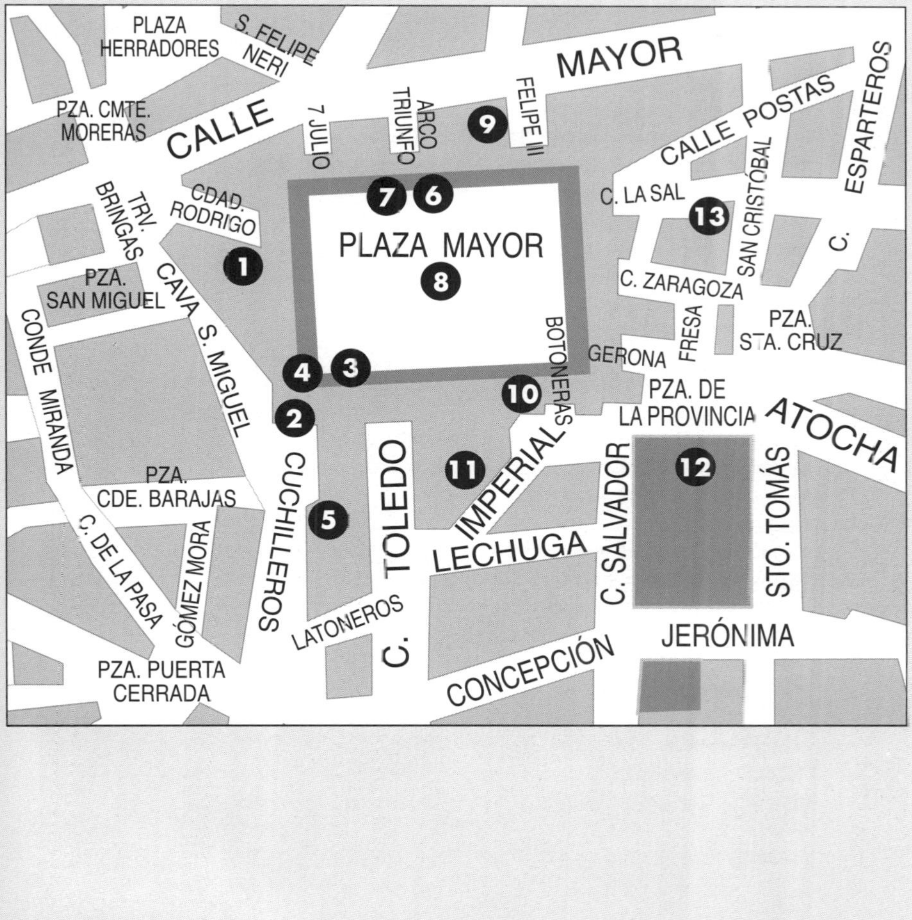
PLAZA HERRADORES
S. FELIPE NERI
MAYOR
PZA. CMTE. MORERAS
CALLE
7 JULIO
ARCO TRIUNFO
FELIPE III
CALLE POSTAS
ESPARTEROS
TRV. BRINGAS
CDAD. RODRIGO
C. LA SAL
SAN CRISTÓBAL
C.
PLAZA MAYOR
PZA. SAN MIGUEL
CAVA S. MIGUEL
C. ZARAGOZA
CONDE MIRANDA
BOTONERAS
FRESA
PZA. STA. CRUZ
GERONA
PZA. DE LA PROVINCIA
ATOCHA
CUCHILLEROS
TOLEDO
IMPERIAL
PZA. CDE. BARAJAS
C. SALVADOR
STO. TOMÁS
LECHUGA
C. DE LA PASA
GÓMEZ MORA
SOMBREREROS
LATONEROS
C.
JERÓNIMA
CONCEPCIÓN
PZA. PUERTA CERRADA
1
2
3
4
5
6
7
8
9
10
11
12
13

Area 3: Mayor

1. **Casa de la Villa** (Plaza de la Villa 5). Authentic Mariblanca statue.
2. **The Narrow House** (Mayor 61). Calderón de la Barca's home.
3. **Calle de Puñonrostro.** Street with a story.
4. **Convento de las Monjas del Corpus Christi "Las Carboneras"** (Plaza del Conde de Miranda 3). Nuns' pastries.
5. **Casa a la Malicia** example (Calle del Conde).
6. **Plaza de la Puerta Cerrada,** mural with inscription from Madrid's first coat-of-arms.
7. **Taberna El Madroño** (Plaza de Puerta Cerrada 7). Tiles with Madrid's coat-of-arms and madroño liqueur.
8. **Casa a la Malicia** example (Calle del Toro).
9. **Colegiata de San Isidro el Real** (Toledo 37). Remains of San Isidro.
10. **Site of "La Cuadra"** (Pretil de Santisteban 3). San Isidro's stable.
11. **Calle de la Cava Baja,** sites of posadas: León de Oro, Dragón, and de la Villa. Also restaurant Casa Lucio (Cava Baja 35).
12. **Museo de San Isidro** (Plaza de San Andrés 2). Miracle well & La Cybeles bear and dragon statues.
13. **Plaza de la Cebada,** Site of executions.
14. **Calle de Isabel Tintero,** Virgen de la Paloma.
15. **Iglesia de San Pedro el Real** (Paloma). Virgen de la Paloma.
16. **Plaza de Cascorro,** El Rastro and statue of Eloy Gonzalo.
17. **Calle de la Ribera de Curtidores,** El Rastro's main drag.
18. **Calle de la Espada.** Street with a story.
19. **Calle de la Esgrima.** Street with a story.
20. **Madrid's medieval** walls (Cava Baja 10), under a glass floor.
21. **Madrid's medieval** walls (Cava Baja 30), large section in the interior patio.
22. **Madrid's medieval** walls (Mancebos 5), can be seen from the street.

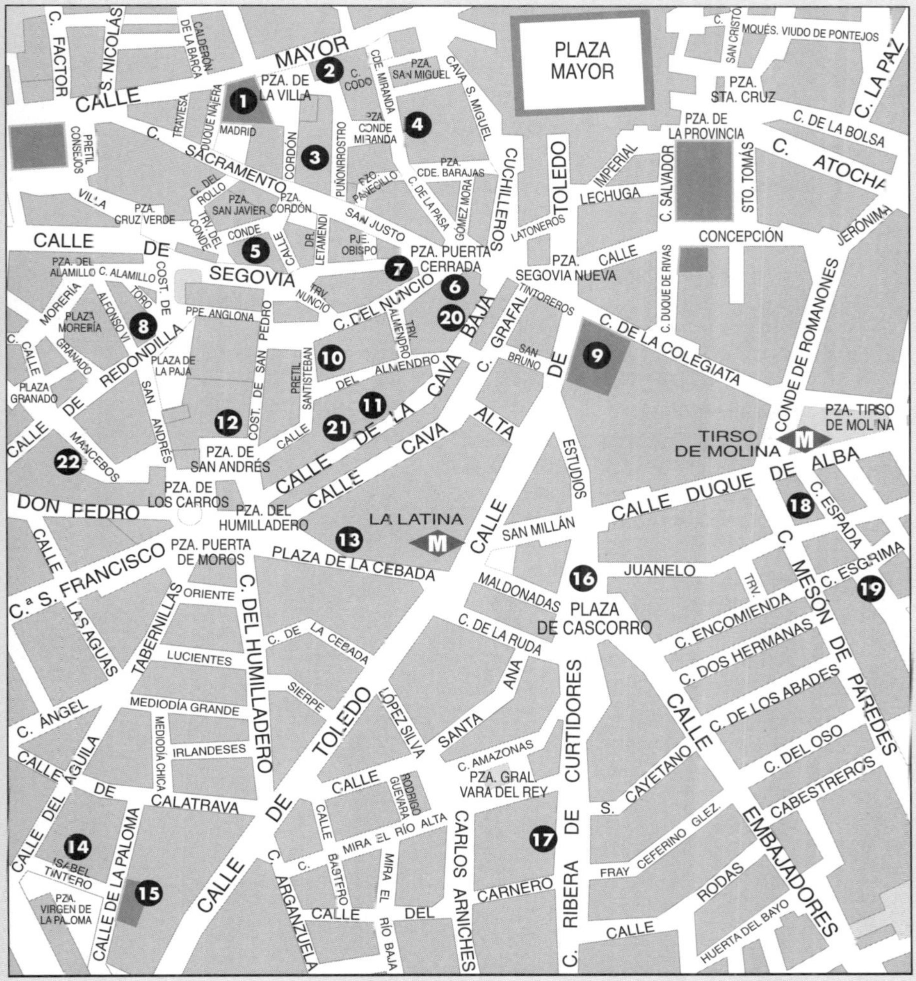
C. FACTOR
S. NICOLÁS
CALDERÓN DE LA BARCA
MAYOR
CALLE
PZA. DE LA VILLA
C. CODO
CDE. MIRANDA
PZA. SAN MIGUEL
CAVA S. MIGUEL
PLAZA MAYOR
C. SAN CRISTO
MQUÉS. VIUDO DE PONTEJOS
C. LA PAZ
PZA. STA. CRUZ
TRAVIESA
DUQUE NÁJERA
MADRID
PRETIL CONSEJOS
C. SACRAMENTO
CORDÓN
PUÑONRROSTRO
PZA. CONDE MIRANDA
PZA. CDE. BARAJAS
CUCHILLEROS
TOLEDO
IMPERIAL
PZA. DE LA PROVINCIA
C. DE LA BOLSA
C. ATOCHA
C. DEL ROLLO
PZA. SAN JAVIER
PZA. CORDÓN
PZO. PANECILLO
C. DE LA PASA
GÓMEZ MORA
LECHUGA
C. SALVADOR
STO. TOMÁS
VILLA
PZA. CRUZ VERDE
TRV. DEL CONDE
CONDE
CALLE
DR. LETAMENDI
PJE. OBISPO
SAN JUSTO
LATONEROS
CONCEPCIÓN
JERÓNIMA
CALLE DE SEGOVIA
PZA. DEL ALAMILLO
C. ALAMILLO
COST. DE
TORO
PZA. PUERTA CERRADA
PZA. SEGOVIA NUEVA
CALLE
C. DUQUE DE RIVAS
CONDE DE ROMANONES
MORERÍA
ALFONSO VI
PLAZA MORERÍA
PPE. ANGLONA
TRV. NUNCIO
C. DEL NUNCIO
TRV. ALMENDRO
BAJA
TINTOREROS
C. DE LA COLEGIATA
C. CALLE
GRANADO
REDONDILLA
PLAZA DE LA PAJA
SAN PEDRO
PRETIL SANTISTEBAN
DEL ALMENDRO
C. GRAFAL
SAN BRUNO
DE
PLAZA GRANADO
DE
SAN ANDRÉS
COST. DE
CALLE DE LA CAVA
PZA. TIRSO DE MOLINA
TIRSO DE MOLINA
M
CALLE
MANCEBOS
PZA. DE SAN ANDRÉS
CALLE
CAVA ALTA
ESTUDIOS
DON PEDRO
PZA. DE LOS CARROS
PZA. DEL HUMILLADERO
CALLE CAVA
LA LATINA
M
CALLE DUQUE DE ALBA
C. ESPADA
CALLE
C. S. FRANCISCO
PZA. PUERTA DE MOROS
PLAZA DE LA CEBADA
CALLE
SAN MILLÁN
JUANELO
C. ESGRIMA
C. MESÓN DE PAREDES
ORIENTE
TABERNILLAS
LAS AGUAS
C. DEL HUMILLADERO
MALDONADAS
PLAZA DE CASCORRO
TRV.
C. ENCOMIENDA
C. DE LA CEBADA
C. DE LA RUDA
LUCIENTES
C. DOS HERMANAS
SIERPE
C. DE LOS ABADES
MEDIODÍA GRANDE
LÓPEZ SILVA
ANA
C. ÁNGEL
MEDIODÍA CHICA
IRLANDESES
TOLEDO
SANTA
CURTIDORES
CALLE
C. DEL OSO
CALLE DEL ÁGUILA
C. AMAZONAS
S. CAYETANO
DE
CALLE
RODRIGO GUEVARA
PZA. GRAL. VARA DEL REY
CABESTREROS
CALATRAVA
CALLE DE
CEFERINO GLEZ.
EMBAJADORES
C. ARGANZUELA
CALLE
MIRA EL RÍO ALTA
CARLOS ARNICHES
RIBERA DE
FRAY
ISABEL TINTERO
C.
BASTERO
MIRA EL RÍO BAJA
CARNERO
RODAS
PZA. VIRGEN DE LA PALOMA
CALLE DE LA PALOMA
CALLE
CALLE DEL
CALLE
HUERTA DEL BAYO
C.

Area 3 - MAYOR

The Plaza Mayor: the ongoing pageant

Madrid's porticoed early 17th century "Great Square" (though it's actually a rectangle measuring 120 X 90 meters) is one of the city's most pleasant spots in which to while away a few hours at one of the many outdoor cafés and restaurants, munch crustaceans, down a *caña* of beer or even to weigh in on a three-course meal. Even if the prices charged are steep and the food levelled down for tourist consumption, lounging in the Plaza Mayor is nonetheless a gratifying experience for most people.

Be warned however that most of the *paellas* served are not authentic, but pre-prepared. Should you want to go really native, try the squid hero sandwiches (*bocadillo de calamares*). Best places to indulge this gastronomical adventure are at La Campana and La Ideal, both on the Calle de las Botoneras, off the southeast corner of the Plaza, or the Casa Rúa on the Calle de la Ciudad Rodrigo, leading off west of the square, towards the Calle Mayor.

Under the arcades of the Plaza Mayor, you'll also still see some of the traditional hat shops, great for buying anything from an authentic Basque beret to a fedora; typical are the stores specializing in philately. It is also here, on the north side, in the Casa de la Panadería, with its painted frescoes, that the municipal Tourist Office is located. The Office organizes a series of highly recommendable guided walking tours through the old part of the city for a minimal cost. Such, for example, as one dedicated to medieval Madrid, or one related to legends of

The Escalerilla de Piedra. A chiaroscuro view of the famous passageway leading out of the Plaza Mayor known as the Arco de Cuchilleros. *Author's photo.*

old Madrid, another to Cervantes's Madrid and still another taken on a bus which covers modern Madrid. Check at the Office for details.

In clement weather, the square is always teeming with a motley assortment of people, including itinerant musicians, artists who will do your caricature, landscape painters, loafers, tourists and locals.

During the Yuletide season, the yearly Christmas fair is set up in the Plaza, with dozens of stands selling ornaments of miniature figures for Nativity scenes, as well as noisemakers, decorations and other paraphernalia. All around the perimeter of the square you'll see evergreen trees on sale, a non-Catholic appendage dating from the 1960's. The Plaza Mayor is also a good spot from which to see the Three Wise Men's cavalcade held each year on Epiphany, January 6th, which starts near the Puerta de Alcalá and winds its way, midst cheering crowds of moppets, down to the Plaza Mayor.

In the summer, a stage is built in the square and many events of the capital's Summer Festival are performed here, ranging from rock concerts to classical plays. The Plaza is also the meeting place every Sunday morning for stamp and coin collectors, who set up stands all around the arcades.

The sparrow cemetery

In the center of the Plaza Mayor you'll notice an equestrian statue of the early 17th century king, Felipe III. Few passers-by realize that the statue has been a cemetery for dozens of sparrows, although no ornithological gravestone or mini plaque marks the "tragic" spot where countless little birds peeped their last peep.

The "cemetery", in fact, was inside the cast-iron horse's belly; it was as though the horse had actually gobbled up the birds. Well, in a way he had.

If you look carefully at the horse, you'll notice that his mouth is soldered closed. But this has not always been the case.

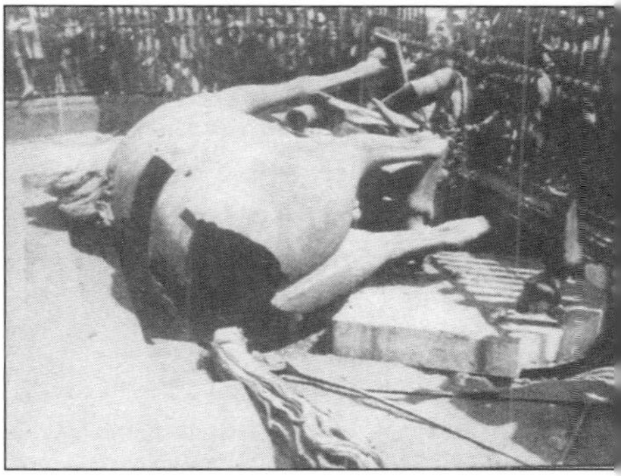

Originally, when the statue was cast in Florence by Juan de Bolonia and finished by Pietro Tacca, the mouth of the horse was open far enough for a small bird to fly in. Birds would perch on the mouth and then fly down through the narrow passage of the throat and deep into the dark bowels of the horse. Once there, they would flutter about the darkness trying to find a way out. Unfortunately when they finally did find the opening, they'd discover that their wingspread prevented them from escaping through the aperture.

For hundreds of years no one was aware of this sparrow death trap. Then, in 1931, when the Second Republic was proclaimed and anti-monarchist sentiment ran high, the celebrations reached such a frenzy of patriotic fervor that a group of people started to deface and vandalize the statue. At this point, a leftwing militant threw a large petard inside the horse's mouth, causing its belly to burst. To everyone's surprise, the air was suddenly filled with hundreds of tiny bird bones, thereby revealing what had been for centuries the deep, dark secret of the "sparrow cemetery".

After the Civil War, restoration work on the statue was undertaken by the sculptor Juan Cristóbal. Among the repairs, the horse's mouth was sealed, thereby preventing any bird from flying into it and suffering the ignominious fate that so many of its predecessors had met.

Felipe III's equestrian statue. (Left) A close look from underneath will reveal that the interior of the horse's mouth has been sealed closed, finally barring entry to an unintentional "sparrow' cemetery." *Author's photo.* (Right) Anti-monarchical crowds destroyed Felipe III's statue during the 2nd Republic. *Author's archive.*

Preacher's corner

El Púlpito. The 17th century "pulpit", known as El Púlpito, from where a friar roused a group of Madrid's citizens to revolt against the occupying French in 1808. *Author's photo.*

One the most typical and best-known nooks in Madrid is at the southwest corner of the Plaza Mayor, known as the Arco de Cuchilleros, so-called because the archway leads down a flight of stairs to the Calle de los Cuchilleros, or Knife-Grinders Street.

In fact, the corner is of such renown that the local Tourist Office even awards a prize called the Arch of Cuchilleros Medal for Madrileños who have demonstrated their love for the city. Curiously enough, the archway, contrary to what most people think, is not *officially* listed as the Arco de Cuchilleros in municipal guides and maps, but rather is called the Calle de la Escalerilla de Piedra (Street of the Little Stone Staircase). That name is also the one seen on the tiled street sign under the left side of the arch.

Until recently, a small tavern stood right next to the staircase which was called El Púlpito (The Pulpit), (pronounced POOL-pito), not to be confused with the same word without an accent (pool-PITO) which means "little octopus". Before the tavern shuttered, there *was* some confusion as to whether the place specialized in octopus or not. But those in the know realized that the tavern took its name from a protective semi-circular metal railing reminiscent of a pulpit which can still be seen on the right side of the stairs.

The earliest records of the "pulpit" date back to 1672 when it was known as *el pulpitillo* (the little pulpit). However, what made it locally famous was when in 1808 a friar from the nearby Convent of San Gil named Antonio (his last name has

been lost in time) delivered a fiery sermon here that incited the citizens of Madrid to rise against the occupying French, just as many of his compatriots had done in others parts of the city, a prelude to the coming Peninsular War.

A few vestiges remain that are associated with the Púlpito, such as two old, cobwebbed street lamps over the archway with the name "Púlpito" on them, or the Bazar Púlpito, a tourist souvenir shop whose owner claims that in pre-Republic days the royal family bought toys there.

The archway played a central part in Benito Pérez Galdós's best-known novel, *Forunata and Jacinta*, for it was here that the eponymous lovers met. Finally, it was also at this spot in 1790 that a tremendous fire broke out which was to destroy half of the Plaza Mayor. The Púlpito tavern is now long gone. The new locale, rather than catering octopus to tourists, sells gifts and "Spanish" knick-knacks.

Escalerilla de Piedra. The street sign showing that the passageway usually referred to as the "Arco de Cuchilleros" is in fact officially named "Calle de la Escalerilla de Piedra." *Author's photo.*

Luis Candelas: Madrid's gentleman bandit

Walking down the long flight of stairs under the archway from the Plaza Mayor to the Calle de los Cuchilleros you'll see on the right-hand side a man who looks like he had just stepped out of the set of a pirate film. He is dressed in the costume of the early 19th century, a *calañés* hat and a bandanna on his head, frilled white shirt, a short red vest, tight-fitting *faja* (sash), trousers, boots and in one hand he holds a *trabuco* (blunderbuss). He is, in fact, the doorman of one of Madrid's best-known and most typical restaurants, Las Cuevas de Luis Candelas, named after the capital's celebrated 19th century highwayman, bandit, swindler and gallant, Luis Candelas. The restaurant, originally just a simple tavern, consists of a bewildering maze of cave-like rooms and cellars. It has been a tourist favorite ever since it was opened in 1949 by an ex-bullfighter, Félix Colomo. His son now runs the establishment.

On the main floor you'll see a framed series of drawings, known as *aleluyas,* illustrating the bandit's life in crime. Upstairs, in a barrel-vaulted room, one wall is covered with a fresco further depicting Candelas' life and adventures. You'll also find a picturesque wine cellar in the maze of old rooms with a tableau which recreates a scene of Candelas counting his loot and sipping a glass of *vino tinto.* In fact, the whole restaurant is decorated with a riot of memorabilia, trinkets, pots, bullfight paraphernalia, posters and drawings, all of which you can ogle as the waiters, also dressed as bandits, serve you the time-honored local dishes – *sopa castellana* (garlic soup), *cordero asado* (roast baby lamb), *cochinillo asado* (roast suckling pig) and *conejo con tomate* (rabbit and tomato stew). The restaurant's guest book features signatures

Luis Candelas. Sketch of the highwayman and bandit Luis Candelas, known as the "gentleman thief" of Madrid. *Museo Municipal de Madrid. Casariego collection.*

Candelas in the movies. Still from the 1926 silent film *Luis Candelas o el Bandido de Madrid.* Shown here are Erna Becker as the bandit's sweetheart and Manuel San Germán as Candelas. This was the first of various films based on the legendary highwayman. *Author's archive.*

from dozens of celebrities who have dined there, ranging from Jimmy Carter to Orson Welles.

Who, then, was Luis Candelas? He is supposed to have been a gentleman-thief, a perfect Mack the Knife, with an added Spanish twist, whose thefts, daring, prowess and knack for breaking out of prisons are legendary. Indeed, the legend has eclipsed the facts, of which there are few.

But Luis Candelas, the bandit hero of Madrid, was real enough. Born in 1806, he grew up near the Calle de Toledo. The first official recognition of his talents came in 1823 when he was indicted for vagrancy. In 1824 his name again appeared on the police blotter, this time for stealing two horses and a mule. For the latter offense he was sentenced to six years hard labor in Málaga, but escaped after eight months. He was recaptured, but was reprieved in 1825.

Before long Candelas had formed a gang with partners in crime who committed misdeeds ranging over kidnapping and housebreaking to murder, though supposedly Candelas himself never sullied his hands with the latter. Legend spins many fanciful tales about the bandit. Among these is one that he inherited a small fortune and began to lead a double life passing himself off as a rich landowner supposedly back from Peru but still continuing his life in crime as a highwayman and bandit. Under the former guise, operating with a respectable alias, he rented a fancy apartment, attended literary salons, and indulged in a long string of romantic involvements with everyone from society ladies to shopgirls. Most of the stories are probably apocryphal. Local lore – with the assistance of penny dreadfuls and lurid sensationalist mass-market pamphlets – have embroidered the facts.

His misdeeds included many thefts that were "confidence" jobs, with Candelas using time-honored ploys and making off with golden watches, stuffed wallets and jewelry. Between these "jobs" he was also active on the high roads, holding up diligences on their way to Madrid and stripping travellers of their possessions.

In Madrid, Candelas and his gang hung out in a tavern called *El Cuclillo* (The Cuckoo) in the Calle Imperial, long since gone, just behind the Plaza Mayor and not far from today's Cuevas de Luis Candelas restaurant.

Notwithstanding the bandit's cunning, he soon fell foul of the police again. After holding up a coach and stealing, among other items, a cloak, he was sighted wearing the garment by its former owner while crossing the Puerta del Sol. This time he was quickly apprehended and sentenced to 14 years of penal servitude in the dreaded El Hacho fortress in the North African port of Ceuta. But while being transported there, Candelas once again managed to give the police the slip.

It's possible that at this point Candelas, who had by now been eluding the police for some 12 years, realized that if he continued with his criminal activities it was only a question of time before the authorities caught up with him. He was almost thirty. Three or four more "jobs" would net him enough money to retire with in some foreign country and play the part of a proper Spanish gentleman in exile, no questions asked. Hence, it was decided in the *Cuclillo* to pull off three housebreaking "jobs" in the space of a month.

The first of the three victims was a rich priest. The bandits entered his house, seized the priest, and bound and gagged him along with others of the household before despoiling him of his valuables. The second in line was a shopkeeper in the Calle de Segovia. And the final and most daring of the "jobs" was pulled off on the Sunday of Carnival, on February 12, 1837, in the house of the official dressmaker to the Queen Regent, María Cristina.

At about 5 p.m. the dressmaker's doorbell rang and a man, posing as a French courier, asked to be admitted. He claimed that he had a letter from France. Since the dressmaker was anxiously awaiting news from her daughter in Paris, the messenger was shown in. No sooner was the door opened than three men forced their way in, two of whom made straight to the room where the dressmaker was sitting. One was tall, sported long sideburns and was elegantly dressed with white vest, jacket and a cape: Candelas in disguise. The second was dressed in the uniform of a lieutenant colonel, very tall, with a cane: Candelas's henchman, Balseiro. The third, who stood guard, was fair of complexion. The men seized the dressmaker, stuffed a handkerchief into her mouth and tied her up. Others of the household were bound as well. The bandits then ransacked the premises and stole whatever valuables they chanced upon. In the course of the theft, the washerwoman, a maid, two elderly women and two friends of the dressmaker rang at the door. All were ushered in and tied up. At about 6:30 p.m., upon hearing a whistle, the thieves withdrew with their loot: a small fortune in jewels.

Restaurant Las Cuevas de Luis Candelas
At the entrance to this restaurant stands a man in the attire of a bandolero. He doesn´t claim to be Candelas but assures us that the "spirit of Candelas lives in him."
Author's photo.

The theft created a sensation in Madrid, and is well documented. Candelas and his mistress had meanwhile set off for northern Spain under assumed names, bound for Gijón, on the Asturian coast. But Candelas' girlfriend balked at fleeing abroad, and the gentleman-bandit set off on his own in the direction of Portugal. Others of the gang had meanwhile been apprehended.

After trying to raise some cash by selling off some of the stolen jewelry in the city of Valladolid, he was rudely shaken awake on the morning of July 18, 1837 in a roadside inn, to stare into the barrel of a rifle. The police had been on his track for days and the loot he had tried to sell had sealed his fate.

Candelas' capture was the talk of Madrid. This time there would be no escapes and Candelas entered Madrid escorted by a heavy guard. His notoriety had caught up with him at last and bribes and influence were useless. Nonetheless his trial dragged on for three months. Vainly his defense attorney pleaded for his life, but at last, near the end of October, sentence was pronounced: on more than forty counts, death by garroting.

On November 4, 1837, Candelas was led to the death cell. A last plea to María Cristina for a reprieve, in which he claimed that he had never killed anyone, failed. Two days later, at 11 o'clock on a dark and cloudy morning, Candelas was conducted to a scaffold outside the Puerta de Toledo. The turnout was enormous and a platoon of soldiers had to clear the way to let the famous bandit, mounted on a donkey, pass. Once at the place of execution, he calmly climbed the steps and seated himself on the executioner's bench. His courage had not failed him. The metal band of the garrotte closed around his neck. A moment before the fatal twist of the screw, he asked permission to make one final statement. Permission was granted. He said: "I have sinned as a man, but I have never stained my hands with the blood of others." And then his final words: *"¡Sé feliz, patria mía!"* (Be happy, country of mine!)

The legend of Luis Candelas' adventures was spread by the populace and by inventive writers of historical fiction, who have made of him a popular hero. One ballad, made famous by the singer Conchita Piquer, went:

Debajo de la capa de Luis Candelas
Mi corazón amante vuela que vuela.
Madrid te está buscando para prenderte,
y yo sólo te busco para quererte.
Y la calle en que vivo está desierta,
y de noche y de día mi puerta abierta,
que estoy en vela para ver si me roba,
ay, Luis Candelas.

Under the cape of Luis Candelas
Flutters my enamored heart.
Madrid is out to catch you,
But I'm only here to love you.
The street I live on is deserted,
And by night and by day my door is open,
For I'm waiting to see if you'll rob me,
Oh, Luis Candelas.

The darker side

It is difficult today to imagine that the Plaza Mayor, with its present cheerful atmosphere should at one time in history have been darkened by the proceedings of the Holy Inquisition. In fact, the square, which was built in only two years (1617-1619) had earlier been a lagoon.

For centuries, the Plaza was a showplace for royal fiestas, coronations, bullfights, jousts, theatre and executions. The spectacles were watched by the king and celebrities from a balcony in the building on the north side of the square, called the Casa de la Panadería (Bakery House), since originally it was the site from where bread was distributed to the townspeople.

Here autos-de-fé' (literally, confessions of faith) were held by the Inquisition in the presence of royalty, arousing strong emotions from the onlookers who could view with righteous satisfaction the sufferings of those sentenced for blasphemy, adultery, witchcraft, religious apostasy and other crimes considered dreadful at the time.

The first auto-de-fé was held in the Plaza Mayor on January 21, 1624 when a man was burnt alive for masquerading

***Auto de Fé* in the Plaza Mayor.** Notice the two cages in the center of the square where the accused were held; also the huge canvas stretched over it to shade viewers and magistrates from the sun as they watched the tortures and executions. *Anonymous 17th century engraving. Museo Municipal.*

as a priest. In 1680, a French ambassador's wife, Madame de Villars, in a letter written to a Parisian friend, Madame de Coulanges, detailed one such auto-de-fé:

"On the last day of June we had here in Madrid something that has not been seen for 48 years: a general *auto* of the Inquisition in which was conducted, with great ceremony, the public trial and condemnation of several people guilty of crimes against religion… For this function, a large stage in the Plaza Mayor of Madrid was erected, where, between seven in the morning and nine at night, people were looking at the criminals and listening to their sentences. Eighteen obstinate Jews, both men and women, two apostates and one Mohammedan, were condemned to be burned; fifty other Jews or Jewesses, arrested for the first time and repentant, were condemned to several years in prison and to wearing what is called a *sambenito,* which is a yellow cassock with the red cross of St. Andrew before and behind (the word comes from *saco bendito* or "holy sack" which is what the cassock resembled); ten others guilty of bigamy, sorcery and other misdemeanors, appeared in large paper hats, ropes around their necks, candles in their hands: the punishment for these things is usually flogging, the galleys, or banishment.

"The following night, those who had been condemned to the fire were burned outside the town, on a specially raised mound where these wretched creatures, before being executed, had to suffer a thousand torments; even the monks who were present there were burning them with small flames from torches in order to convert them. Several people, who had climbed on to the mound, struck them with swords and the populace showered them with stones..."

The writer expresses a certain admiration for some of the criminals, who right up to their death had a "bearing worthy of a better cause, and some even threw themselves on to the fire", thereafter pointing out that the tortures do not greatly diminish the number of Jews to be met with in Spain and especially in Madrid where, while some of them were being punished so ferociously, others were employed in finance, well-considered and respected and nevertheless recognized as being from Jewish families.

Though there is certainly no doubt of the Spanish Inquisition's horrors, some historians allege that its misdeeds have been given greater publicity than equally horrendous excesses, such as witch-burnings in Germany, beheadings in England and assorted persecutions, pogroms, "ethnic cleansing" and atrocities in other countries. In part, some scholars argue, the blackening of Spain's image was the result of a deliberate smear campaign supported by north-European Protestant countries.

One reputable French scholar on the Inquisition, Jean Plaidy, avers that the Supreme Council of the Inquisition even protected many people from charges of witchcraft. "In 1555 when many people were arrested on suspicion of witchcraft in the Guipúzcoa (Basque) area, the Suprema reproved the tribunal and expressed fear that many innocent people might be involved… Even in Britain – usually so much more moderate than other European countries – the total number of witches done to death is in the neighborhood of 30,000… There is no doubt that many old women in Spain avoided torture and hideous death because of the existence of the Spanish Inquisition".

Nevertheless, the image of Spaniards in the guise of mustachioed, leering villains, from the times that the Duke of Alba invaded the Netherlands in the 17th century to Hollywood swashbuckling movies about the Spanish Main to visions of atrocities invented by Hearst and the yellow press during the Spanish-American War, have kept the legend of Spanish cruelty alive for centuries. After all, one *Pit and the Pendulum* is worth a thousand disavowals in propagandistic tugs-of-war.

In addition to the Plaza Mayor itself, other nearby sites are associated with the Inquisition. Just off the square, in the short Calle de Felipe III, you'll come to one of Madrid's many Irish pubs, called Moore's, a favorite hang-out for tourists and expatriates. Beneath the place where Hibernian cheer flows, several underground rooms and chambers can be visited which *supposedly* were once used by the Holy Office for its dastardly deeds and Poe-like excesses.

Rather more documented is the site where the Inquisition had its feared Tribunal. It was located at the Calle de Torija 14 (see Area 4 map, Pg. 167) in a building constructed in 1735. A plaque on the façade says in Spanish: "This building was the site of the Supreme Council and Tribunal of the Inquisition from the 1780's to its abolition in 1820." The building now houses the more peaceful Convento de las Reparadoras, a convent.

In point of fact, the Inquisition was abolished by Joseph Bonaparte as soon as he took over the kingdom in 1808. However, when the tyrannical King Fernando VII returned to power in 1823 he actually *revived* the Inquisition, though it was then officially referred to as *Juntas de Fé*. But it was just as intransigent as its earlier version. As such it lasted for ten more years, finally being abolished in 1833 upon the death of the king.

Whiffs of the Holy Office can also be discerned in a site on the corner of the Calle de la Cabeza and the Calle de Lavapiés. Here was located the crown's Ecclesiastical Prison. The present building dates back to the late 18th century, and the part which used to house prison cells is now the Taberna del Avapiés (see Area 2 map, pg. 85), serving out wine and beer rather than punishments. Should you happen to hear any muffled groans, they probably come from those laboring in the kitchen rather than from the ghosts of former inmates.

The Plaza Mayor was also the site of the occasional public execution which for many years was a major source of public entertainment throughout Europe before the advent of movies, radio and television. On such occasions, during celebrations and spectacles, the owners of apartments with balconies overlooking the square were required to cede them to officialdom. When the balconies were not requisitioned by the authorities, their owners often rented them out for those who wanted a good view of the goings-on.

After 1790 these grim activities were moved elsewhere. Indeed, one of the ways that early 19th century travellers could while away a morning in old Madrid was to watch an execution, since these were held in public places and charged no admission price.

The most common ways of executing criminals were by hanging and by garroting, the latter method seemingly peculiar to Spain, and vividly portrayed in one of Goya's *Caprichos*. The Spanish name of the instrument used is the *garrote vil*. "*Vil*", or ignoble, because death by strangling is considered to be a humiliating and dishonorable death, but not as ignominious as hanging; most dignified is being shot by a firing squad. The garrotte consists of a wooden bench or chair placed in front of a tall stake, to which is attached a thick metal collar. This is placed around the victim's neck. To the back of the collar is attached a mechanism with a large screw and a long handle. When the executioner gives a vigorous twist to the handle, the screw tightens the metal collar and the prisoner's neck is instantaneously snapped.

Plaza de la Cebada: A lovely day for a hanging

If you leave the Plaza Mayor from the south side and go down the Calle de Toledo about five blocks you'll come to the Plaza de la Cebada, or Barley Square, the most common place to hold executions in the early 19th century. In those days the square was the site of an outdoor market (now a modern enclosed market building takes its place) with a fountain in the center. The square was surrounded by wooden tenements from where locals commanded excellent views of the activities. As in the days of the guillotine during the French Revolution, or hangings in London's Tyburn, such festive occasions were announced the preceding day in the local gazettes.

We include the following description of the execution of two robbers, written by an American naval officer, Alexander Slidell MacKenzie, the author of an excellent travel book *A Year in Spain* written after his sojourn in the capital in 1828.

MacKenzie had seen a similar execution two months earlier in Montpellier, France, and had been disgusted by it. Nonetheless, he decided that he might see "the national character brought into strong relief" by watching one in Madrid and decided to stifle his repugnance.

So just before 10 a.m. he went to the Cárcel de la Corte (City Prison) on the Plaza de la Provincia 1, (now used as the Ministry of Foreign Affairs) where there was already a crowd of people waiting for the prisoners to be brought out. Seeing that there was no action yet, MacKenzie went to the Plaza de la Cebada.

"The balconies of the surrounding houses were crowded with groups of either sex, formed into a panoramic view, probably not unlike what the Plaza Mayor may present on the occasion of a bull feast," wrote MacKenzie. "The area below was thronged by the lower classes, blended in one vast and motley collection. There was an abundance of sallow mechanics, tinkers, and cobblers, with leathern aprons and dirty faces; or of thin-legged tailors, intermingled with gaily-dressed Andalusians or with sturdy athletic peasants and muleteers from the neighboring plains of Castile and La Mancha…"

When MacKenzie got to the Calle de Toledo, he saw that all eyes were turned in one direction. "It was some minutes before we discovered, first the *celadores*, with their white belts and sabres, moving upward and downward – next their horses, spurred and reined into impatience, in order to intimidate the crowd and clear a way for the coming of the procession. Behind the *celadores* were soon after seen the glittering points of many bayonets, vibrating with a measured motion from right to left, and only seeming to advance as they grew brighter above the sea of heads which intervenes… Presently the large bearskin caps of the grenadiers emerged, until at last the whole was apparent, to the very feet of the soldiery. It was now, too, that might be heard the death-dirge, chanted by the humble monks who attended the criminals, swelling gradually above the hum of the multitude.

"The criminals were three in number, instead of two; but the first, though an accomplice of the others, had either been found less guilty at the trial, or else had made his peace with justice by becoming a witness against his companions. At all events, he was not to suffer death, but only to be conducted under the gallows and remain there during the execution. He was seated upon an ass, with his arms pinioned beside him. His head was bent forward so as nearly to touch the neck of the animal, and his long hair hung down on every side so as to form a complete veil about his features… The second criminal was dressed in a shroud; a living man in the garment of the dead. He sat bolt upright on an ass, and his feet were bound tightly together under the belly of the animal… His hands were tied with a cord, and made to clasp a copper crucifix. But when it was pressed to his lips by the anxious and tremulous hands of the poor monk who walked beside him, he refused to kiss the image of the Savior; nay, he even spit upon it… The third criminal was dressed like the last…

"The procession had now filed into the square and took

possession of the area reserved immediately about the gallows. The first culprit was posed beneath, and the other two were dismounted from the backs of the asses and made to sit upon the last step of the ladder. The hangman now came to take possession of his victims. Getting upon the step next above them, he grasped the smaller and more guilty miscreant under the arms and retreated upward, dragging him after step by step, and pausing an instant between each, which was marked by the vibration of the ladder. At length the hangman stood on the highest step – his victim was a little lower. They had been followed the whole way by a humble monk, in a loose garment of sackcloth, and girded with a scourge... After once again refusing to kiss the crucifix, the last moment of his life had now arrived. The hangman took two of the cords which dangled from the beam; and having once more convinced himself that they were of equal length, he opened the nooses and placed them about the neck of the malefactor. This done, he let himself down a single step, and seating himself firmly upon the shoulders of his victim, he grasped him tightly about the neck with his legs. He then drew powerfully upon the cords. The strangling malefactor made a convulsive but ineffectual attempt to reach upward with his pinioned arms, and then writhed his body to escape from the torture. This moment was seized upon by the hangman, who threw himself over the edge of the ladder, when both fell downward together. They had nearly turned over, when the ropes arrested their fall; and as they tightened, they struck across the face of the hangman and threw his hat aside among the crowd. But he clung to his prey with a resolute grasp, recovered his seat, and moved upward and downward upon the shoulders of the malefactor. Nor was he left to his own efforts: his assistants below reached the legs of the victim, and drew them downward with all their might.

"When this had continued a few minutes, the hangman stood erect upon the shoulders of his victim, and attempted to climb up by the cords, as he probably had been wont to do; but whether he had been stunned by the stroke of the ropes, or had grown heavier and less active since the last execution, his attempt proved abortive, and the loud cries of the multitude, outraged at the brutality, restrained him from a second effort. He then slid down by the body and legs of the criminal, until his feet rested upon the ground; and having tied a rope about the ankles of the dead man, he was drawn aside, so as to make room for his companion."

Madrid's narrowest house

Ramón de Mesonero Romanos, in addition to trying to save the house that Cervantes had lived and died in, as mentioned earlier in the book, also sought to prevent another historic building from being torn down, located near the Plaza Mayor. The house in question, on the Calle Mayor 61, was the former home of the famous Spanish Golden Age writer, Pedro Calderón de la Barca, author of *La Vida es Sueño* (Life is a Dream) and *El Alcalde de Zalamea* (The Mayor of Zalamea), among many others. On this occasion, unlike his unsuccessful bout in trying to save Cervantes' last dwelling, Mesonero was prepared to put up more of a fight for his cause.

Don Ramón showed up at the house just as the demolition squad was beginning to knock down walls. At first he tried to reason with the workmen, imploring them to stop. But the workers paid no heed to the elderly meddler and continued to swing their sledge-hammers at the masonry. Realizing that courteous requests and polite reasoning were proving ineffective, Don Ramon started to strike out at the men with his cane, thereby interrupting the demolition efforts. He then kept guard until nightfall, staunchly threatening anyone who would touch a brick of the hallowed building.

The next morning, Mesonero petitioned friends in City Hall, asking that an injunction be issued to stop the work of demolition and preserve the historical building. This time the appeals were effective. Work on tearing down the house was halted. Thus, thanks to Mesonero's efforts, if you now walk up the Calle Mayor to number 61, you'll come to the house that Calderón de la Barca lived and died in.

The Narrowest House. The "Casa Estrecha" or Narrow House measures only five meters (15 ft.) in width. It is here that the writer Calderón de la Barca lived, wrote and died. *Author's photo.*

The building is also of interest for quite another reason: it is possibly the narrowest house in Madrid, and is known as the "Casa Estrecha" (the Narrow House) since it is only five meters (15 feet) wide. That may be small, but even more astonishing is that, this being Madrid, part of the façade was taken up by a tavern only nine foot wide! The locale has now been converted into a souvenir shop.

We might also mention that over the past there have been other contenders for the questionable honor of being the narrowest house in the city. One was called the Casa de las Cinco Tejas (House of the Five Tiles) which was so narrow that the roof was only wide enough for five roof tiles to fit in side by side. It stood in the Calle de Santa Ana near the Rastro, but sadly enough Don Ramón didn't consider it worth being saved since it was not associated with any literary luminary. It was torn down in 1851.

Yet another narrow house was the well-known Casa del Ataúd (Coffin House), so called because its shape resembled a coffin. It was located right at the corner of the Calle de Alcalá and Calle del Caballero de Gracia and was torn down when the Gran Vía was built.

Cloistered nuns: from relics to pastries

Walking south of one of the busiest and most bustling squares in Madrid, the Plaza del Callao, you'll come to a large brick building constructed in the mid-16th century called the Convento de las Descalzas Reales (Convent of the Royal Barefoot Sisters) (see Area 5 map, Pg. 207). The convent has played host to many illustrious royal guests, and up to the 18th century it was customary in Madrid to bring the bodies of deceased kings and princes here to receive their last benedictions and responsories. The building and its furnishings are considered to be one of the artistic jewels of the capital.

But the guided tours are limited to only a part of the building. The reason, incredible though it may seem considering its proximity to the hectic modern-day activity all around it, is that sections of the large edifice are still occupied by 23 reclusive Franciscan nuns who are not allowed to have any direct communication with the outside world. If you are in the last morning tour, near the end of your visit you'll hear a bell ringing at about 1:30 p.m. This is to warn all visitors that they must tarry no longer, for the nuns are about to leave their restricted area for meals, prayers and other activities.

This is not the only convent in Madrid where cloistered nuns still live, much as they did at the time of the Inquisition. There are 37 other nunneries in the city still inhabited by 515 sisters. However, only the Descalzas Reales and the Convento de la Encarnación (Convent of the Incarnation), on the Plaza de la Encarnación 1, near the Royal Palace, (see Area 4 map, Pg. 167) are partially open to the public, thanks to the artistic treasures found in them.

One of the highlights of the Convento de la Encarnación is a crypt filled from wall to wall with glass cabinets containing an impressive number of ornate reliquaries. Fingers of saints, skulls, hair, teeth, pieces of arms and other parts of the human skeleton – all are on display here. The collection has been growing ever since the chamber was first opened in 1616.

Perhaps the most famous and revered reliquary in the convent is a vial which is said to contain the coagulated blood of San Pantaleón, a saint who lived near the end of the 3rd century AD in ancient Rome and who was the court doctor for the Emperors Diocletian and Galerius.

The story goes that one day Pantaleón came upon a child who had just died of a snakebite. The doctor, who had heard of the God of the Christians but who was skeptical of his powers, decided to put the new Deity to the test and asked Him to save the child and kill the serpent. Lo and behold, the child miraculously came to life again and the snake was struck dead. Pantaleón was so astounded that he decided to

Nuns' Pastries. Seen here is the rickety intercom found beside the door that leads to the Corpus Christi Convent where cloistered nuns still sell pastries. The sign reads:

OPENING HOURS
Sale of Pastries and Visiting Hours
Mornings from 9:30 to 1
Afternoons from 4:00 to 6:30.
Author's photo.

convert to Christianity. When the Emperor Galerius found out about his conversion, he was so incensed that he had him tortured and then publicly decapitated. The execution occurred on July 27th in 305 AD.

After the deed was done, several Christians carefully gathered his spilt blood in vials and kept them as relics. Later, the doctor was sanctified.

Once a year on the feast day of the saint, July 27th, the coagulated blood inside the vial is seen to turn liquid and remains that way for approximately 24 hours. On the day the blood liquefies, the number of people crowding in to see the "miracle" is so great that only a small proportion of them manage to get close enough to the vial to see it. Those who can't push in, however, can see the liquefaction on closed-circuit TV screens that are put up inside the convent.

The vial in Madrid is not the only one reputed to have the saint's blood in it. There are others in Rome, Amalfi, Salerno, Chieti, Bari and Venice, each with its own religious characteristics, though not all are said to liquefy on July 27th. The one in Salerno remains liquid throughout the entire year.

Yet another convent abuts on a popular street for nocturnal bar-hopping, the often boisterous Calle de las Huertas, now closed to vehicular traffic. The entrance to the convent, called the Convento de San Ildefonso, occupied by the Trinitarias Descalzas nuns, whose founding dates back to 1612, is on the Calle de Lope de Vega 18 (see Area 2 map, Pg. 85). It is here that Cervantes' last remains were buried, as mentioned earlier in the book.

Other convents with cloistered nuns in the center of town, all from the 16th and 17th centuries, include the Convento de las Comendadoras de Santiago, on the Plaza de las Comendadoras, the Convento de San Plácido in the Calle de San Roque 9, the Convento de Santa Isabel on the Calle de Santa Isabel and the Convento de las Monjas del Corpus Christi on the Plaza del Conde de Miranda 3, to mention just a few.

The latter convent is known familiarly as "Las Carboneras" (The Coal Women) due to a painting of the Immaculate Virgin they accidentally found in a coal bin, which is now displayed in the church. It is in the Carboneras that a 50-year-old tradition is maintained whereby you can buy pastries made by the ten cloistered nuns now living there.

Steep yourself for a few brief minutes in the atmospheric Madrid of the past by proceeding to the convent where you'll find a sturdy wooden door a few steps to the right of the entrance to the church. You ring an outside bell, after which the door will be opened and you pass down several dimly-lit passageways and past a small inner courtyard before coming to the "*torno*". This is a revolving wooden turntable window, through which you tell the attending sister what pastries you want, though you are unable to see her. There is a price list next to the window with the products for sale: *pastas de coco y almendra* (coconut and almond biscuits), *mantecados de yema* (egg-yoke cookies), *mantecados de Jerez* (sherry cookies), and *naranjínes* (orange-flavored sweets), just to mention a few. You then place your money on the turntable which revolves and presently the bakeries appear. Contrary to what some might think, the nuns are often pleased to talk to the customers and will even answer questions about their life in the convent.

Curious to say, it wasn't until 1950 that Pope Pius XII authorized the sale of home-made goods by the nuns. Since then the custom of purchasing pastries and other items from the sisters has been popular in other convents around the

The "torno." The wooden *torno* or turntable that conceals sight of the sisters but allows them to sell their goodies. Note the chain on the door. Its purpose is to permit the nuns to close it from inside the convent and hence not be seen. *Author's photo.*

country, each group of nuns specializing in their own type of bakeries and sweets.

Pastries made by cloistered nuns are also on sale in the Segundo Monasterio de la Visitación de Santa María, better known as the Convento de Las Salesas Nuevas on the Calle de San Bernardo 72 (see Area 5 map, Pg. 207). Our favorite pastries here are called "Santa Eulalia" named after Sister Eulalia who was in charge of the baking oven. These pastries are made of flour, sugar, margarine and a bit of brandy. The latter ingredient may help to brighten the sisters' spirits while in the confinement of the convent and during the cold winter months in Madrid. Indeed, during the Christmas season, for Epiphany (January 6th), the nuns make typical pastries called *roscones de reyes* which are so popular that customers reserve them months ahead of time. Each of these ringlike *roscones* has a "surprise" in its dough, usually consisting of a small porcelain figure. Traditionally, when eating it, the person who winds up with the piece containing the "surprise" is expected to pay for the whole *roscón*.

FIST-IN-THE-FACE STREET
(Calle de Puñonrostro)

Contrary to what one might suspect, the name of this short street right behind Madrid's City Hall was not so named because of a street fight or due to some mugger punching his victim in the face in the then dark alleyways of the capital. Its name dates back to the 16th century when a house was located on it which was owned by the Count of Puñonrostro, hence the street came to be known by the same name.

The Posada del Peine: Madrid's original flophouse

In Madrid there was never the equivalent of a "skid row" in the city. However, there have always been poor parts of Madrid, the so-called *barrios bajos* (down-under neighborhoods), which served as inspirations for both novels and *zarzuelas* (short musical comedies). In the 19th and early 20th centuries one of these areas contained dozens of what were called *posadas* (inns) where those bringing produce for sale to the capital from the provinces put up for a night or two. Most were muleteers, teamsters, farmers and the humblest of travelling salesmen.

Usually, you entered these inns through a large doorway, a little like an English coaching inn, which led into a spacious tamped-earth courtyard. Here the horses could be tethered and watered at a trough, fed, and the wagon unloaded. Around the sides of the courtyard you could access a row of no-frills small rooms, each furnished with a bed and a chair. Climbing up a flight of wooden stairs, you came to a kind of outdoor gallery which ran all around the courtyard where more rooms accommodated the weary teamster or itinerant pedlar.

Until just a few years ago some of these *posadas* were still doing business, especially those on the street called the Cava Baja, just off the Plaza Mayor. There you can still make out some of the faded old signs such as the Posada del Dragón, the Posada del León de Oro and the Posada de San Isidro.

As the tourist trade turned from a controllable trickle into an avalanche in the 1960's, fancy restaurants started opening on the Cava Baja. One of these took over a former *posada*, subsequently called the Mesón del Segoviano, popular with students and tourists, and transmogrified it into what is now Casa Lucio, on Cava Baja 35, a hang-out for politicos and besuited businessmen on expense accounts. Reservations here are hard to book, though the fare consists mostly of the standard old dishes that have been served for 100 years in Madrid, except at double the price, such as *callos a la madrileña*

Vestiges of the former Posada del Peine. Some telltale signs of the old guest house still remain on the façade of the building, such as the ceramic tiles on the corner of the Calle de Postas. *Author's photo.*

(tripe, Madrid style). One of their specialities, *huevos estrellados,* is made by dropping several raw eggs on piping-hot deep-fried potatoes. The dish must be served within three minutes, otherwise it is considered to be *passé.*

The nearby Posada de la Villa, Cava Baja 9, supposedly dating back to 1642, now an expensive tourist venue of fairly recent vintage, also keeps the *ambiance* of the old Madrid, and its three floors of dining rooms, decorated in the traditional Castilian manner, serve up an excellent roast baby lamb (*cordero asado*). But watch out for the tab on that "house wine", which on our last visit turned out to be rather expensive Marqués de Riscal reserve. A number of celebrities including José María Aznar, Roberto Carlos and Bruce Springsteen have dined in the restaurant over the past decades and the management has carved the names of these customers on the backs of the chairs in the dining rooms.

The original *posadas,* in contrast, were strictly for the local teamsters and hardly suited to foreign visitors, who usually stayed at the better hotels and boarding houses. However there *was* one inexpensive inn that bridged the gap between smelly hostelries and posh hotels, even achieving a modicum of international repute and being listed in British guidebooks.

It was called the Posada del Peine (Comb Inn), between the Plaza Mayor and the Puerta del Sol. The Posada claimed it had been opened in 1610. It boasted over 150 rooms in its five stories, the higher priced ones with the customary French windows enclosed by small metal-grilled balconies with wooden shutters. It got its name in the old days because as a courtesy to its guests a comb was placed in each of its rooms, but to avoid it being stolen was tied to the sink.

Posada del Peine's clock tower. Years back, this was the most characteristic architectural element of the posada. Recently (2010), a new clock has been installed. *Author's photo.*

An unexplained curiosity was that in Room 126 could be found a cupboard which concealed a narrow secret staircase leading up to a hidden room on the upper floor of the building. What its purpose was remains unknown, though it may have been used for hiding fugitives during the stormy 19th century.

The best description of the Posada del Peine that we have come across is not from a local writer, but from Edith A. Browne, a Briton who stayed there in 1909 with her travelmate, Salome, who dedicates to it a section of her otherwise slight children's tome, *Peeps at Many Lands*. Browne was the sort of lady who "liked to be as the natives, to sleep in native hotels or inns, live on native fare, travel with the natives..." Upon her checking with friends in England somebody had heard of an inn where a bedroom could be had for only one *peseta* a night, about 25 cents American, or 10 pence British, at a time when most regular hotels cost four times that amount, including light and attendance. The women thought there was something fishy about such a place.

Since the ladies had a couple of hours to spare upon first passing through Madrid en route to Toledo, previous to making a stay in the capital, they decided to cast an appraising glance at the Posada.

"We found that so-called inn without much difficulty. It was quite an imposing-looking establishment, and we came to the conclusion, as we mounted a broad flight of steps leading to the bureau, that the place had changed hands, and been raised to the dignity of an hotel. It did not seem at all probable that the rooms were now a *peseta* a night.

"A well-groomed man in white uniform came forward to greet us in the office. In answer to our inquiries, he informed us

Interior of the present Posada del Peine. The original wooden staircase, wrought-iron banister and even part of the brick wall with its iron grilles on the windows have been preserved in the refurbished hotel, now called the Petit Palace. *Author's photo.*

that the *best* single bedrooms were 1 *peseta* a night, the *best* rooms with two single beds 1 $^1/_2$ *pesetas*. We asked to see one of the latter. He selected a key, led us down a wide corridor that looked spotlessly clean, and opened the door of an equally clean-looking, fresh-smelling room. Certainly there was no superfluous furniture in that room, no attempt at decoration; but this is an advantage, rather than a drawback, in a strange apartment. It was large and airy; the walls had just had a new coat of whitewash. There were two iron bedsteads, with snowy-white coverlets, a couple of chairs, a table, and an enamelled washstand. Impressed by the courteous manners of our cicerone, the spaciousness and cleanliness of the establishment, and the atmosphere of peace and quietude, we booked the room for a specified date, and took the first opportunity of rejoicing over our good luck in hearing of the place and getting a room there.

"One Saturday night we arrived back in Madrid. We had come up by the last train, and it was very late, but we were perfectly at ease, seeing that we knew where we were going to stay. We drove straight to our destination. This time, instead of finding ourselves on the threshold of an empty doorway, we stood on the curb looking in bewilderment at a crowd of men, women, and children who blocked up the entrance. We called someone to take our luggage, dismissed the cab, and edged our way through the crowd, only to find ourselves caught in another throng that was wending its way upstairs. That broad flight of steps, which we had previously mounted in solitary state, was now packed with men in shirt-sleeves, soldiers of the line, women with babies in their arms, and ragamuffin children. We were carried up with the stream, never dreaming that we should not break clear before we reached the bureau.

"Suddenly we were brought to a standstill at the back of

a queue. As we took our turn to move forward and came nearer to the office, the truth dawned on us. We looked at each other, but said never a word; silently we agreed to see the thing through. In due course our turn came to have a key handed to us over the counter, and we found our own way to our room. But we did not have to let ourselves in; that little service was undertaken as a personal act of grace by an attendant, who had already taken up his official position for the night on a bench just outside our door. Whilst the key was being turned we had leisure to watch a pedlar let himself in at a door opposite, and notice a peasant, his buxom wife, and several children, enter a room on our right.

"Left to ourselves in our own apartment, I broke the silence – that is to say, the silence between us two; but I had to raise my voice to make myself heard above the din without.

"'Do you know we're in a doss-house?' (the British expression for a flophouse. Ed.)

"'A first-class one,' came the cheery reply.

"'And evidently a favourite.'

"'Saturday night, you see – soldiers on week-end furlough, country cousins in town for Sunday... By the way, perhaps there's a bull-fight to-morrow... if so, we're in luck... and that would easily account for a specially busy night here.'

"'Are you really prepared to stay in this place?'

"'The room looks just as clean as when we first saw it. Besides, we can't go out into a strange town and look for an hotel at this time of night.'

"That settled the question, and I proceeded to turn down the snowy coverlets and examine the beds. The sheets were clean, inasmuch as they were not begrimed, but obviously they had been slept in. I called the attendant, and told him to bring all fresh bedclothes for both beds, at the same time slipping a coin into his hand. He returned presently with the desired luxuries, remade the beds, and went away smiling, as though he were highly amused by our eccentric ideas; but he came back unbidden over and over again, each time with something new that he had thought of to make us more comfortable.

"We went to bed, and, tired out, fell asleep. An odd rebel

or two defied Keating (a famous Victorian anti-bug-powder. Ed.) and woke us up in the early hours of the morning. We made tea, got out the biscuits, sat down side by side at the table, had a festive picnic, laughed over past adventures in the night, told ourselves how we should laugh over the present one when we were well on the other side of it, and, growing drowsy, leant our arms on the table for pillow, bent our heads down on them, and dozed off into a semi-slumber. But when morning came we were quite sure we had not dreamed that people had been on the move in the building all through the livelong night. Nevertheless, we both agreed that we had often passed a night in far more uncomfortable and 'lively' surroundings, and been obliged to pay through the nose for the experience into the bargain.

"Considering its clientèle, that doss-house was remarkably clean, and it was certainly conducted in a most orderly manner. Massed in memory with all the native Spanish inns at which we stayed, it has a place of honour for its freshness of atmosphere, and, judged by comparison, even its sanitary arrangements now seem to me to have been planned on some sort of hygienic system."

From the Calle de Postas, on which the inn is located, you can still see its name from former times on a pretty ceramic strip on the side of the building, as well as a clock tower on the roof erected in 1892 which for many decades was its signpost. The clock has long since disappeared, but the small structure is still intact, with the name of the Posada prominently displayed underneath it.

The inn shuttered its doors in 1970 and stood abandoned for over three decades. However, in 2005 it was refurbished and modernized and reopened as the four-star Petit Palace Posada del Peine. Fortunately some of the old structural features have been maintained, such as the wooden beams, parts of the brick walls with iron grilles and the original wooden staircase with the wrought-iron banister. Although the new designer look, including flat TV screens and hydroshowers bear little resemblance to the legendary Posada of the past, you may still get an inkling of what it may have been like. By the way, the combs in the bathrooms now have no strings attached. You can take them with you.

The Rastro: a flea market for all tastes

Every Sunday morning until midday, the center of Madrid closes some of its streets to vehicular traffic. Among these is the Ribera de Curtidores (Strand of the Leather Tanners) where a huge flea market springs up which spills out into all the side streets around it. Here you can buy anything and everything choosing from a bewildering jumble ranging from authentic junk to expensive antiques. The array includes handicrafts, old clothes, sunglasses, army surplus, leather goods, furniture, hardware, vinyl records, sporting goods, DVDs and CDs, pets, rocks, back-issue magazines, and a huge spectrum of seemingly useless household debris.

This flea market is known as "El Rastro" which literally means "the trail" and refers to a trail in blood. Long ago, the Plaza Vara del Rey, off the Ribera de Curtidores, was the site of a slaughterhouse. It was from here, once the animals were killed, that the offal was dragged off to loading wagons, leaving a visible trail of blood on the ground. This eventually gave rise to the name "El Rastro", or The Trail.

The Rastro can be divided into different areas, each of which specializes in a certain kind of merchandise. In the upper reaches of the Ribera de Curtidores, around the Plaza de Cascorro, you'll tend to find a riot of outdoor stands mostly selling arts and crafts, sunglasses, T-shirts, clothing and leather goods.

Further down on the left side, the street is lined with modern furniture shops, while on the right you'll see a row of sporting goods outlets. Turning into a side street on the right, the Calle de las Amazonas, will bring you to the Plaza del General Vara del Rey, the site of one of the most popular outdoor emporiums in the market, where a large selection of

Palulú in the Rastro. These edible (or chewable) sticks are the roots of the shrub from which licorice is extracted. *Author's photo.*

minerals, fossils, shoes, paintings, coins and clothing, as well as a few records and books are on sale.

Returning to the Ribera, on the lefthand side, you'll come to the Calle de San Cayetano which specializes in original paintings, art reproductions and etchings. Then, a few steps further down the Ribera, on the left, beckons the Calle de Fray Ceferino González, known popularly as the *Calle de los Pajaritos* (Street of the Birdies). Not so long ago, all sorts of domestic animals, especially birds, could be bought from street vendors there, but the practice has now been outlawed. Presently, the animals can only be sold by licensed shops, although many continue to display the cages with pets in them on their storefronts. Well worth a look, at Number 10 of this same street, is the Naturaves Mundo Azul, selling all sorts of birds which range from partridges to huge macaos.

Those seeking high quality artifacts and authentic antiques should head for the two indoor "galleries" halfway down the Ribera de Curtidores, one on the left, called the Galerías Piquer, at Number 29, and another on the right, the Nuevas Galerías, at Number 12. Each features two floors of shops ranged around a large courtyard and are crammed with a wide variety of collectibles. Other antique shops are located on the Plaza Vara del Rey and the surrounding side streets.

It is in the Rastro that you'll sometimes still see people chewing on what appears to be a stick from a tree. What in fact they have in their mouths is popularly called *palulú,* the root of the shrub from which licorice is extracted. As you chew and suck on it, the root gives off its licorice taste. At the time of writing, there is a tiny shop selling the *palulú* on the Calle de Mira el Sol, off to the right from Ribera de Curtidores, on which street you'll also come to a number of stands hawking hardware equipment. The street then leads into a sprawling square, the Plaza de Campillo del Mundo Nuevo, a good place to browse for magazines, books and movies on DVD.

If you're put off by modern computers and electronics and have a soft spot for vintage office equipment such as typewriters, adding machines and rolltop desks, head up to the Calle de la Arganzuela that leads out of the Campillo del Mundo Nuevo, and at number 39 you'll come to the Antigüedades de Oficina. And a little bit further up that street is another shop for the nostalgia-minded called El Museo del Teléfono Antiguo which specializes in antique telephones, gramophones and radios.

Finally, if you've succumbed to the fashion among collectors and decorators for furniture from the 1950's and 1960's, a few shops specializing in this genre have sprung up in la Rastro. Such, for example, as the huge L.A. Studio on Calle de la Arganzuela 18 (across from the Callejón del Mellizo) and El 8 on the Calle de Mira el Rio Alta 8.

Finally, in case you haven't been forewarned elsewhere, be on the alert for pickpockets, who infest the area. Our personal recommendation is to leave your wallet and valuables in your hotel safe the day you visit the Rastro. The best time to go is around 11 a.m. or earlier on a Sunday morning, before the crowds get really thick.

Plaza de Cascorro: a forgotten suicide mission

One of the most common meeting places in the crowded Rastro – an easy place to lose sight of those accompanying you — is the Plaza de Cascorro (a block from the Metro station La Latina), the site of a monument to the soldier Eloy Gonzalo. The square takes its name, "Cascorro", from the battle he fought in. If you look at the statue, you'll notice that in one hand Gonzalo is holding a box or bin, in the other a torch, and that a rope is tied around his midriff. What purpose did this paraphernalia have and what was the soldier up to?

Eloy Gonzalo statue.
The statue of Eloy Gonzalo stands in Madrid's flea market, El Rastro. Note that he carries a torch, a bin of gasoline and has a rope tied around his waist. All three items played a key role in his heroic deed in Cascorro, Cuba.
Author's photo.

Eloy Gonzalo's background was not an uncommon one in the penurious Spain of the 19th century. As a newly-born infant, he was found in 1868 on the steps of a Madrid church called La Inclusa on the Calle de O'Donnell, a religious institution dating back to 1572 which cared for abandoned children. Eloy was soon adopted by a family from a village near Ávila who provided him a home and cared for him lovingly. When Eloy reached manhood, both his foster-parents died, once again leaving him homeless. Times were hard and Eloy chose to enlist in the army. But misfortune seemed to dog him wherever he went. In the army, a quarrel with an officer over a woman landed him in front of a court martial which sentenced him to 12 years in prison for military insubordination.

He began his term in Valladolid, but as a consequence of Spain's war with Cuban insurgents, and the great number of Spanish casualties resulting from warfare and illness there, a law was passed in which military prisoners would be pardoned if they volunteered for overseas duty. To Eloy Gonzalo the chance to fight for his country and possibly even return as a hero seemed far preferable to enduring the degrading conditions of prison life.

After minimal additional training, Eloy was sent off to Cuba in 1896 where his unit entered action against the insurgents in the small village of Cascorro, about 60 kilometers (40 miles) from Havana. The Spanish regiment consisted of only 170 men who found themselves surrounded in three positions by 3,000 of the enemy. The imminent defeat of the Spaniards seemed assured. Their captain, Francisco Neila de Ciria, concluded that the only options left were either to surrender or to sneak up at night and set fire to a building being used by the Cubans as a stronghold. A volunteer was called for, though everyone knew that it was a suicide mission. Eloy, mustering his strength and valor, took a step forward, arguing that since he had no family or loved ones he was willing to give up his life for his country. However he attached one condition. In case he were killed, he was to have a proper Spanish burial. To insure this, he asked that a rope be tied around his midriff so that his body could be dragged back to his own lines and would not fall into the hands of the enemy. The commanding officer agreed and in the still of the night Eloy crawled up to the stronghold with a canister of gasoline and a long rope tied around his waist, with his rifle slung over his shoulder. Upon reaching the enemy, he doused the building with the gasoline and set it ablaze.

With the flames of the building now making him a perfect target, he was seriously wounded. However, his comrades somehow managed to drag him back to his own lines. Thanks to his action, the Spaniards were able to hold out until a relief column broke through to liberate them after being surrounded for 13 days.

When news of the events got back to Spain, Eloy Gonzalo was hailed as the hero of the day. His humble Madrid origins, doubtless coupled with a dash of patriotic hyperbole in the press, endeared him to the Madrid populace. He was promptly awarded the Military Merit medal. Unfortunately, the young soldier was not to enjoy his popularity for long in far-off Cuba, for only nine months after his heroic deed he died in a hospital there as a result of his wounds.

The statue raised in memory of Eloy Gonzalo's heroic deed, which now peers over the hundreds of bargain-hunters that mill around the Rastro, was inaugurated by King Alfonso XIII in 1901. Eloy Gonzalo also has one of Madrid's major avenues named after him. Not bad for an orphan and a jailbird!

SWORD AND FENCING STREETS
(Calle de la Espada and Calle de la Esgrima)

Back in the 17th century, there was a house with a yard behind it nicknamed the House of the Inquisitor. The property was rented by a fencing master who there opened a fencing school and, to publicize his business, hung a huge sword over the outside of the yard. He proudly claimed the sword had once belonged to a French grandee and had been wielded in countless battles and adventures.

It was in this fencing school that the playwright Lope de Vega and his brother took fencing lessons. When the owner of the yard later decided to build a house on it, he took possession of the sword outside the fencing master's establishment in lieu of money owed him by his tenant, but left it hanging over the entrance to the yard. But litigation over the construction of the new building caused work on it to be halted. Meanwhile, for many years, the sword continued to hang in its former place. It was thus that the street eventually came to be known as the Calle de la Espada.

Upon the fencing master being evicted from the yard, he found another nearby site where he opened a new fencing school. This was in the yard of a book dealer. The fencing master soon turned the site into a lively place for thrusts and parries that always attracted curious passers-by. Soon the street came to be called the Calle de la Esgrima, or Fencing Street. In fact, on occasions some of his more high-spirited students would amuse themselves by skirmishing with idlers who wandered into the yard. The resulting complaints prompted the authorities to henceforth bar entry to outsiders not connected with the school.

But when the fencing school was closed, one item associated with it did survive for posterity. For the sword that had hung over the yard in the Calle de la Espada was eventually acquired by the Duke of Alba, who was interested in its historical associations and who hung it in the private collection of armor in his Madrid mansion.

San Isidro: Madrid's miracle man

Incorrupt body of San Isidro. Although more than 800 years have passed since the death of San Isidro, what is supposed to be his body still remains. It is only displayed publicly on very special occasions. *Author's archive.*

Even the most devout visitors to Madrid can be excused for feeling some perplexity when it comes to deciding who is the city's patron saint. Is it Our Lady of the Almudena, the oldest of them? Is it San Isidro? Or is it the most popular of the three, the Virgin of the Dove, or, in Spanish, La Virgen de la Paloma? In fact, there are still further contenders for that honor, among them the Virgin of Atocha and the Virgin of the Maravillas.

However, only the first three mentioned are honored by having a public holiday set aside for them in the capital. And agreement that San Isidro is the *male* patron saint is unanimous.

Isidro was born in 1082, before the Christians reconquered the city from the Moors. He began working as a well digger and then as a tiller of the soil, under the orders of Iván de Vargas, one of the richest and most powerful land owners in Madrid. Isidro was a humble servant and there wasn't anything particularly extraordinary about him except possibly his stature, which was 1.80 meters (5'11"), extremely tall in those days. Nonetheless, the Church has attributed to him hundreds of miracles. In his 90 years on this earth - certainly most unusual in those days — he married María de la Cabeza who also was made a saint and who bore him a son, Illán, also reputed to have performed many miracles. After having been buried, he is said to have resuscitated in 1212, 40 years after his death, in order to be able to give King Alfonso VIII some pointers on how to win the battle of Navas de Tolosa. Not bad at all for a simple farmer!

As one walks around Madrid, at every turn there seems to be something related to San Isidro. To visit all the sites associated with him would require a virtual pilgrimage. However, we shall mention only a few.

The best place to start on such a tour is at the Plaza de San Andrés 2, at the Museo de San Isidro. The building stands on the site of Juan Vargas's house, Isidro's master, and was formerly the mansion of the Counts of Paredes. Still remaining from the original building is a beautiful 16th century Renaissance patio. The museum displays a large variety of paraphernalia related to the saint, such as paintings, sculptures and a chapel constructed in the 17th century with an oval fresco on the roof painted by Zacarías González Velázquez. In the fresco, you'll see a banner that reads *Hic obdormivit in domino* (Here he slept with the Lord), signifying that this is the site where San Isidro supposedly died. However, perhaps the most curious attraction in the museum is an old glass-covered well, quite impressive in depth, for it descends 20 meters (60 feet). It is here the saint was reputed to have performed one of his most famous miracles.

Miracle Well in the Museo de San Isidro. Legend has it that San Isidro's baby fell into a very deep well and that after fervent praying the water level suddenly rose bringing the child up alive, safe and sound. *Author's photo.*

This concerned Isidro's baby son. Apparently the infant fell into the well and was on the verge of drowning. Upon Isidro appealing to the Lord, the water of the well miraculously rose, thereby saving the child.

Some experts now claim that another well, only recently discovered in 1997, is the authentic one. This second well is located in the Hermitage of Santa María de la Antigua in Carabanchel Bajo, somewhat out of town on the other side of the Manzanares River. An ancient inscription on it reads: "Pozo de San Ysidro" (San Isidro's Well). However, it's anyone's guess which one of the two is the real McCoy.

Aside from the exhibits relating to San Isidro, the museum sponsors temporary exhibitions on the second floor. Most of the building is dedicated to a survey of the city's history, tracing its development from its origins to the time it became the capital of Spain. On view are bones from paleolithic times, mosaics from Roman villas, Islamic pottery, paintings, maps, graphics, and various models of buildings and churches including a huge model of the streets and houses in the city, based on a famous map drawn up by Pedro de Texeira in 1656.

Downstairs in the museum, you'll come to an archeological and paleontological laboratory as well as a large room with showcases exhibiting some of the artifacts that have been found in excavations in and around the city.

Closely associated with the Saint is the nearby Church of San Andrés. Inside it you can visit a chapel dedicated to Isidro which is built over what is believed to have been the site of an earlier primitive chapel where he was buried. The present chapel was begun after his canonization in 1622 but not completed until 1657. Various paintings depicting scenes from the Saint's life decorate the sides and front of the church.

Miracle Fountain in the Ermita de San Isidro. From this fountain flows the "miraculous" water that allegedly cures all types of ailments. The inscriptions tell of the many miracles attributed to the water. *Author's photo.*

But let us return to San Isidro's alleged miracles. One of the most famous of these is said to have occurred on the opposite bank of the Manzanares River, near the Segovia Bridge, and is now marked by a hermitage (Paseo de la Ermita 78). At the time, the land owned by the Vargas family extended from what is now the Casa de Campo park all the way to this hermitage, near the village of Carabanchel. In fact, centuries later, King Felipe II purchased the Casa de Campo lands from descendants of the Vargas in order to use it for his own pursuits. It was there, in Carabanchel, that Isidro spent much of each day plowing the fields.

One day Isidro's master, Vargas, paid him a visit. It being a very hot day, Vargas asked Isidro to give him a drink from his canteen. However, seeing that the canteen was empty, Isidro struck a rock on the ground with his stick and said, "When it pleased God, there was water here." At that instant, a stream of water spurted out of the ground. Years later, a modest chapel was raised beside the spring from where the water had come.

In the 16th century, when the Emperor Carlos V and his son Felipe were struck by fevers and when all else failed to cure them, they were said to have drunk the water from the spring and miraculously recovered. In appreciation of this, Carlos's wife, Isabel of Portugal, in 1528 built a more elaborate hermitage on the spot, depicted in one of Goya's painting, *La ermita de San Isidro*, currently in the Prado. The structure was later destroyed during the Spanish Civil War, but after the conflict the present one was built in its place.

The spot at which the water spurted out has ever since been an active fountain and still today is thought to have curative powers. Even now, on the saint's feast day, May 15th, enormous crowds of people still cross the river to flock to the hermitage to drink the supposedly curative waters. But we'll let you in on a little secret not commonly known: the water coming out of the fountain doesn't flow directly from the natural spring, but first runs through a filter, as prescribed by the health authorities. Should you wish to fill your canteen with some of the "miracle" water, you can do so on Sunday mornings, when the fountain is open to the public from 10:30 a.m. to 2 p.m.

Nearby, you can walk over to the traditional Pradera de San Isidro (San Isidro Meadow) which during the week in May when the saint is honored becomes a funfair, providing the usual rides, refreshments, food and picnic facilities.

Also associated with Isidro is a place where the oxen that he ploughed the earth with were kept, known as La Cuadra (The Stable.) These oxen were also associated with a miracle, since on one occasion they performed the task of plowing the fields when he was absent. This odd site is not in the countryside, but smack in the oldest part of the city, on the Pretil de Santisteban 3. From the 17th century on, a small chapel marked the spot where the stable had been, and this was respected and incorporated into the new buildings that subsequently rose on the site. When the present late 19th century apartment building was constructed, one of the ground rooms in it was again maintained as being the site of the former stable. Its proprietor is an elderly lady, Doña María Teresa Pérez Balsera, now in her 80's, a descendent of the Vargas family, who personally cares for the shrine throughout the year. Only on May 15th, the room is opened to the public. It contains a small ornate altar, with polychromed statues of San Isidro and his wife, Santa María de la Cabeza, as well as several modern paintings of the saint performing miracles. On that day, a sizeable number of devotees crowd into the small chapel to offer their homage to the city's patron saint. Should you just happen to be in Madrid, you can talk to Doña Pérez, who dutifully surveys the day's activities and who will be happy to reminisce about the history of the stable with you.

Doña María Teresa Pérez Balsera. In her 80's, this descendant of the Vargas family maintains and cares for the small chapel that marks the site of the stable where San Isidro's "miracle oxen" were allegedly kept in the 12th century. *Author's photo.*

San Isidro's body reputedly now lies in an ornate gold and silver casket in the Colegiata of San Isidro el Real on the Calle de Toledo 37. As a final miracle, San Isidro's body is considered to be incorrupt, meaning that without having been embalmed his body has not disintegrated - although it is in quite bad condition - and can seldom be viewed. In modern times, the body was on public display in 1947, when the faithful brought it out during a drought in order to plead for rain. It was also publicly visible in 1969, on the 350th anniversary of Isidro's beatification, in 1972 to celebrate the centenary of his birth and again in 1985 during celebrations for the first centenary of the diocese of Madrid. It will most probably be displayed again in 2022 celebrating the fourth centenary of his canonization, even though in 2012 it will be the 800th anniversary of the Battle of Navas de Tolosa where, as mentioned earlier, he appeared miraculously after his death.

ISIDRO'S "DUMMIES" AND "SMARTIES"

On the feast day of San Isidro, May 15th, it is estimated that between 3-4 million *rosquillas de San Isidro* are sold, and many more are devoured during the saint's weeklong festivities. These ringlike pastries can be purchased in any of the many pastry shops in the city. They come in four main variations. The first are called *tontas*, the "dummies", made of dough dunked in eggs and are the simplest and least tasty, hence their name. Then there are the *listas*, the "smarties", spongy and lemon-flavored, the *Santa Claras*, with meringue on them, and finally the *francesas*, the French ones which are made with almonds.

The Virgen de la Paloma: from retrieved canvas to street fair

The most *castiza* of Madrid's female patron saints is, without a doubt, the Virgen de La Paloma, whom many girls born in Madrid are still named after. In fact, the madonna is so popular that Madrid's best-known *zarzuela* was named after the *verbena* (street festival) still held in her honor, the Verbena de La Paloma.

The *zarzuela*'s action takes place, not surprisingly, on the feast day of La Paloma, August 15th, and concerns a jealous young printer's apprentice who has a tiff with his girlfriend. She, in a huff, goes off to the street fair with another girl and an old rakish pharmacist in defiance of the apprentice. This infuriates the lad, giving rise to one of the best-loved duets in this musical genre. But it all ends happily with a charming choral number after the misunderstandings have been cleared up. The *zarzuela*, with music composed by Tomás Bretón and libretto by Ricardo de la Vega, which premiered in 1894, is as familiar to Spaniards as are the musicals of Cole Porter or Jerome Kern to Americans. Several films have been based upon the *Verbena de la Paloma* and its characters are stock figures in the lore of the city, the piece being *the* favorite in the whole repertoire of Spanish *zarzuelas.*

Virgen de la Paloma. The Paloma (Dove) is considered to be the most popular of Madrid's Holy Virgins, although curiously she is not a wooden sculpture, but rather appears as a painted Image on a canvas. *Author's archive.*

The madonna of the patron saint in question refers not to a statue or wood-carving, as is usually the case, but rather to an anonymous 18th century painting of little artistic value. Although the actual Virgin depicted in the painting is that of the Virgen de la Soledad, it has popularly been called the Virgen de La Paloma, because at first it was displayed in a house on the Calle de la Paloma. This street got its name of "Paloma" when, as an image of another Virgin – the Virgen de las Maravillas – was being transported to a small church on that same street, a dove followed it and then, with seemingly religious devotion, started to roost in the temple and remained there until it died. The street thus came to be officially listed as the Calle de la Paloma, in memory of the feathered friend.

The painting of the Virgen de la Paloma hangs high over the altar of the Church of San Pedro El Real in what used to be a typical 19th century working class neighborhood. The story goes that the painting, dirty and in poor condition, was accidentally found by a man searching for firewood in the courtyard of the church. He removed the frame, in order to burn it, and gave the painting to some kids, one of whom was the nephew of a certain Isabel Tintero. Upon seeing the painting, she gave the lad a few coins in exchange for the portrait. She then carefully cleaned it, had it reframed, and hung it at the entrance to her house on the Calle de la Paloma, flanked by two nosegays and a small lamp.

Apparently, shortly after finding the painting, Tintero's

Isabel Tintero street plaque. Several children searching for firewood found the painting of the Virgin and sold it to Isabel Tintero for a pittance. *Author's archive.*

sister-in-law decided to lay her new-born child before the Virgin, asking for Her blessings. This started a trend. Such was the fame and popularity of the madonna throughout the city that Tintero had to set aside a part of her own house to accommodate the crush of visitors. Voluntary contributions enabled a small chapel to be built for Her in 1795. But even then the space wasn't large enough and the Virgen was finally transferred to the next door church, San Pedro El Real, where it still remains today.

The Virgin is especially revered by women expecting children and those who have recently given birth. Newly-born children are brought to the sacred Image and their mothers seek Her blessing. At the present time, a Mass is still held every Saturday morning for expecting mothers and their infants.

La Paloma's popularity continued to increase over the years, even among Spanish royalty, and became a special favorite with two queens, María Luisa de Parma (Carlos IV's wife) and Isabel II. On one occasion, the former supplicated Her divine assistance when her son Fernando was very ill. Her prayers were answered. Unfortunately so, because Fernando VII turned out to be one of the most dastardly kings Spain ever had.

According to one of the city chroniclers, the portrait represents a nun from a cloister in Burgos and dates back to the 17th century. Supposedly the father of the girl had the picture painted shortly before she entered a convent so that he might have something to remember her by. She is depicted wearing the same apparel she was henceforth to wear in the cloister: a

Firefighters and the Virgin. Side by side with La Paloma, firemen parade proudly through the crowded streets. *Author's archive.*

white dress with a black shawl in the Flemish style. Indeed the young lady lived so piously that she was subsequently beatified. Permission was later obtained to shower further honors upon her and her portrait was hung in the convent in which she had lived. Numerous copies were made by enthusiasts who wanted to propagate her name. One of these finally got to Madrid and fell into the hands of the aforementioned Isabel Tintero, who, by the way, has the street in front of the church named after her. (Notice the illustration on the tiled street name, in which she is shown purchasing the painting from the children.)

In May of 1936, just before the outbreak of the Civil War, the painting was secretly removed from the church to prevent it falling into the hands of anti-clerical Republicans, and passed from house to house, finally being hidden between wooden boards on the headpost of one of the worshipper's beds. Thereupon it passed to the basement of a building on the Glorieta de San Bernardo and finally, at the end of the war, was placed in a private chapel belonging to the bishop of Madrid before finally returning to its original site.

August 15th is the national feast day for each city's local saint, which in Madrid is the Virgen de la Paloma. People in the neighborhood rise early and the shops and houses are decorated with small lanterns and strips of colored paper and bunting. Mass is held in San Pedro, which is always so crowded one can't get in. A group of firemen (La Paloma is their patron saint) then take down the painting from up high on the altar and carry it on a float through the streets. In earlier years, when the firemen didn't have a fancy float adorned with flowers and Manila shawls (typical of turn-of-the-century Madrid) they placed the painting on a fire truck.

The Mayor and the Virgin. Alberto Ruiz-Gallardón, the city's present mayor (2011) examines the afamed painting of the Virgin. *Madrid's City Council archive.*

The streets are filled with people as the procession follows along, with the locals looking out of every window. Then there is dancing of *pasodobles* (two-steps) and concerts featuring popular musical groups in the nearby Vistillas Park. Some of the locals dress up in the typical Madrid garb of the 19th century, while hawkers and street vendors dispense *churros* (fried dough) accompanied by hot chocolate and the bars spill out into the streets, setting up stands dispensing all sorts of food and drink to slake the thirst of the parishioners.

It is usually *very* hot at this time of the year in Madrid, and though much of the city has emptied out and many stores and restaurants are closed, in the neighborhood of La Paloma the crowds are thick as the festivities continue into the wee hours of the morning. Many of those living in the neighborhood have the choice of either joining the merry-making or, because of the noise level, not falling asleep until dawn.

Area 4: Royal Palace

1. **Convento de las Reparadoras** (Torija 12). Site of the Inquisition's Tribunal.
2. **Jardines de Sabatini**. Statues from Royal Palace's cornice.
3. **Convento de la Encarnación** (Plaza de la Encarnación 1). San Pantaleón's liquefying blood.
4. **Palacio Real.**
5. **Statues from Royal Palace's cornice** (Plaza de Oriente).
6. **Statues from Royal Palace's cornice** (Plaza de Oriente).
7. **Equestrian statue of Felipe IV** (center of Plaza de Oriente). Galileo's balanced statue.
8. **Arab watchtower** (Plaza de Oriente). Entrance to underground parking lot.
9. **Botillería del Café de Oriente** (Plaza de Oriente 4). Ancient ruins under glass floor.
10. **Restaurant Foster's Hollywood** (Plaza de Isabel II, 3). Arab remains in the cellar.
11. **Plaza de Ramales**, Marker of Velázquez's remains.
12. **Virgen Rinconera** (corner of Plaza Ramales and Vergara). Last of the corner Virgins.
13. Former site of **Iglesia de San Juan** (Plaza de Ramales). Ruins and outline on floor.
14. **Calle del Espejo**. Street with a story.
15. **Plaza de la Armería** (part of the Royal Palace). Statues of Montezuma and Atahualpa.
16. **Catedral de la Almudena** (Bailén 8). Virgen de la Almudena.
17. **Cuesta de la Vega**, Virgen de la Almudena, lost and found.
18. **Casa Ciriaco**, (Calle Mayor 84). Site of assassination attempt on Alfonso XIII.
19. **Parque de Emir Mohamed I**, remains of Arab defensive wall
20. **Cuesta de los Ciegos**. Street with a story.

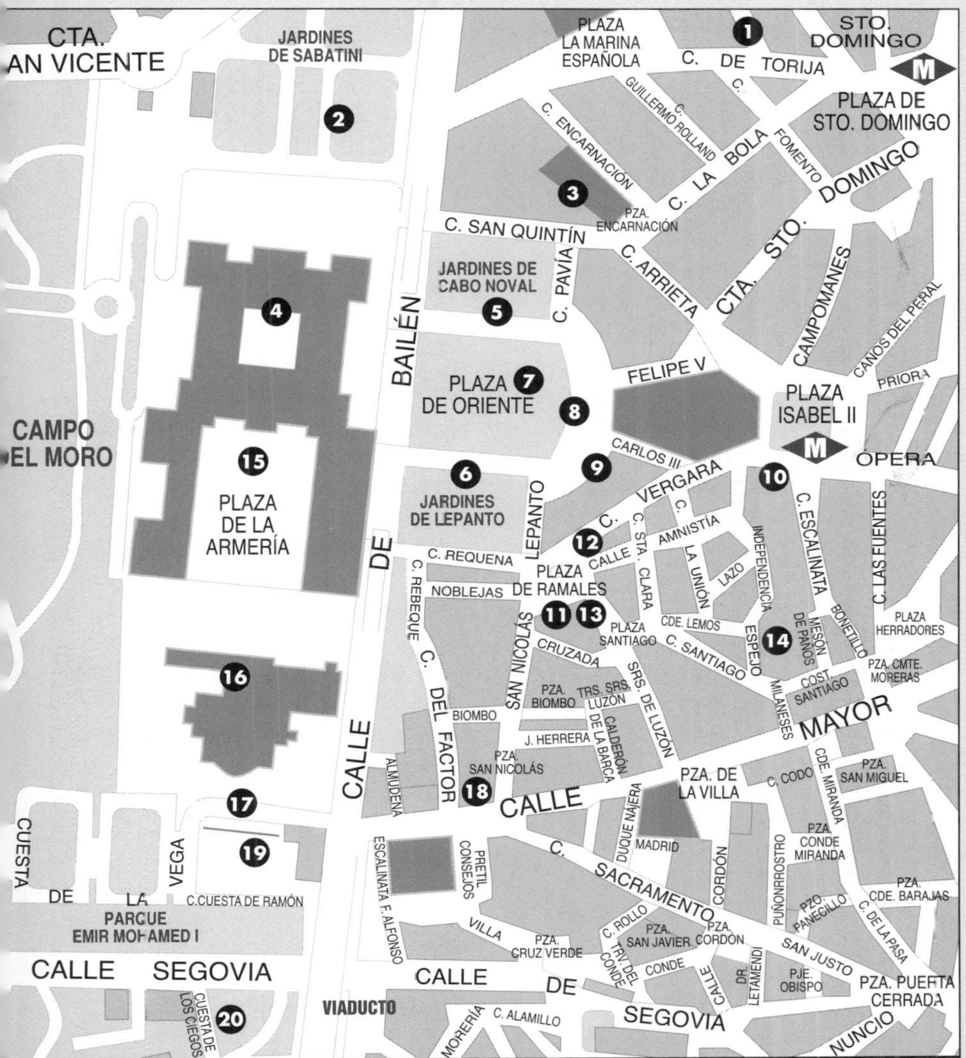
CTA.
AN VICENTE
JARDINES
DE SABATINI
PLAZA
LA MARINA
ESPAÑOLA
C. DE TORIJA
STO.
DOMINGO
PLAZA DE
STO. DOMINGO
C. GUILLERMO ROLLAND
C. ENCARNACIÓN
C. LA BOLA
FOMENTO
DOMINGO
PZA.
ENCARNACIÓN
C. SAN QUINTÍN
C. ARRIETA
CTA. STO.
CAMPOMANES
CAÑOS DEL PERAL
JARDINES DE
CABO NOVAL
C. PAVÍA
BAILÉN
PLAZA
DE ORIENTE
FELIPE V
PLAZA
ISABEL II
PRIORA
CAMPO
EL MORO
CARLOS III
ÓPERA
PLAZA
DE LA
ARMERÍA
JARDINES
DE LEPANTO
LEPANTO
C. VERGARA
C. ESCALINATA
C. LAS FUENTES
DE
C. REQUENA
CALLE
C. STA. CLARA
AMNISTÍA
LA UNIÓN
LAZO
INDEPENDENCIA
PLAZA
DE RAMALES
C. REBEQUE
NOBLEJAS
CDE. LEMOS
PLAZA
SANTIAGO
C. SANTIAGO
ESPEJO
MESÓN DE PAÑOS
BONETILLO
PLAZA
HERRADORES
SAN NICOLÁS
CRUZADA
PZA. CMTE.
MORERAS
C. DEL FACTOR
PZA.
BIOMBO
TRS. SRS.
LUZÓN
SRS. DE LUZÓN
MILANESES
COST.
SANTIAGO
MAYOR
BIOMBO
J. HERRERA
CALDERÓN
DE LA BARCA
CALLE
ALMUDENA
PZA.
SAN NICOLÁS
PZA. DE
LA VILLA
C. CODO
CDE. MIRANDA
PZA.
SAN MIGUEL
CALLE
DUQUE NÁJERA
MADRID
PZA.
CONDE
MIRANDA
CUESTA
DE LA VEGA
ESCALINATA F. ALFONSO
PRETIL
CONSEJOS
C. SACRAMENTO
CORDÓN
PUÑONRROSTRO
PZO.
PANECILLO
PZA.
CDE. BARAJAS
C.CUESTA DE RAMÓN
PARQUE
EMIR MOHAMED I
VILLA
C. ROLLO
PZA.
SAN JAVIER
PZA.
CORDÓN
SAN JUSTO
C. DE LA PASA
PZA.
CRUZ VERDE
TRV. DEL CONDE
CONDE
CALLE
DR. LETAMENDI
PJE.
OBISPO
CALLE SEGOVIA
CALLE DE SEGOVIA
PZA. PUERTA
CERRADA
CUESTA DE LOS CIEGOS
VIADUCTO
MORERÍA
C. ALAMILLO
NUNCIO
1
2
3
4
5
6
7
8
9
10
11
12
13
14
15
16
17
18
19
20
M
M

Area 4 - ROYAL PALACE

Where kings lodged royally

"You are more comfortably lodged than I!" Napoleon Bonaparte is said to have told his brother Joseph when he visited him during the French occupation of Madrid in 1809. He was referring to the impressive structure of the Royal Palace which dominates the western confines of Madrid and can be seen from miles away as you approach the city from the Extremadura highway.

After the previous royal residence of Spain's kings, the Alcázar, burned down in 1734, Spain's first Bourbon king, Felipe V, decided to build a new, far more sumptuous palace on the same site on top of the ruins of the former palace. The Italian architect Philippo Juvara put forth a design for a huge palatial complex, but it was rejected as being too expensive. Instead, the plans of another Italian, Giovanni Bautista Sachetti, were accepted and the new palace constructed.

After Felipe's death, the building was continued under Carlos III who then used it as his royal residence. As such, it continued to be the home of kings until the abdication of Alfonso XIII in 1931. The palace is now a museum and its many treasures, combined with its historical importance, have made it one of the most frequently visited tourist sights in the city. In May 2004 the monarchy again made use of it, since it became the venue for the royal wedding of Prince Felipe and former TV anchorwoman Letizia Ortiz.

The area around the palace is one of the most scenic and pleasant in the city. Beside it stands the modern Almudena

The Royal Palace. One of the statues meant to top the ledge of the Royal Palace now seems reconciled to instead adorn the pretty Plaza de Oriente. *Author's photo.*

Cathedral; on the palace's other side it is flanked by the pretty Sabatini Gardens, and directly in front of it is the handsome Plaza de Oriente with its landscaped gardens, statues, the Teatro Real and several elegant cafés with tables and chairs placed outdoors in the clement months. The whole square has been closed to traffic for a number of years. The cars, instead, pass through a long tunnel that connects either side of the Calle de Bailén.

The topheavy gallery of unwanted kings

In the gardens in front of the palace on the Plaza de Oriente you'll see two rows of larger-than-life stone statues of obscure Spanish kings and queens; eight more can be found in the Sabatini Gardens to the right of the palace. Of this same series, an additional 13 decorate the Paseo de Argentina, a promenade in the Retiro Park, six stand in front of what until 2005 was the Army Museum, (see Area 7 map, Pg. 259 for site of both groups of statues) and others can be found in Toledo and as far away as Burgos, Logroño and even Vitoria in the Basque region.

Who commissioned all these obscure kings and queens, totalling over 100, and why are they scattered all over the city? Was it some "cheaper by the dozen" scheme of a mad monarch? Or an obsession by a lover of statuary gone awry?

If you examine any of the statues at close range you'll see that the sculpting is rather unrefined and detail is kept to a minimum. On some, the head seems to have been sculpted separately; one might think that it was dropped on the shoulders of the statue haphazardly and is interchangeable with others. This is a sure sign that either the artists were terrible or that the statues were meant to be seen from a great distance, not as they are presently displayed. Seen from a great distance? From where?

The story dates back to the time when the palace was

Royal Palace cornice. In the close-up of the pedestal you can read "GUNDE-MARO M.A. 612." This is where the statue of King Gundemaro, who died in 612 AD, was meant to be placed. So where is the statue now? *Author's photo.*

being enlarged in the reign of King Carlos III. At that time, the architect who was modifying the palace, Francesco Sabatini, came up with the idea of crowning the cornice of the palace with statues of all the kings and queens of Spanish history that ruled various regions of Spain from 417 AD (the Goth, Ataulfo) up to the 16th century, 108 in all.

The king gave his approval and the massive enterprise was carried out by more than 20 sculptors. In fact, the statues, each almost twice the height of a normal man, took years to complete. However, when the task of placing the statues on the cornice of the palace began, the extremely superstitious queen mother, Isabel de Farnesio, objected. It seems Isabel had repeatedly awoken in the middle of the night in a cold sweat, tormented by a recurring nightmare. In her dreams, she saw Madrid being shaken by a ferocious earthquake. This caused the huge stone statues to topple and crush her to death. The dreams were so vivid and disturbing that they could not be ignored. Isabel was convinced that these were warnings either of her own death or of

MONTEZUMA AND ATAHUALPA

Montezuma and Atahualpa in front of the Royal Palace? Curiously, in the long list of statues of Spanish monarchs meant to decorate the palace, Carlos III decided to include two rulers of pre-Columbian civilizations which had been conquered by the Spaniards: Montezuma from the Aztec empire and Atahualpa from Peru. The statues can now be seen in prominent positions on the second floor ledge on the north side of the inner courtyard of the palace, the Plaza de Armería, close to where visitors enter to start their tour of the building.

the fall of the monarchy and begged her son King Carlos III to halt work on them and to place the statues elsewhere. Carlos III obliged, although a few remained on the cornice.

Whether these nightmares were the real reason for taking down most of the statues or not may be debated. It seems probable that the tremendous aggregate weight of the 108 stone figures, each more than two and a half meters (8 feet) in height, was deemed too heavy a load for the building. Or, that the aesthetic effect of all those statues crowded on the top of the building was not pleasing. Either way, the general consensus of local historians is that most of the statues were never placed on the roof. A document dating from 1760, during the reign of Carlos III, orders the statues to be stored in the underground vaults of the palace.

It was not until 1842, under the reign of Isabel II, that the statues were finally removed from the vaults and distributed throughout Madrid. Even so, dozens were left over and hence were dispatched to the aforementioned cities all around Spain. Whether or not the locals were happy with having them foisted upon them is not recorded.

If you look at the façade of the palace, you can see the empty ledges where the missing statues were to be placed. Moreover, if you examine these ledges more closely, using binoculars, you'll notice that the date and name of the missing kings and queens are actually inscribed in the stone. The earliest dates start from the left side and ascend as you move towards the right of the building.

We have tried to locate some of the statues missing from the niches. For example, on one of the ledges is written "Gundemaro 612". Upon searching through the statues in the Retiro Park in the Paseo de Argentina, one, indeed, is seen to be that of Gundemaro. Doubtless,

Statue of Gundemaro in the Retiro Park. The missing statue is in the Retiro Park along with 12 others that were meant to be placed on the cornice of the Royal Palace. *Author's photo.*

the remainder, corresponding to each of the empty niches, can be found among the others scattered around Madrid and the rest of the country.

Galileo's royal balancing act

In front of the Royal Palace in the Plaza de Oriente, in addition to the two rows of ancient Spanish kings, you'll also see an imposing monument topped by the equestrian statue of King Felipe IV. The entire weight of the statue rests solely upon the horse's hind legs. These touch the ground to achieve a sculptural equilibrium which, at the time it was made in the mid-17th century, was considered to be an impressive balancing act. In fact, four great artists were involved in designing and constructing the monument: Diego Velázquez, Pietro Tacca, Juan Martínez Montañés and, most surprisingly, the renowned astronomer Galileo Galilei.

In order to emulate the monument to his father, Felipe III, which now stands in the Plaza Mayor, King Felipe IV had ordered an equestrian statue to be made which was to be based on Velázquez's famous painting of himself, now in the Prado Museum. However, it was one thing to *paint* the king mounted on a rearing horse, as Velázquez had done, quite another to actually construct an equestrian statue imitating that very pose and trying to balance the great weight of the metal on the horse's two hind legs.

Chosen by the king to execute the sculpture was Pietro Tacca, a well-known sculptor from Florence who had, in fact, also sculpted his father's statue. Basing himself on two sketches by Velázquez, Tacca went to work on the project. But he immediately saw that he must grapple with a daunting challenge: the front of the horse was simply too heavy to sustain the statue only on its hind legs. Even if the horse's tail were somehow anchored to the base, it was not enough to counterbalance the tremendous weight at the front. Knowing the king would not accept excuses, Tacca sought advice from others in order to find some sort of solution to the problem. But who was there ingenious enough to solve this dilemma?

Felipe IV's equestrian statue. Due to the heavy frontal weight of the statue, help had to be sought from no other than the famous Italian astronomer Galileo in order to properly balance it. *Author's photo.*

Finally it occurred to the desperate sculptor to seek out the advice of the most famous physicist and astronomer of the time: Galileo Galilei. He wrote to him and received the following reply:

"...The problem you face is indeed a curious one and I am approaching it in the manner of riddles such as I was accustomed to solve when I was a young man. The idea of collaborating with you and the master Velázquez is a proposition far too tempting to pass up.

"Let me tell you that you will need eight tons of bronze for your statue, since the back part (of the horse) must be solid metal. I will send the pitch, angles and calculations to you as soon as possible. Doubt not that I will dedicate as much effort to solving this problem as I would to my most important scientific inquiries."

Galileo solved the problem by concentrating much of the weight in the solid hind part of the statue, which thus acted as a cantilever, an innovative practice since metal statues at that time were usually hollow. But the distribution of the weight had to be exactly calculated, which required considerable mathematical knowledge.

A full-sized clay model was completed in Florence and transported the great distance to Madrid to be approved by Felipe IV before they proceeded with the casting process. Upon arrival in the Spanish capital, the model was deemed to be magnificent, however the head did not bear sufficient likeness to that of the king and lacked the monarch's regal bearing.

A solution to the problem was found when Diego Velázquez recommended that a friend of his in Sevilla, Juan Martínez Montañés, could re-sculpt the king's head.

The king agreed and the model was stored in the base-

Juan Martínez Montañés. This painting by Diego Velázquez shows Montañés sculpting the substitute head of the monarch (bottom right), which by the way is far too small compared to the real head of the statue. *Author's archive.*

ment of the Alcázar (predecessor to the present Royal Palace). Montañés came to Madrid posthaste and the first thing he did was to cut the head off the king… the statue that is, using it as a guide to measure the dimensions for the new substitute head. For six months a headless horseman bided his time in the deep vaults of the palace as Montañés painstakingly sculpted the new head of Felipe IV. Velázquez was following the process so carefully, that he even executed a painting of Montañés working on the head, which can now be seen in the Prado Museum. Curious to note, Montañés made the sculpture in wood, not clay, for he was a wood carver. To insure complete likeness and the satisfaction of the monarch, he even had the wood polychromed.

Once the new head was approved by the king new head, it was dispatched to Florence, (Italy), where it quickly replaced the old one. A deep hole was dug into the ground where the cast would finally be made and then filled with melted bronze. Once poured, it took 27 days for the metal to cool off. It was then removed from the hole, and artisans skillfully burnished and polished the sculpture. Finally, in 1640, seven years after the beginning of the ordeal, the statue was carefully loaded on a ship and transported to Spain.

Upon arriving in Madrid, as the enormous crate was opened, the king and Diego Velázquez stood in awe and amazement as they gazed at the extraordinary work of art, a masterpiece of sculpting and casting, whose elegance far exceeded the king's most sanguine expectations.

The statue was presently placed in a prominent spot in front of the huge Palace of the Buen Retiro (which formerly stood in the front of the Retiro Park), considered at that time to be the most elegant and fashionable location in the city. Later the statue was moved in front of the Alcázar, and subsequently back to the gardens of the Parterre in the Retiro Park. Moving the statue in past centuries was a huge undertaking and it took 14 oxen hitched to a moving platform to just shift the statue from one site in Madrid to another.

Finally, in 1843 the statue was transferred to its present site and placed on a base with two reliefs, one depicting a ceremony in which Felipe IV is awarding Velázquez the Cross of the Order of Santiago (St. James) and the other showing an allegory of the monarch as patron of the arts and literature.

Even today, the equestrian statue of Felipe IV on the Plaza de Oriente is considered one the best sculptures of its kind ever made.

The elusive bones of Diego Velázquez

Diego Rodríguez de Silva y Velázquez is one of the best-known and admired painters in the world. In the Prado you will find many of his most-renowned works: *Las Meninas, Los Borrachos* (The Drunkards), *La Rendición de Breda* (The Surrender of Breda) a.k.a. *Las Lanzas* (The Lances) as well as many other of his paintings and portraits. It might be expected that the tomb where the painter's remains rest would be a place much visited and greatly revered. Therein lies the rub.

Fairly close to the Royal Palace, in the Plaza de Ramales, you'll find a small, rather ugly monument consisting of a pillar topped with an iron cross representing the Order of Santiago. This underwhelming column marks the site where Velázquez's remains more or less are buried. We emphasize the "more or less", for with the passing of time the exact location has long since been forgotten and lost. The painter's remains may still be somewhere in the general area, under the asphalt, but no one knows exactly where. Here's the reason why.

Velázquez died on August 6, 1660 and was buried with much pomp in the Church of San Juan Bautista (St. John the

Baptist) which was located on the site now occupied by the Plaza de Ramales. Funerary documents of the time confirm that his body was on public display for a day. Thereafter the coffin was deposited in the church's Chapel of the Order of Santiago, of which he was a member "...dressed in a tunic, with the scarlet insignia on his chest (the cross of the military order. Ed.), a hat, sword, boots and spurs." We even have a description of the coffin: "...lined in fine black velvet surrounded with golden handles, and adorned by a cross with gold fastenings and hinges and two keys." So much is certain and beyond doubt.

The church survived for another 150 years until the time of the French invasion in 1808. After Napoleon's brother became king, it was decided that the neighborhood surrounding the palace was far too cluttered with rundown buildings and old churches. In less than a year, a dozen buildings had been torn down, one of these being the Church of San Juan Bautista. Unfortunately, no one bothered to mark Velázquez's resting place! Hence the site where his remains were buried was soon forgotten and all that is known is that *somewhere* beneath the square rests the body of the famous painter. The small column erected in his honor thus didn't mark the spot where he was buried, but only the general area.

In the summer of 1999, work began on building a parking lot under the Plaza de Ramales. As the bulldozers started digging down into the square they came across various archeological remains. Work on the parking lot was ordered to be stopped. Clearly, before the digging could proceed, a team of archeologists would have to examine and survey the terrain and decide what was of historic value. Suddenly, 400 years after Velázquez's burial, it seemed there might be a chance of discovering the painter's remains. Having a description of the coffin and of how he was dressed could make the task easier. Several exhaustive searches were undertaken and the archeological excavations proceeded cautiously, with hopes of finding the artist's lost remains.

But when nothing relating to Velázquez was found, new theories were spun and formerly-forgotten discoveries remembered, such as a pair of mummies from the 17th century, the time Velázquez lived, that had been found several years earlier in 1994 when the Convent of San Plácido (Calle de San Roque 9) (see Area 5 map, Pg. 207) had undergone restoration. The theory proposed at that time went as follows:

During the French occupation, Joseph Bonaparte issued a royal decree which ordered all bodies that had been buried in churches in the center of Madrid to be exhumed and transferred outside the city as a precaution for preventing possible epidemics. However, there were exceptions to the rule. If the remains were of an important or well-known person, they could be transferred to a cathedral or major church in the city. Thus one conjecture sustains that Velázquez's remains may have been removed and placed in the Church of San Plácido at the time the Church of San Juan Bautista was demolished.

Monument to Velázquez in the Plaza de Ramales. The unimpressive monument marking the approximate resting place of the painter Diego Velázquez. The exact location has been lost over the years. *Author's photo.*

Could the two mummies be those of Velázquez and his wife, who were buried side by side? There were many indications that seemed to support this theory. Of the two mummies, one male and one female, the male was dressed in almost the same manner in that which Velázquez had been buried, with the gear of the military Order of Santiago on him, hat and sword included. The approximate age at time of death was 61 for Velázquez and 58 for his wife, which corresponded with the mummies. Since the coincidences couldn't just be shrugged off, a commission of 13 experts was gathered, which included members of the Madrid autonomous government, the Culture Ministry, the Archbishopric of Madrid and various university professors.

With great expectations, the bodies were taken to the Complutense University of Madrid to be examined by forensic anthropologists. Every conceivable test was run. First the morphology of the skulls was analyzed. These seemed to match the known descriptions of both husband and wife, as well as their appearance on paintings. Next, DNA tests were done on the bodies. Bizarre as it may sound, the present Prince of Spain, Felipe de Borbón, happens to be a blood-descendant of Velázquez on his mother's (Queen Sofía) side of the family, albeit the link is very remote. If the body were really that of the painter, some theorized, then it would carry some of the same DNA as the prince's. Unfortunately, as it turned out, establishing this link was discarded when it was realized that the bloodline was far too remote to yield any positive results.

Another tack was attempted by the investigators based on fingerprints. When the painting known as *Las Lanzas* was restored, it was discovered that Velázquez unwittingly had left a perfect fingerprint on the wet part of the canvas, probably as a result of handling the painting. Once again, unfortunately the condition of the mummy's fingers was far too deteriorated to provide a conclusive match. Still another lead was the analysis of the bones for traces of lead, since lead was an integral component of oil colors used in the 17th century. The lead could be absorbed through the skin and affect the bones and could indicate that the corpse was that of a person who handled oil colors.

Tests however were inconclusive and failed to shed any new light on the conundrum. Moreover, the commission was made up of so many organizations and expressed so many diverse opinions, that it seemed impossible to reach a verdict. Some investigators urged further tests to be run, while others felt it was all a wild goose chase and reminded their colleagues that according to the original funeral documents Velázquez had been buried with "boots and spurs" and since the mummy was found wearing shoes and tights the whole endeavor was flawed from the start.

After shedding little light on the subject, the investigation was closed at the end of 1999. All seemed to have been forgotten, when suddenly in the summer of 2004 a revealing new document came to light. It concerned the "assets" of a certain Don Gaspar de Fuensalida, a very close friend of Velázquez's. The document mentions that Fuensalida paid 3,000 ducats in aid of the Convent of San Plácido when its founder fell into the hands of the Inquisition. Such a donation would give Don Gaspar certain privileges in the Church, including burial rights. Thus the new theory now was that Don Gaspar, having been a friend of Velázquez, used these privileges to bury the painter and his wife in the Convent of San Plácido where the mummies were recently found. All this seemed to give new weight to the argument that the mummies were actually those of Don Diego and his spouse.

Hence new voices were raised urging the case to be re-opened with further testing on the mummies and the creation of a more select and scientifically-orientated commission rather than the politically- and religiously-motivated group that was previously in charge. But this, too, petered out.

As forensic science advances, it may enable further clues to be uncovered, perhaps finally some day resulting in the discovery of the exact location of Diego Velázquez's body. In the meantime, whenever we stroll past the Plaza de Ramales, we can't help thinking that maybe, just maybe, right under our feet might rest the remains of the world- renowned artist.

Should you be in the Plaza de Ramales, you might want

VIRGENES RINCONERAS

Don't miss seeing what is probably the last of the Vírgenes Rinconeras in the city. It is an ornate statue found in a niche in a building on the corner of the Plaza de Ramales and the Calle de Vergara. These madonnas were traditionally placed on the outsides of buildings and over doorways by the faithful in thanks for having their prayers answered, or even just as a sign of piety. This Holy Virgin is known as "La Dolorosa". Many can still be seen in provincial Spanish cities, but virtually none survive in Madrid.

The ground floor of the house is taken up by the Café de las Austrias, a pleasant stopping-off place for a coffee or a drink.

to cast a glance at the archeological ruins of the Church of San Juan Bautista which have been excavated. You can actually look down through glass plating at the foundations of the church where Velázquez was originally buried. You may notice that embedded in the sidewalk are various black stones and granite slabs that look like seats. These are actually markers tracing the outline of the former church.

Alfonso VI "the Brave." During this king's successful siege of Madrid, the nickname for Madrileños, "Gato", was coined. *Historia de la Villa de Madrid.*

Why Madrileños are called "Gatos" or "Cats"

It is common knowledge to most Madrileños that those born in their city are nicknamed *gatos* (cats). Calling someone a *"gato, gato"* (cat, cat) or a *"gato de muchas generaciones"* (a cat of many generations) means that at the very least both his/her parents were born in the capital. The origin of the term dates back to early medieval times.

In 1083, centuries before the various kingdoms of Spain were unified and became a single country, Alfonso VI, King of Castile, the pre-eminent warrior spearheading the Reconquest, was planning to retrieve Toledo from the Moors. At that time Toledo was the most important city in Spain. But only 60 kilometers (40 miles) away lay the strategically crucial military and tactical Moorish stronghold Magerit, which was none other than the old name for Madrid.

Alfonso VI, distinguished by the eponym "the Brave", realized it would be a mistake to conquer Toledo while leaving a Moorish fortress to his rear. Hence he brought his army up to the walled fortifications of Magerit, invested it, and prepared for battle. But he gradually came to realize that taking the city would be a far more daunting task than he had at first imagined, since the enemy's defenses seemed impregnable and no weak points could be found. Despite these misgivings, the night before the battle, he gathered his troops together and roused their spirits in preparation for the next day's assault on the city's walls, though he knew his chances of conquest were slim.

After retiring to his tent, he pondered over the battle plans, desperately searching for a solution of how to breach the city's stout defenses. Just when he was about to give up and retire to his bed, the guards brought in a teen-aged boy who was so eager to fight against the Moors that he had slipped past the guards and into the camp. The boy was courageous and much liked by the troops. The king, amused at the boy's persistence, asked him what his name was. The boy said, "They call me Gato" (Cat), which was the name the soldiers had given him due to his agility and nimbleness at clambering up walls others couldn't scale. This gave Alfonso an idea, which he shared with Gato.

MIRROR STREET
(Calle del Espejo)

Here's a case where the name of a street is, in fact, a misnomer. At the time the Moors occupied Madrid they built watchtowers to warn them of any approaching Christian army attempting to conquer the city. One of these was located on the street in question. These watchtowers in Latin were known as *specula*, which in Latin also means "mirror"; hence when the Christians finally retook the city the name "Mirror Street" stuck. In fact, the line of the original Arab defensive walls of the city ran along this street.

The next day, just before dawn, carrying a very long rope on his shoulders, the boy started to scale a wall that rose up so steeply that it seemed impossible that anyone could climb up it. The enemy had left it virtually undefended. Using a knife, Gato painstakingly dug small holes between the bricks of the wall and, advancing catlike, he managed to stealthily climb up near a watchtower. After securing one end of the rope, he threw down the other end so that the soldiers could climb up, silence the guards posted by the Moors, and then launch a surprise attack. And so, legend goes, it was thanks to the nimble and fearless Gato that the battle was won and Alfonso the Brave conquered Magerit. Gato became such a famous local hero that as time went by the term "gato" came to be identified first with any brave person from Madrid and eventually spread to mean anyone born in the city. Eventually, the boy changed his family name to "Gato", which became one of the most renowned surnames in the city, along with such other illustrious lineages as the Escarabajos (beetles) and the Muertos (dead men). For many centuries the descendents of the Gato family included in their coat-of-arms a picture of a cat climbing a wall, in homage to the original Gato.

The Virgin of the Almudena: lost and found

The massive modern church standing next to the Royal Palace, the Cathedral of the Almudena, stood uncompleted for over a hundred years since its first stone was laid by King Alfonso XII in 1883. What was long considered the city's "white elephant" was at last consecrated in 1993, though the final touches for it, such as a huge decorative mural, were still being completed just prior to the marriage of Spain's heir to the throne, Prince Felipe, in 2004.

The original statue of the Virgin, which according to hagiographers had been brought from the Holy Land to Madrid by the Apostle Santiago (St. James) or by one of his disciples in 38 AD, has long since been lost. The one presently located in the cathedral appears to have been carved in the 16th century and is made of pinewood. Some sources claim that fragments of the original Image can be found inside the present one, although this claim has never been substantiated. Others argue that there was a third "intermediate" Virgin that preceded the present one. Be that as it may, our story concerns the original statue that reputedly stood in Madrid at the time when the Iberian Peninsula was being conquered by the Moors.

Old Virgin de la Almudena niche. This photo from 2007 shows a stone life-sized replica of the Virgin where it supposedly appeared. Presently (2011) the wall is being repaired. *Author's photo.*

The Moors had swept up the Peninsula in a matter of months and now threatened Magerit, present-day Madrid. Upon hearing of the approach of the conquering Moorish armies and fearing that the Muslims would destroy all Christian relics and images, the townspeople of Madrid hid all sacred objects for safekeeping in what was then a small village. One of its most revered madonnas, later known as the Virgin of the Almudena, was among those hidden in a secret place. Flanked by two lighted candles, its hiding place was then sealed up. After the village fell to the Moors, the exact spot where the Virgin had been hidden was passed down by word of mouth from one generation to the next until finally, in the 11th century, when the Moors had been expelled from the central part of Spain, the Image could finally be recovered.

Legend has it that a girl by the name of María had been told of the hiding place by her mother. But there was a problem. Her mother had died and María could no longer remember the precise location where the Image was hidden. At the time, King Alfonso VI "the Brave" had just reconquered Toledo from the Moors after previously having successfully conquered Madrid (with the help of "Gato"). Now the king returned to Madrid anxious to see the famous Virgin that had been hidden for so

View of the Almudena, 19th century. This is what the niche and statue (on bottom right of photo) used to look like in the past. *La Ilustración Española y Americana.*

many centuries. When Alfonso was told that the person who was the keeper of the secret location had forgotten the exact place, his anger and fury were such that he vowed that if the Virgin were not found within two weeks he would begin to tear down the defensive walls that had meanwhile been built by the Moors until the sacred statue was found, thereby leaving the city at the mercy of any future attacks from its enemies.

Needless to say María was in a panic, to put it mildly. The only thing she could think of doing was to pray night and day for a miracle to occur.

The deadline for her finding the Virgin finally arrived on November 9, the day that Alfonso had vowed to start tearing down the walls. However, before starting to undertake the destruction, he organized one final royal procession along the fortifications to implore Divine intervention for the discovery of the hidden Virgin. All Madrid gathered near the walls for the occasion. María, too, attended, heartbroken and in despair at her own guilt and disgrace. The procession proceeded for some time, but no sign of the Virgin was revealed. Suddenly, as the cortege was slowly making its way up the steep Cuesta de la Vega, passing in front of a grain shelter, María let out a piercing cry. The procession came to a halt as the king and his court wondered what the commotion was about. Just at that precise moment… yes, you guessed it… a miracle occurred. Before the incredulous eyes of María's fellow townspeople, the wall began to crumble. As it did so, it revealed not only the intact image of the Virgin but even that of the candles, which were still burning. For almost 400 years the Image had been hidden, and now the city had miraculously recovered it! Since the Virgin was discovered next to a granary, it was given the name "Almudena", from the Arabic *almud,* a measure of wheat. Other sources claim it is derived from *almudayna,* meaning "in the wall". Clearly, the word's etymology is blurry. In either case, it is noteworthy that the actual spot on which the miracle supposedly occurred can still be seen today.

Nuestra Señora de la Almudena. A 19th century illustration of the Almudena statue now on view in the Cathedral. *Author's archive.*

Thus, if you walk down the Cuesta de la Vega (about a block south on the Calle de Bailén from the cathedral), you'll come on the right to a niche high up in the ancient defensive walls of the city where a stone replica of the sacred Image has been placed. It is here where more than ten centuries ago the Virgin was hidden and later refound. As a plaque next to it indicates, the rosary is still prayed here each Saturday at 7:30 p.m. in honor of the Almudena and flowers are regularly placed there by devotees. A few steps to the right, you come to an entrance to the cathedral's crypt, which in its interior contains a copy of the Almudena statue. The 16th century "authentic" one can be seen behind the altar of the main nave of the cathedral.

Due to work on the expansion of the museum of the royal collections, at the time of writing, the stone replica of the statue of the Virgin in the wall has temporarily been moved to the left side of the entrance to the crypt.

BLIND MAN'S HILL
(Cuesta de los Ciegos)

In the days when the Vistilla Heights still looked out on fields, two blind men were wont to station themselves at the foot of the hill and beg for alms. Francisco de Asís, later made a saint, would occasionally drop a coin into their hat upon passing. One day, the holy man was returning with an amphora of oil which he had received in exchange for a basket of fish he had brought to his prior. He gave some of the oil to the blind men, who, upon rubbing it on their eyes, miraculously regained their vision.

Another less saintly derivation of the name of the street avers that near the bottom of the hill once stood a shelter for the blind. It would seem that for a while it was also known as the "Cuesta de Arrastraculos" (Hill of the Sliding Buttocks), since the local kids used to slide down it as though they were on sleds.

A search for the hidden walls of the city

Imagine you're parking your car in an underground garage, and as you're looking for an empty space suddenly you drive past an ancient Islamic watchtower which was originally part of the walled Moorish defenses of the city. Well, that is exactly what could happen right smack in the center of Madrid.

These defenses, dating back to the 9th century, were later rebuilt and enlarged by the Christians in the 12th century. Most of them have disappeared. However, other short stretches of the walls have been excavated in modern times. Indeed, remnants of the walls were uncovered in the most unexpected places, such as in the basements of taverns or restaurants, and even beneath the ground floors of private houses.

Moorish fortifications. The best-preserved fortifications constructed by the Moors in the 9th century, beside the Almudena Cathedral. *Author's photo.*

The best-preserved segments of the defenses that once protected the Moorish inhabitants of the original Magerit against incursions are located behind the Cathedral of the Almudena, proceeding down the steep Cuesta de la Vega, opposite the niche containing the statue of the Virgin of the Almudena. Standing on small metal observation points recently built, you can peer down and see the excavated brick foundations and remains of what used to be Moorish dwellings. A bit further down, turning a corner, you'll be treated to a good view of a long stretch of the original wall that once ran around the city. The walls were anywhere from three to five meters (15 feet) tall, and every 20 meters (60 feet) there was a watchtower. The base of one of these, jutting out, is still visible.

The remains of the walls, once associated with war and

Christian fortifications. In front of the rest rooms in the basement of a hamburger restaurant (Foster's Hollywood) you can see a small section of the city's 12th century Christian fortifications. *Author's photo.*

violence, provide a venue for art and music events, since the city now uses the site behind the excavations, the Park of Emir Mohamed I, as one of the places where the annual summer festival is held.

Among the most curious sites to view other remains of the wall is the public parking lot located under the Plaza de Oriente. Access to it is in front of the Botillería del Café de Oriente, through a staircase (you can also opt for a glass enclosed elevator) that leads down one flight of stairs. Turning left, past the toilets, a 50 meter (150 foot) walk will bring you to the ruins of a section of the Moorish wall (located in front of parking lot N° 42 – as marked on the pillar). There, in the middle of this impersonal and modern parking lot, bustling with cars and hurrying businessmen, behind a huge protective pane of glass, like a vision out of the remote past, appear the remnants of an 11th century Islamic watchtower. It is one of the few archeological remains saved from destruction when the parking lot was built, thanks to strenuous objections from cultural entities.

To view more ruins of the wall in the Plaza de Oriente, you can enter the aforementioned Botillería del Café de Oriente. Once inside the café, descend the spiral staircase that leads to the rest rooms and you'll come to a chamber with glass doors called El Ajibe (The Cistern), used only for special events by the café. Here you'll discover that the entire floor of the room is made of glass, allowing you to view what used to be the foundations of the Moorish wall underneath. The owner of the establishment has added his own decorative touches, such as a modern stone well and various old amphoras that he brought from Sevilla. The large clay ones date back to the 15th and 16th centuries, while the older green ones are Roman, from the third century AD.

Instead of looking at the Moorish ruins through a glass

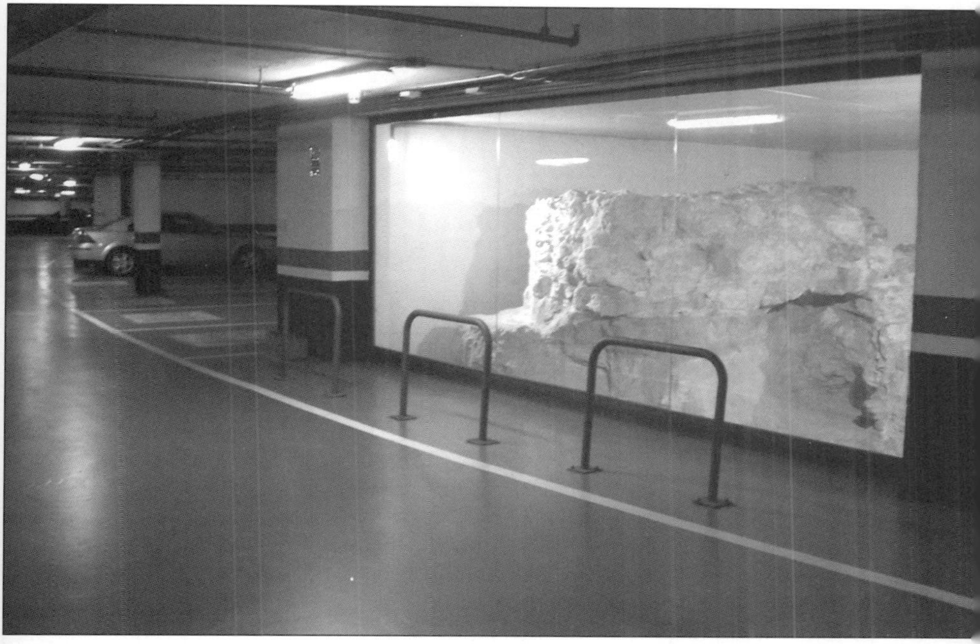

plate, you might prefer to inspect them while munching on a hamburger. You can do this in a restaurant specializing in American food called Foster's Hollywood located on the nearby Plaza de Isabel II, 3 (known as "Opera" since it is the site of the Opera House). There, in the dining area in the basement, just before you get to the rest rooms, you'll see a part of the old wall cropping out. If you are so inclined, treat yourself to burgers 'n history.

Moorish watchtower. Yet another unlikely place to find ruins is the subterranean parking lot located in the Plaza de Oriente where an 11th century Islamic watchtower has been excavated. *Author's photo.*

Further sites where parts of the wall can be visited (see Area 3 – Plaza Mayor map, Pg. 117 A) are:

Cava Baja 10: One of the tenants must buzz open the front door. The 12th century (second Christian wall) is down the hallway, below a glass floor covering.

Cava Baja 30: Here too you must be buzzed in by one of the tenants. Past the entrance in the inner patio you come to one of the largest remains of the wall that has been preserved (11th-12th century).

Calle de los Mancebos 5: A section of the Christian wall can be seen from the street behind an iron fence. Quite a curiosity.

FELIPE IV'S NEGLECTED WALL

Should you want to hunt down other remains of old walls, head over to the Ronda de Segovia 95 (near the Puerta de Toledo) where you'll find a sizeable remaining chunk of what was known as the Cerca de Felipe IV (Felipe IV's Enclosing Wall). As the city grew and started to sprawl over areas beyond the old Christian and Moorish walls, the king realized that a new enclosing wall was needed, not for defensive purposes, but so as not to leave Madrid open for anyone and everyone to come into and leave at will. With such a new wall, traffic would be properly controlled, transit taxes collected and miscreants and carriers of diseases better surveilled. Hence in 1625 Felipe IV had a wall built made of brick and mud which remained in situ as late as 1868. By that time the city had again expanded far beyond it and thus made its existence unnecessary. In fact, the perimeter of that wall in modern Madrid is where the present "rondas" and "bulevares" form what may be considered the first "ring road" of the capital.

Anarchists and royalty

When one speaks of terrorist attacks in Madrid, the images conjured up to Spaniards are those of March 11, 2004 when 191 people were killed on trains near the Atocha Railway Station and those perpetrated by the Basque ETA terrorist group over the past decades. The Spanish capital, in fact, has been no stranger to terrorism and political assassinations over the past century.

The second worst single attack in Spain, in terms of victims claimed, was not the work of the ETA, but rather that committed by a lone anarchist. It occurred on May 31, 1906 on the Calle Mayor and left 28 people dead and around 100 injured. However, unlike the attack at Atocha, the aim of the

Alfonso XIII's assassination attempt. This photograph was taken only seconds after the bomb exploded. *ABC, June 1, 1906.*

terrorist in this case was not to create mass mayhem, but rather to assassinate King Alfonso XIII on the day of his marriage to Victoria Eugenia de Battenberg, a niece of Queen Victoria.

Alfonso was born the son of King Alfonso XII and Maria Cristina of Hapsburg in 1886 and was proclaimed King by the Parliament in 1902. Both his mother and the ruling politicians of the time had urged him to marry and provide a successor to the throne. They bombarded him with a series of pictures of eligible female candidates. But Alfonso had a will of his own. "I'm not going to marry a photograph," he told them, and presently started scouting about for a suitable consort on his own. He began his quest in Paris in 1905, aged 19. After not finding anyone to his liking in the French capital, he travelled on to England, where he was introduced to Victoria Eugenia, better known by her nickname of "Ena", born in Balmoral in 1887, and took a strong fancy to her. Though Spanish conservatives at the time favored a Central European wife, the King followed his own inclinations and after other meetings and an exchange of affectionate letters, he announced his engagement to Ena, a move which greatly pleased the liberal faction in Spain. In order to tie the marriage bonds, however, Ena first needed to convert to Catholicism, which she

Alfonso XIII's assassination mementoes. (Left) Markings found on a tree in the Retiro Park shortly before the wedding. They read, "Alfonso XIII will be executed on the day of his wedding. A redeemer." On the left you can read the word "dinamite". (Right) Fragment of the anarchist's bomb kept in the Army Museum. *Author's archive.*

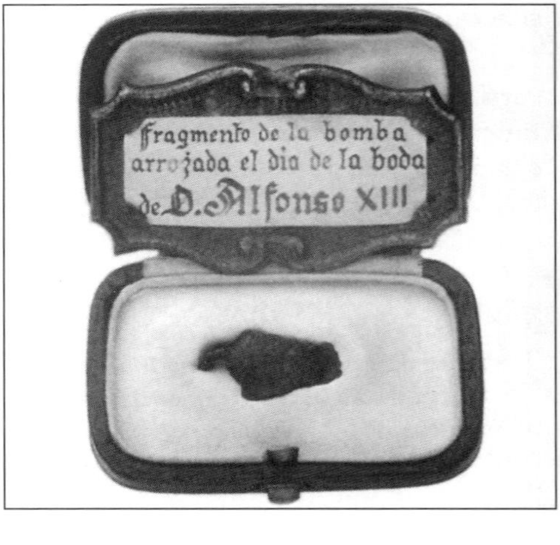

subsequently did in the chapel of the Miramar Palace in San Sebastián. After that, she came down to Madrid for her wedding to Alfonso, briefly putting up in the best hotel Madrid had to offer in that era, the Hotel Paris on the Puerta del Sol. She was all of 18 years old. The city was bedecked in gala for the great occasion, and there seemed no ill foreboding for the event, despite stirrings of anarchist and republican extremist activities in the country. Nonetheless, a week before the royal wedding, someone had carved into a tree in the Retiro Park: "Alfonso XIII will be executed on the day of his marriage" and signed it "An Irredentist." (One who cannot be redeemed).

Anarchist's balcony. On the Calle Mayor, the balcony from which the anarchist Mateo Morral threw the bomb camouflaged in a bouquet of flowers is still marked by a palm. *Author's photo.*

The day of the nuptials arrived. The solemn marriage ceremony went off without a hitch at the Jerónimos Church, behind the Prado Museum, and the royal cortège then wound its way slowly through the streets of the city, heading towards the Royal Palace, where a huge banquet was scheduled to be held.

The newly-married royal couple, sitting in a closed carriage, drove up the Carrera de San Jerónimo, crossed the Puerta del Sol and then entered the Calle Mayor, greeting the cheering crowds on either side of the street. Then, barely one block away from the intersection of the Calle Mayor with the Calle de Bailén, on the last leg of their trip before reaching the Palace, their procession was stopped dead in its tracks by a tremendous explosion. From the top floor of a building on the north side of Mayor, a bouquet of flowers was thrown down at the monarch's carriage. However, instead of falling straight down on top of it, it first bounced off a trolley-car wire, thereby causing it to shear off to one side of the carriage. Then, when the bouquet hit the ground, a powerful bomb concealed within

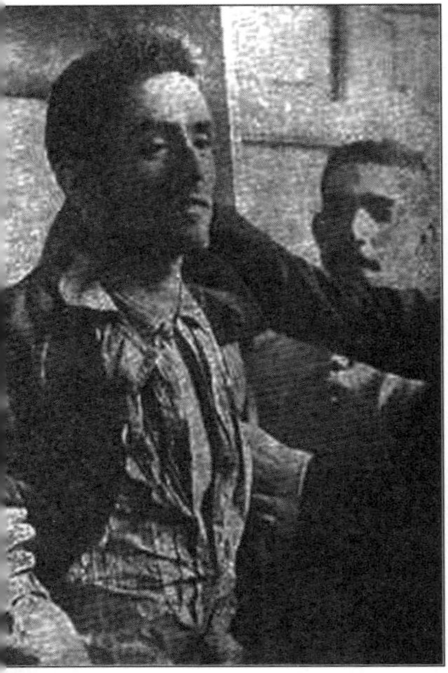

Anarchist's cadaver. In the morgue of the clinic of the Buen Suceso, the body of Morral is held up so it can be photographed. *Author's archive.*

it exploded deafeningly causing a scene of mayhem all around the royal carriage. Horses reared and the screams of injured spectators, well-wishers, bystanders, mounted guards and security men rent the air, as the dead and injured mingled in a scene of Dantesque horror. The final tally would be 23 killed outright and close to a hundred (the official figure was never agreed upon) injured.

By some fabulous chance of Fate, though the young queen's white dress was splattered with blood, she as well as the king had escaped unscathed. Alfonso calmly descended from the carriage with her, and slowly continued the last leg of his journey to the Royal Palace in another carriage.

The author of the terrible attack was a dedicated 26-year-old anarchist by the name of Mateo Morral, the son of a wealthy Catalan industrialist, who had broken off with his family and had been bankrolled by a group of other militant anarchists to pull off the assassination of the king in Madrid.

In the confusion caused by the blast, Morral managed to get out of the building and lose his way in the crowds outside. It seems he then made his way to the Madrid offices of an anarchist newspaper called *El Motín* ("Mutiny") and sought out its owner, José Nakens, who helped him to find a hiding place on the outskirts of the city in the house of a staunch anti-monarchist.

The following day, Morral donned a blue working man's overall, such as are still commonly worn by service workers today, pulled a worker's cap over his head to escape detection, and headed towards the railroad station in Torrejón de Ardoz, about 15 kilometers (9 miles) past today's Barajas Airport. However, on the way there, he stopped at a humble roadside inn and ordered some food. His incongruently polite manners and Catalan accent aroused the suspicions of one of the people in the bar, who urged the innkeeper's wife to summon the authorities. Shortly thereafter, a Civil Guard appeared at the inn and took Morral into custody for questioning. The anarchist offered no resistance. However, after marching off a short distance, the people at the inn saw with surprise and horror as Morral suddenly swung around, pulled out a pistol, and fired a shot pointblank at the Civil Guard, who crumbled to the ground. He then pointed the gun at his own chest and pulled the trigger. Morral immediately became a martyr for those who believed in his cause.

King Alfonso XIII was to rule Spain for many years after that. However, in 1931 the Republic was declared and he was forced into exile. After living in various European countries, he finally settled in Italy. He died in Rome in 1941.

Monument to the victims of Alfonso XIII's assassination attempt. Across the street from the balcony where the bomb was thrown, a statue has been erected in homage to those who died in Spain's second bloodiest terrorist attack. *Author's photos.*

The building in front of which the attempted assassination occurred, and from which the anarchist's bomb was hurled, is that still standing at Calle Mayor 88. The room from which Morral threw the bomb has been marked by a palm branch over its balcony. On the ground floor is one of Madrid's oldest remaining restaurants, Casa Ciriaco, known at the time of Morral's attack as Baliñas. On one of the walls in Casa Ciriaco, you can see a framed photograph of the assassination attempt that was published in the newspapers at that time. In fact, many photos of the event were taken at the critical moments.

You might wonder how, in that early era of photojournalism, when few people possessed cameras, anyone actually had the presence of mind and the means to take such a spectacular shot. The reason the event was so well documented is that the monarchist daily *ABC* had the day before offered 25 pesetas (about $300 by today's reckoning) for each quality photograph of the day's event accepted for publication. Hence, a number of snapshots of the fatal moment were taken.

A year after the assassination attempt, Madrid authorities erected a statue in remembrance of the victims, crowned by a figure representing the Madonna of All-Saints, which rose above three marble columns of different colors, representing the social classes of the victims: the aristocracy, the military, and the townspeople. On the base was inscribed the names of those who had lost their lives. The monument was erected on the site of an old fountain. The cost was raised by popular subscription.

During the Spanish Civil War, when Communist and Anarchist influences were all-powerful in Madrid, not only was the statue destroyed, but the name of the Calle Mayor was changed to that of Mateo Morral in honor of the would-be regicide. When the city was taken by the Nationalist troops, the name of the street reverted to the Calle Mayor. Later, in 1963, a simple monument with an angel was erected across the street from Mayor 88, commemorating the victims of the attack. Since then, the staff of the Casa Ciriaco restaurant have placed a laurel wreath on the monument every May 31st in memory of those who died during the attack.

A royal scheme to turn Madrid into a seaport

New York has its Hudson, London its Thames, Paris its Seine and Madrid… has its own *little* river: the Manzanares. You could easily miss seeing it, since it's more like a drying-up creek than a full-fledged river. It's so small and often so shallow that over the centuries it has been the butt of innumerable insults and slights. Here's what a few classic local writers had to say about the bedraggled waterway:

Lope de Vega: "The Manzanares is more like an apprentice to a river than a river itself... the bridges that cross it seem to be vainly searching for the river... It might be better for Madrid to either buy a new river or sell its bridges."

Góngora: "...The bridge is hurting, for the people say that the Manzanares is a river requiring only half a bridge."

Quevedo: "...The Manzanares is so emaciated and squalid that the frogs and mosquitoes there die of thirst."

The river was maligned not only by local Spanish authors, but also by famous foreign travellers who saw it. When the French invaded Madrid during the Peninsular War, one general said, "Not only have the Spaniards run away, but even the river has absconded". The novelist Alexandre Dumas, when visiting Madrid in 1846, was taken on a tour of the city by his Spanish hosts. After an exhausting day of sightseeing, which included a walk along the banks of the Manzanares, he stopped to get a drink of water. After emptying half a glass, he pushed the glass aside and said to his Spanish guide, "Here, I think your river needs it more than I do!"

It seems that in the early 1900's one of Madrid's aldermen delivered a speech in which he commented on the statistics of people who had drowned in the Manzanares. With puffing pride he explained that 29 people had drowned there in the preceding three years, a greater number than those drowning in the Seine in Paris. However, he did have to add a minor clarification to this surprising statistic: those who died in the Manzanares did so because when diving into the shallow river they hit their heads on the rocks and then drowned.

But enough of insults! The Manzanares, although small, runs for more than 60 kilometers (40 miles). And it was around this river that the first prehistoric settlements in Madrid sprang up. Recent archeological excavations have uncovered rich

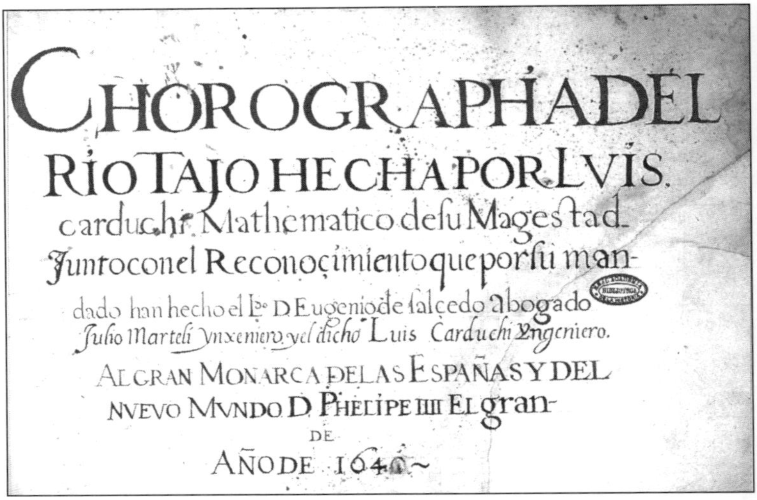

CHOROGRAPHA DEL
RIO TAJO HECHA POR LVIS
carduchi Mathematico de su Magestad.
Junto con el Reconoçimiento que por su man-
dado han hecho el Lº D. Eugenio de Salcedo abogado
Julio Marteli ynxeniero y el dicho Luis Carduchi Yngeniero.
AL GRAN MONARCA DE LAS ESPAÑAS Y DEL
NVEVO MVNDO D. PHELIPE IIII EL gran-
DE
AÑO DE 164[illegible]~

Title page for Carduchi's project. Cover of the 1641 series of 62 sketches by Luis Carduchi illustrating his in-depth study for making the Tagus River navigable. *Real Academia de la Historia archives.*

Paleolithic and Neolithic sites giving us a clue as to the people, their culture and the animals – elephants, deer and even rhinoceroses – that lived here at the time.

The Manzanares has been the subject of many of Goya's paintings, such as *Baile a la orilla del Manzanares* (Dance on the Bank of the Manzanares) and *La pradera de San Isidro* (The San Isidro Meadow), both in the Prado Museum. Throughout the centuries the river provided the common washing site for the Madrileños' dirty laundry, where thousands of private washerwomen each day cleaned and hung to dry the townpeople's clothes. During the Spanish Civil War the river was the dividing line between the Republican defenders of the capital and the Nationalists, who besieged the city for most of the war.

The Manzanares River, despite its being belittled by all and sundry, nonetheless played a key part in a scheme to convert Madrid into a seaport. A *seaport?* Yes, a seaport.

Originally, Madrid had been chosen as the capital of the country precisely because it lay at the center of Spain, more or less equidistant from the various seaports in the Peninsula. Of course, the problem was always how to transport the merchandise from afar to a city that essentially had to import everything it used, from food to manufactured goods, making life in Madrid as expensive as London or Paris. Which is why for centuries there has been a yearning to somehow connect the city to the sea. Moreover, the yearning was not merely an idle wish. Surprisingly, on several occasions, work on converting Madrid into a seaport was actually undertaken.

The project dated back to the 17th century, when Spain possessed a huge, powerful and wealthy empire that stretched halfway around the globe. In the New World its domains spread from Florida and California to the tip of South America. Spanish galleons plied the oceans, transporting gold, silver and spices from the colonies to the Spanish Main and then to the homeland. But one nagging problem recurred constantly: the ships could only travel as far as the major ports in Spain, such as Cádiz, Sevilla, Sanlúcar and Lisbon, the latter at that time under Spanish control. From there, the cargoes had to be transported overland to Madrid and to other inland cities, a complicated and costly endeavor. Even as late as 1775 it took a diligence *two weeks* to travel from Cádiz to Madrid, using execrable roads and facing the dangers and inconveniences that any trip involved in those days.

Memoria
RELATIVA A LA NAVEGACION
del Rio Tajo.
PUBLICASE DE REAL ÓRDEN.
MADRID,
IMPRENTA DE DON MIGUEL DE BURGOS.
Año de 182[illegible].

Title page for Cabanes's project. Cover for Francisco de Cabanes's research on the Tagus River, printed in 1829. *Biblioteca Municipal de Madrid.*

To attempt to solve this major drawback, an enterprising Italian in the employ of Felipe II by the name of Juan Bautista Antonelli conceived a daring and bizarre plan: to open an inland water route all the way from the Atlantic to the center of Madrid.

Antonelli, an engineer and architect who had built fortifications in Cartagena, Oran and near Gibraltar, as well as El Morro in Puerto Rico, presented his revolutionary scheme to the king. It called for the widening of the Tagus River, which begins in Lisbon, and making it navigable as far as Madrid. The Tagus flows into the Jarama River which then connects with the Manzanares, known in those days as the Guadarrama River. Thus, by means of a complicated series of dams, sluices and constructions on the banks of the rivers and the widening of existing bridges, the ships from the Indies would be able to navigate all the way from Lisbon to Toledo, the latter a mere 70 kilometers (42 miles) from the capital, navigating then up the Manzanares, right to the very Villa de Madrid.

Antonelli assured the king that the technology at the time was up to accomplishing this feat and that the success of the scheme was only a question of money, of which there certainly was no shortage at the time. Sound crazy? Well, the king didn't think so and authorized Antonelli to start work on the project without further delay.

The Italian engineer drew up the plans for the mammoth endeavor and began prospecting the rivers in small boats. Availing himself of a moment when the waters of the Manzanares stood high, he actually paddled in a canoe most of the way from Lisbon to Madrid. Initial constructions were undertaken between the towns of Abrantes and Alcántara, with excellent results. But the grandiose scheme was doomed to failure for reasons quite unrelated to the technical and engineering problems. For Felipe had meanwhile cast his eye on the conquest of England and the court's first priority was the building and outfitting of the famous Armada, the largest and most impressive fleet of warships ever assembled in Spain. On the 29th of May of 1588, the fleet totalling 130 ships set sail from Lisbon, stopping in La Coruña, with 30,000 men on board to invade England. It encountered the British fleet off Plymouth in July, commanded by Charles Howard. Following engagements at Calais, the Armada was dispersed and after running into storms and making a landing in Ireland, the surviving ships headed back to Spain. About half the Spanish fleet was lost and only around 10,000 of those originally on board managed to return. It was the greatest naval disaster Spain had ever suffered.

Antonelli died shortly before the defeat, but gave all his

detailed plans with the solutions to the navigational problems of the Tagus River to his cousin. This new bearer of the project sought an interview with the king, enthusiastically laying his plans and calculations on the table before the monarch. But he had arrived too late; for Felipe had lost all interest in the scheme. What would be the point of building the waterway when there were hardly any ships left and Spain's coffers had been depleted by the disastrous loss of the Armada? The naval catastrophe had submerged the entire court into despairing gloom and the project of an ocean link with Madrid was virtually abandoned. Antonelli's downcast cousin withdrew, realizing that his scheme was now only an unattainable chimera.

But though shelved for decades, the project was never quite forgotten. In 1641 a mathematician, Luis Carduchi, wrote a detailed book containing extensive full-color illustrations, in which he again examined the possibilities and feasibility of navigating the Tagus as far as Madrid and presented it to King Felipe IV. But nothing came of the matter.

Then in 1770, in the reign of Carlos III, the king ordered a navigable canal to be built from the Toledo Bridge to the Jarama River, thereafter to connect with the Henares or Tagus Rivers. Work on the canal actually began, and two leagues, 10 kilometers (6 miles) of it were built. It was known as the Royal Manzanares Canal.

In 1814, in the reign of Fernando VII, work was again taken up on the canal, extending it another four kilometers (2.5 miles) to the town of Vaciamadrid, where it linked with the Manzanares River at a point about three kilometers (2 miles) before it flows into the Jarama.

Nine locks and four water mills were constructed for it as well as various transport boats. In addition, some buildings intended to be used for offices and a boathouse and even a small chapel were added near the Toledo Bridge. The entrance to the canal was protected by a large metal gate. Trees were planted along the banks. But work on the canal was never completed.

In 1829, the project was once again revisited in depth by

Boat house. View of the boat house of the Royal Canal of Manzanares. *José Avrial y Flores, lithograph by Carlos Palmoroli.*

the hydraulic engineer Francisco Xavier Cabanes and in 1834 by Manuel Bermúdez de Castro. These were only a few of the most important attempts at furthering the waterway. Presently, the canal can be visited and its ruins, old locks and small buildings be seen. There is even a boat ride that takes you from the fourth lock to the dock in Vaciamadrid. The area, known s the Parque Lineal del Manzanares, was declared in 2009 an endangered historic site.

However, the dream of linking Madrid to the sea was never attained. Only a few small sections of the Tagus, Jarama and Manzanares Rivers have ever been navigable – short stretches where boats could be sailed but which proved of hardly any practical commercial advantage to anyone. Moreover, as Spanish roads improved and especially with the inauguration of railroad service starting in 1851, the need for such a waterway became moot.

If you should happen to be in the western part of Madrid, behind the Royal Palace or down the road past the Toledo Gate, you may want to cross one of the bridges over the Manzanares River such as the handsome Toledo Bridge (closed to vehicular traffic), or better still you can take the cablecar (Teleférico) from the Paseo del Pintor Rosales across the river to the Casa de Campo park. But whether crossing the Manazanes on foot or in the air, you can look down the length of the river and imagine what it would have looked like in past centuries with several Spanish galleons docking on its banks, unloading the riches and treasures brought all the way from the New World.

Area 5: Gran Vía

1. **Convento de las Salesas Nuevas** (San Bernardo 72). Nuns' pastries.
2. **Plaza de Dos de Mayo**. Former site of the Monteleón arms depot.
3. Futbolín. **Bar La Leyenda** (San Bernardino 8).
4. Futbolín. **Bar Marx Madera** (Madera 9). Hang out for "leftwingers".
5. **Convent of San Plácido** (San Roque 9). Possible Velázquez remains found here.
6. **Hotel TRYP Washington** (Gran Vía 72). Last building to be constructed on the Gran Vía.
7. **Calle de Leganitos**. Where a bull ran loose.
8. **Convento de las Descalzas Reales** (Plaza de las Descalzas Reales). Museum.
9. **Calle de la Salud**. Street with a story.
10. **Casa del Libro** bookshop (Gran Vía 29).
11. **SER** (Gran Vía 32). Radio network station.
12. **Hotel TRYP Gran Vía** (Gran Vía 25). Hemingway stayed here.
13. Former **Aleixandre Jewelry Shop** (Gran Vía corner with Montera). Now a McDonald's.
14. **Oratorio del Caballero de Gracia** (Caballero de Gracia 5). Street with a story.
15. **Calle de la Reina**. Luxury houses built on speculation before Gran Vía was built.
16. **Cultural Center for the Armed Forces** (Gran Vía 13). Frascuelo's saber and restaurant on 2nd floor.
17. **Calle de Barbieri**, ex-Calle del Soldado. Street with a story.
18. **Chicote** cocktail lounge (Gran Vía 12). Former site of the Museo de Bebidas.
19. **Calle de Victor Hugo** (corner of Gran Vía). Site of Loewe.
20. **Plaza del Rey**. Site of the Spanish Culture Ministry.
21. **House of the Seven Chimneys** (Infantas 31). Site of ghostly apparitions.
22. **Site where construction of Gran Vía began** (Marqués de Valdeiglesias corner with Alcalá).
23. **Circulo de Bellas Artes** (Alcalá 42 – entrance through Marqués de Casa Riera).
24. Former site of the **Hotel Suecia** (Marqués de Casa Riera 4). Hemingway stayed here too.

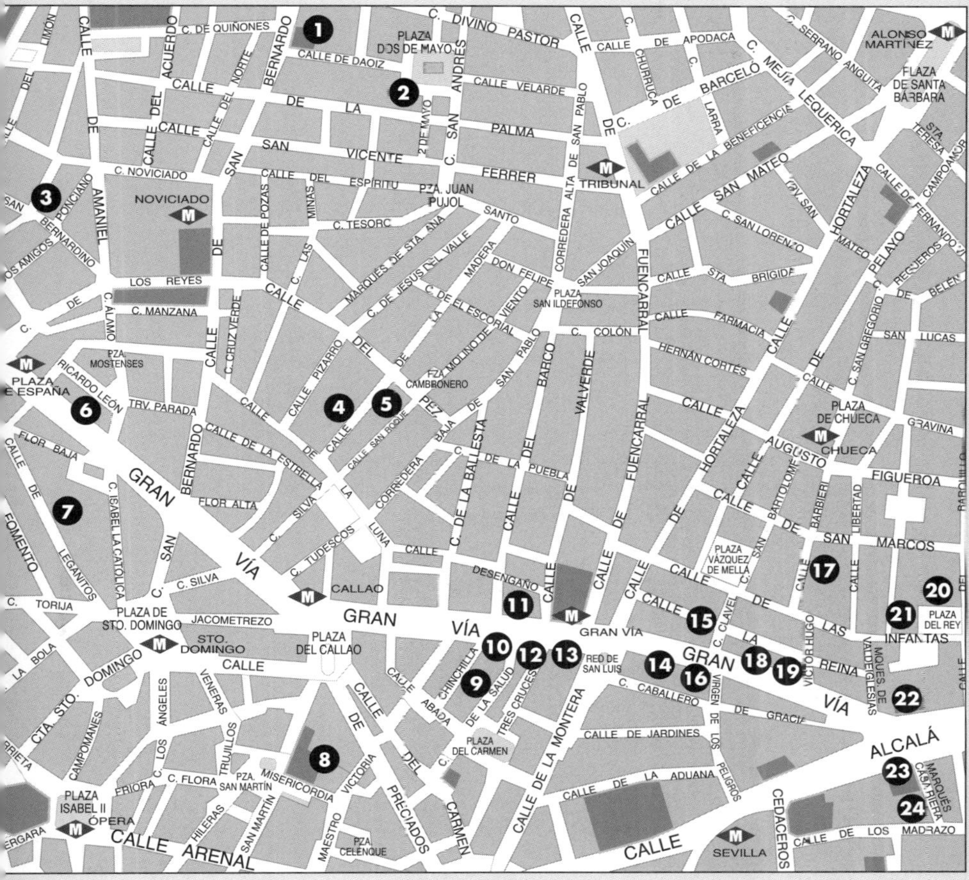

Area 5 - GRAN VIA

Madrid's Great White Way

The center of Madrid in the 19th century looked substantially different from the way it does today, not only in the shops, transportation, lighting, hotels and cafés, but also in the lay-out of the streets themselves. At that time there was no Gran Vía, which may be hard for present-day visitors to imagine. For the Gran Vía was an afterthought, an avenue that was bulldozed through the old part of town, destroying everything in its path.

The *project* for cutting a wide swath through the center of the city dated back to 1862, about the time the rebuilding of the Puerta del Sol was completed. At the time the idea of building an elegant new avenue was an attractive one, especially after similar projects had been carried out in Paris by Haussmann. Moreover, modernizing the city by building such a prestigious thoroughfare would alleviate the traffic-choked narrow streets, such as the Calle del Caballero de Gracia and the Calle de la Montera, and allow easy transit from east to west. The dingy old buildings that lay in the path of the new avenue would be replaced by handsome, spacious new ones that the capital of Spain could be proud of. In addition, of course, the construction of such a radical thoroughfare would fatten the purses of many politicians and constructors, as is always the case when such projects are undertaken.

The plans for building a Gran Vía or "Great Way" were infinitely more complicated than just remodelling a square. The bickering and political influence-pulling and jockeying to

The Gran Vía. An early Sunday morning view of the Gran Via which cut a swathe through a whole section of old streets and houses in the old part of the city. *Author's photo.*

Federico Chueca. Author of the *zarzuela* (operetta) *La Gran Vía* in which actors representing small Madrid streets and squares complain in song about plans to build a "Gran Vía". *Author's archive.*

obtain the fat contracts to handle the mammoth undertaking via the usual bribes was monumental and dragged on for years.

In fact, the project was so often brought up and not acted upon that a famous *zarzuela* (operetta) was written by Federico Chueca in 1886 called *La Gran Vía* which so well poked fun at the controversial scheme that it immediately became a resounding hit, and is still popular with Spanish audiences. This short *zarzuela* didn't have much of a story, but that didn't seem to matter since its musical numbers were catchy, especially the title piece which parades out in front of the limelight a dozen actors and actresses dressed up as Madrid streets and squares. In chorus they sing about the much-bruited plan to build a Gran Vía, and express their fear that this unnecessary Great Way will humiliate all the existing smaller streets in the city and that it would be preferable instead to take better care of their welfare instead of launching into new projects.

One of the most popular songs in the musical is that sung by the Calle del Caballero de Gracia (Charming Gentleman Street), which in the 19th century was one of the main, elegant thoroughfares of the city, lined with hotels and restaurants.

Caballero de Gracia me llaman,
y efectivamente soy así;
pues sabido es que a mí me conoce,
por mis amoríos, todo Madrid.

Es verdad que estoy un poco antiguo,
pero poniéndome mi frac,
soy un tipo gentil,
de carácter jovial,
a quien mima la sociedad.

They call me the Charming Gentleman,
And truly that's what I am:
For it is common knowledge that all Madrid
Knows me for my love affairs.

While it's true that I'm a little old,
When I dress up in my tuxedo
I'm a catching fellow,
With a jovial manner,
Spoiled by one and all.

GENTLEMAN OF GRACE STREET
(Calle del Caballero de Gracia)

The now totally marginalized Calle del Caballero de Gracia, which runs from the Calle de la Montera to the intersection of the Gran Vía and the Calle de Alcalá, before the construction of the Gran Vía, used to be one of the most fashionable and transited streets of the city. In the 19th century it was considered to be an "elegant" thoroughfare, lined with restaurants, inns and shops. In fact, a plaque still marks the place where the inn that the French writer Théophile Gautier, author of the amusing *Voyage en Espagne*, stayed in. Further up the street you can still visit the Oratorio, a chapel which has entrances on both the Calle del Caballero de Gracia and the Gran Vía. It was at one time one of the most "fashionable" sites to say one's prayers.

Who, then, was this "charming gentleman" that the street was named after?

His name was Jacobo de Grattis (not "Jacobo de Gracia" as is mistankenly written on the plaque), an Italian from Modena, who had come to Madrid in 1580 to represent Pope Gregory XIII. He was a gallant and powerful gentleman, very much of a lady's man, who owned most of the buildings on the street in question, each with a small garden behind it. One of the buildings was the residence of the Venetian ambassador, another was that of the French ambassador.

De Grattis, according to pious legend, was about to seduce a young lady, Leonor, who lived in the French ambassador's house. But at the moment of truth, the gallant Grattis suddenly saw a "sign from God" and desisted from his dastardly deed. Later he returned to Rome, took orders in the priesthood and upon returning to Madrid used his money to fund works of charity.

All the houses on the north side of the street, other than the Oratorio, were demolished when the Gran Vía was built.

Work on the Gran Vía begins. After 48 years of delays and procrastination, on April 4, 1910 Alfonso XIII signs the document that marks the start of construction on the first stretch of the Gran Vía. *Author's archive.*

Work on the first part of the Gran Vía (between Alcalá and the Red de San Luis) didn't begin until 1910, a half century after the initial plan had been drawn up. On April 4, King Alfonso XIII, wielding a small silver pickaxe, dislodged a chunk of a window in an old house in which the parish priest of the adjacent Church of San José lived, whereupon a band struck up a celebratory *pasodoble* (two-step) and work began in earnest on the much-heralded avenue. The exact spot was at the site of the building to the left of San José, now the site of a souvenir shop. The first stretch of the Gran Vía was originally called Conde de Peñalver, the name of the then-mayor. His name now is given to a large street in the Salamanca district.

The second stretch of the Gran Vía, at first called Pi y Margall, runs from the Red de San Luis to the Plaza del Callao.

Gran Vía under construction. View of the first public works on the Gran Vía dating November 17, 1910. Seen are the Calle del Caballero de Gracia on the left and the Gran Vía on the right (going towards Callao.) The triangular space in the center is the site where the horologer Grassy is presently located. *Nuevo Mundo, Nov. 17, 1910. Photo by José Campúa*

The final part, originally named after the politician Eduardo Dato, extending down to the Plaza de España, wasn't completed until 1931, *over twenty years* after work on the project had begun! In all, 14 entire streets were eliminated and 311 houses torn down. Eleven lots with buildings on them and 33 empty ones were swallowed up as well as 274 street lamps removed; tons upon tons of water mains, sidewalks, paving stones, earth, and rubble were dislodged. The result transformed the whole center of the city and affected not only the parts actually torn down, but also other streets that henceforth lost their importance such as the Calle del Caballero de Gracia, Calle de Jacometrezo, Calle de la Montera, Calle de San Miguel and others which previously were main thoroughfares but were now relegated to streets, or even sections of streets, of relatively minor importance. So the fears of their being eclipsed which were expressed about them in the *zarzuela* were, in fact, prophetic and came to pass.

Over the years, the Gran Vía became the hub of Madrid nightlife, as new hotels, film palaces, cafés, restaurants, luxury shops and later airline offices and department stores opened. The Gran Vía also became the home of Spain's largest radio network, the SER, founded in the 1920's, as well as one of Madrid's top bookshops, the Casa del Libro.

One of the most emblematic buildings on the Gran Vía is that housing Spain's telephone company, Telefónica, the largest privately-owned company in the country. The building, on Gran Vía 28, erected in 1926, was at that time the highest in the city. In the Civil War it was used as a lookout post by Republican forces during the multiple-year siege of Madrid, from where the defenders could peer out with binoculars and see the Nationalist forces entrenched just beyond the Manzanares River in the Casa de Campo Park. Being of great strategic importance and a prime target, the building had sandbags piled high all around it.

On the second floor of the Telefónica building, the company has installed a quite ambitious museum which is well worth a visit. The exhibits trace the development of the telephone in Spain, showing 75 models used through the years. Perhaps most curious is a large room with 20 switchboard operators sitting at a giant console. It's a few seconds before one realizes that the ladies are manikins. The ground floor is used by Telefónica for all sorts of public exhibits.

After Franco won the Civil War, the Gran Vía was officially named the Avenida de José Antonio Primo de Rivera, in honor of the founder of the Falange; but even during the dictatorship all locals still referred to it as the Gran Vía. After Franco's death, the avenue officially reverted to its former name.

Pedro Chicote. Standing in his world-famous Museo de las Bebidas (Drink Museum), containing more than 18,000 different bottles, "Perico" Chicote points at one of his "treasures". *Author's archive.*

Today, the first stretch of the Gran Vía, from its intersection with Alcalá to the Red de San Luis, is the tamest and least interesting, though it does include Chicote, at Gran Vía 12 , a bar that opened in 1931 and became one of the most famous gathering places in the city, a favorite hangout for journalists, literati, bullfighters, hookers, and a motley assortment of drinkers and carousers from all walks of life. In 1946 its owner, Perico Chicote, opened a Museo de Bebidas (Drink Museum), as part of the bar, which contained over 18,000 different bottles. Among the most curious was a prized bottle of Courvoisier brandy from 1811, tagged "Bottle 42" (out of 100), specially made for Napoleon. Another showpiece was a bottle of "Diamante" (a brand of Spanish wine) used by Pope Pius XII in a Mass. There was a very old bottle of Johnny Walker that dated back to 1820, the first year the Scotch was distilled. Other curiosities included bottles with radios, watches, ashtrays attached to them and others that even lit up.

Just about every celebrity of the time had a drink or two, in some cases many more, in Chicote's, including Ernest Hemingway, Ava Gardner, Rita Hayworth, Lana Turner, Josphine Baker, Salvador Dalí, *Manolete,* Dr. Alexander Fleming, Douglas Fairbanks and a long etcetera.

On December 25, 1977, when film buffs the world over mourned the passing of Charles Chaplin, Madrid also mourned the death of Perico Chicote, known locally as the "alchemist of drinks". His memorable collection of bottles was subsequently purchased by a famous and later scandal-ridden financier, Ruíz Mateos, and exhibited for a short while to the public. The collection was then auctioned off and bought at a very low price by a private collector in 1983. The bottle museum was found in a warehouse outside Madrid and resold in the greatest secrecy to an American. The collection is currently owned by Arturo Fernández, the owner of the gigantic restaurant and hotel company Grupo Arturo Cantoblanco.

Chicote's remained open after the founder's death, passing from one management to another without much success, until finally it was relaunched in 2002 as a modern jet-set venue. At present it is one of Madrid's most fashionable hangouts for actors, producers, media types, fashion designers and literary celebrities and is now a worthy scion of Perico's original bar.

The second and third stretches of the Gran Vía are its most vital and colorful, usually filled with a lively throng of Madrileños and tourists who crowd into the rows of movie houses and theatres lining the street, cram into fast-food eateries, or shop in a wide variety of stores. On the corner of Gran Vía and Montera, in the Red de San Luis, you'll see an elegant-looking McDonald's with wooden panelling on the outside and a luxurious marble staircase inside. The site used to be occupied by the fashionable and expensive jewelry store Aleixandre, the former "Tiffany" of Madrid. When the store closed and it was known that the buyers were the McDonald's burger chain, there was a great public uproar of protest in the city. However McDonald's maintained the former aesthetic appearance of the store thereby mollifying its harshest critics. Nevertheless, those aware of its former history still feel a twinge of guilt when ordering a Big Mac with Coke and fries in what was once such a fancy setting.

The busiest corner on the Gran Vía is at the Plaza del Callao, named for a naval battle in 1866 at the Peruvian port of the same name, though exactly who won the encounter depends on the history book you read. On this square you'll see the large FNAC building (selling CD's, books - many in English — DVD's, and hi-fi equipment). From here you can proceed towards the Puerta del Sol, where you'll see various branches of El Corte Inglés department store. Since Callao is also an important subway junction, as well as a crossroads and entertainment hub, it is usually teeming with people.

You may notice that the Gran Vía doesn't run in a straight line, which may seem surprising given the fact that it was artificially laid out. The reason it is disjointed arises from the consideration that had to be given to preserve certain churches, which would have had to be razed if a straight line of demolition had been followed. In the first stretch, the Church of San José had to be respected, as well as the Oratory on the Calle del Caballero de Gracia, and in the third stretch, the Church of San Francisco de Borja which, however, was later torn down and replaced by the Lope de Vega theatre.

Furthermore, if you walk along the Calle de la Reina, which runs parallel to and behind the Gran Vía in its first stretch, you'll see a row of quite luxurious houses. This is a welcome example of real estate speculators winding up with egg on their faces, since the houses were built on the assumption that the Gran Vía would run along that street. As it turned out, this was not the case.

The first house to be built on the new Gran Vía (1915-1916) was the one on the corner of the Calle de Victor Hugo, now occupied by the elegant Loewe fashion shop, formerly the site of a tea house. The last built, in 1954, was the one located at Gran Vía 72, presently occupied by the Hotel Washington.

Aside from gala premieres of films and musical shows as well as parades and demonstrations passing along it, the Gran Vía in 1928 had an unwelcome, uninvited visitor. No, it was not General Franco and his troops – that came in March 1939 – but a 600 kilo (1,320 pound) fighting bull.

A bull rampages through the Gran Vía

In a country where bulls are a part of many fiestas, it is not surprising that on occasions a fighting bull has escaped from a stockyard and may even have run loose in the streets of some small village or *pueblo*. Far stranger is what occurred in Madrid in 1928. That year not only did a bull break out of a stockyard, but he actually managed to get as far as the most crowded street in Madrid, the Gran Vía.

It all began on the crisp Monday morning of January 23, 1928 at 8 a.m. in the neighborhood just past the Manzanares River known as Carabanchel Bajo. When several fighting bulls and cows were being driven through a corral, one of them, followed by a cow, managed to escape from the attendants. These bulls are specially bred over many generations for the sole purpose of fighting in an arena; they are fierce, strong and fast animals that will charge and attack even if wounded. So it was a serious matter when one of them had escaped.

What the caretakers of the stockade had most feared came to pass: the savage black bull started to head towards the Puente de Segovia, the bridge that leads right to the center of Madrid. He and the cow crossed the bridge, knocking over a

Dead bull on the Gran Vía. This is the bull that ran amok in the streets of the Gran Vía in 1928 and injured several people. The *torero* Diego "Fortuna" confronted the bull with only a coat, a hat and a cane and later killed him with a sword that was rushed to him. *ABC, Jan. 24, 1928.*

bicycle rider on the way and then rammed his horns into the metal door of a taxi cab, puncturing it and nearly ripping it off as the driver watched helplessly.

Out of the various routes that the bull could now take coming off the bridge, most leading to unpopulated areas, he decided to choose the one that headed straight into the center of town, about a half mile away. He trotted down the Paseo de la Virgen del Puerto, which runs along the side of the Manzanares River, and then turned up the hill that leads into the Plaza de España.

At this point, several *espontáneos* (would-be amateur bullfighters) tried to distract the bull, while passers-by scrambled for safety. The news that a wild bull was roaming through the streets spread like wildfire, and shopkeepers locked their doors, street vendors quickly closed their stands and anyone with a horse and cart lost no time in speeding from the scene, for horses are a favorite target for fighting bulls.

Meanwhile, a few of the amateur *toreros* managed to distract the bull; some were knocked over but not hurt. The bull, still being trailed by the cow, next decided to charge up the Calle de Leganitos. There a 66-year-old woman called Juana López saw the bull coming and tried to run away, but couldn't do so fast enough, nor could she duck into any of the stores or doorways, which had all been shuttered. The bull attacked her and threw her into the air and gored her badly. A passer-by who tried to help her was also injured, as well as a 77-year-old man.

Next the bull headed for the narrow Corredera Alta de San Pablo, just when that street was most crowded due to a market held there. Panic broke out upon seeing the charging bull and people started to scatter and take shelter behind street stands or anywhere they could, while the bull rampaged thrusting its powerful horns into street stands, sacks, dry goods and anything it came across. A hard-of-hearing fruit seller, innocently pushing along his cart, didn't hear the warning shouts from others and became the next victim. After being gored from the rear, the vendor remained lying unconscious on the ground as the bull furiously ripped his fruit cart apart. One of the wheels of the cart got hooked on the horns, giving the bull a nightmarish appearance as he continued his death spree. He next attacked a 16-year-old messenger. Although the boy was tossed about several times, the wheel on the bull's horns prevented the boy from being gored and he was quickly dragged to safety.

The bull and cow then started eating some bananas and cabbages that they found strewn in their path. Once they had eaten their fill, they decided to head towards the Gran Vía.

By now it was 11 a.m. Having shaken off the wheel, the bull arrived at the lower stretch of the Gran Vía, in those days called the Avenida del Conde de Peñalver. Upon seeing him, pedestrians fled in terror. A few individuals started to confront the animal, but then thought better of it when they saw his size and ferocity.

And what were the police doing all this time? Well, two municipal guards apparently *tried* to establish order, but their efforts were in vain. A third policeman, out of uniform, was caught by the bull and suffered minor injuries.

Just happening to be walking down the Gran Vía with his wife at that moment was a certain Diego Mazquiarán, better known as *Fortuna* (his nickname, meaning "fortune"), a well-known matador in his thirties. *Fortuna* had not performed well in the past few bullfight seasons. The last time in the arena, he had been gored and the cartilage in his knee was badly injured. He was still recuperating from the injury both physically and emotionally.

Quickly sizing up the situation, *Fortuna* led his wife to the side and took off his coat. He then slowly walked up to the bull and, using his coat as a cape, did a few passes, hoping thereby to stop him from causing further damage. Someone from the nearby Military Casino sent him a sabre, but this weapon was useless. Instead, *Fortuna* sent off a boy in a car to the nearby Calle de Valverde where he lived in order to fetch his *estoque* (sword).

For about fifteen minutes *Fortuna* kept the bull busy, while the crowd cheered. In fact, all the windows and balconies around the scene were crowded with onlookers watching the dramatic events unfolding. From one balcony, a group of young seamstresses cheered the *torero* each time the bull charged his coat. Police on foot and on horseback had a hard time trying to control the crowd of gawkers watching the spectacle.

When the boy sent for the sword finally showed up, he was greeted by a huge ovation, followed by cheers as *Fortuna* lined up the bull with his coat for the kill. When the bull was in the correct position, the *torero* managed to deliver a half sword-thrust, which however failed to kill the animal. Thereupon the crowd's cheers suddenly turned to panic as they saw the wounded bull heading towards them. *Fortuna* quickly executed two or three more passes to distract the bull, and prepared his sword for a final thrust in the bull's nape. At last, the *torero* thrust his sword into the bull the second time, killing him on the spot.

The crowd went wild, the seamstresses on the balcony and everyone else waved white handkerchiefs, signifying that

Fortuna should be awarded the bull's ear as is done in bullfights. Standing next to the dead bull, *Fortuna* was overcome by emotion. Several men from among the spectators raised him on their shoulders and carried him to a café on the Calle de Alcalá. There he was toasted and a petition drawn up that he be awarded the Cruz de la Beneficencia (Cross of Charity), the highest medal a civilian can receive, which in fact was subsequently bestowed upon him.

Of course, given the publicity, and having been awarded the medal, the matador was now eagerly sought out by bullfight impresarios and within a few days had 18 fights lined up for the next season. Sadly, *Fortuna*'s career was to be shortlived, for he died only eight years later, but was still famous enough to be included among the *toreros* who officiated the opening of Madrid's present bullring in Las Ventas in 1931.

Curiously, the same year that *Fortuna* killed his bull on

A HANDY MILITARY VENUE

Among the first buildings built on the Gran Vía is one at Number 13 over whose doorway you'll see a small plaque with the Latin inscription: *Si vis pacem, para bellum* (If you want peace, prepare for war). It houses the Cultural Center of the Armed Forces, inaugurated by King Alfonso XIII in 1919. It was from here that the bullfighter Fortuna obtained the sabre he used to first try to kill the wild bull that had rampaged down the Gran Vía. Aside from its use by the military, this historic building is also a good place in which to have a set-price budget meal. Should you want to do so, walk past the concierge, and up a wide staircase, flanked by photos of Alfonso XIII and military mementoes, which leads up to a spacious second floor restaurant that is open to the general public. The three old-fashioned dining rooms (one with a view of the Calle de la Virgen de los Peligros), draw a mixed clientele of businessmen, non-uniformed military people, families and public in general.

the Gran Vía, another "loose" bull showed up in the Calle de Atocha. The casualties in this case were one person seriously gored and four others with minor injuries. Since no bullfighter happened to be in the area at the time, the job of finishing off the bull had to be undertaken by a Civil Guard, who followed the rampaging bull in a taxi, and then ungallantly shot the bull dead with his pistol.

More recently, in 1973, a matador by the name of Luis Segura, aided by his brother, tried to pull off a publicity stunt by killing a bull that had supposedly escaped from its corral and run as far as the Plaza de España. When it was learned that the bull had been placed there purposely by the *torero*, he was taken to court and wound up in the clink.

In any case, should you be near the Gran Vía or the Plaza de España, you might want to take a look at the narrow Calle de Leganitos where *Fortuna*'s bull ran amok and try to imagine what it would be like to suddenly see a 600 kilo (1320 pound) fighting bull running up the street charging at you.

Ghosts in the House of the Seven Chimneys

Behind the Gran Vía, on the Calle de las Infantas 31 (beside the Plaza del Rey), stands an old mansion with four freestanding columns in front it. If you raise your eyes to the top of the 16th century structure, you'll see that on its roof is a row of seven cylindrical chimneys. The building from which they jut out is still known locally as La Casa de las Siete Chimeneas (The House of the Seven Chimneys), though now it houses the offices of the Culture Ministry. An old legend is associated with it which dates back to the century when the house was built. At that time, its location was on the fringe of the small city. In the legend the seven chimneys were equated to the seven deadly sins. And for good reason.

The mansion was ostensibly built by a huntsman in the court of King Carlos V for his daughter Elena. Rumor had it

House of the Seven Chimneys. Legend has it that a spectre in the form of a maiden, wronged by the king, appeared nightly on the roof of this old mansion. *Author's photo.*

that in fact the girl was the mistress of Carlos V's son, later King Felipe II. And that it was the latter who ordered the mansion to be built.

Soon after its completion, Elena married an army captain by the name of Zapata. Spain at that time was at war, and shortly after the nuptials the captain received orders to depart for Flanders. There he took part in the battle of San Quentin.

Two weeks later, Elena received tragic news: Zapata had died in the line of duty. The bereaved widow was distraught. She could not sleep or eat and, grief stricken, was daily wasting away. Her hair unkempt and her nails having grown long, she spent the days weeping disconsolately. Finally, her deep grief reached its unhappy conclusion as she died of a broken heart.

But now comes a strange twist to the story. Some there were who claimed that before she passed away, while in her tormented state of mind and ill health, she gave birth to a baby girl. But what had become of the infant? No one knew. To complicate matters further, the house servants swore that Elena had not died of grief; they claimed that she was *murdered,* and swore that her body showed marks of several stab wounds.

Suspicions of foul play increased when, shortly after her death, her body mysteriously disappeared, making any kind of investigation difficult. Could her death and the disappearance of her body have been part of a plot to cover up her amorous involvement with the prince, the future king Felipe II? However, instead of suspicions for the possible murder falling on Felipe, they were heaped upon Elena's father, who was detained and interrogated by the police. Several weeks after the excruciating interrogation and, maligned by the false accusations, the shamed and broken old man's inert body was found hanging from a wooden beam in the House of the Seven Chimneys.

These events naturally became the subject of daily gossip in Madrid. Rumors about the goings-on grew increasingly wilder and more fantastic. To squelch them, the prince finally ordered a full-fledged investigation of Elena's death, which uncovered — nothing. Rather, the investigation raised more questions than it answered. For it failed to allay speculation of a possible conspiracy and suggested that since no one had seen Elena's body being taken out of the house there could only be only one possible explanation: that the body had been hidden and walled up somewhere inside the house, in the manner of Edgar Allen Poe's *The Black Cat*. Pressure built up to such a degree that a search was finally authorized. However after ransacking the entire house, once again, nothing was found.

As time went by, the rumors slowly began to dwindle, until, in the middle of a cold wintry night, a farmer returning home claimed to see a shape moving amongst the seven chimneys. It was a strange ghostly figure shuffling to and fro on the roof of the house. He averred it was that of a pale woman in a silken white dress holding a torch who made her way to the edge of the roof and knelt down. The figure pounded her chest in grief and then pointed westwards towards the Royal Palace, the Alcázar, where Felipe, now having been crowned king,

House of the Seven Chimneys. This is what the building looked like in the 1920's and 1930's. *Author's archive.*

lived. The figure then mysteriously vanished.

Apparently, the specter reappeared for many months in an identical fashion and was unexpectedly seen by others passing in front of the old house. So who was this apparition? Some believe that it was Elena's ghost condemning the king for having had her murdered and hidden her body instead of allowing a proper Christian burial. Others aver that it wasn't a ghost at all. They said it was Felipe and Elena's illegitimate daughter, raised as an orphan, who had gone mad upon discovering who her real parents were. It was she who walked on the roof each night to accuse the king for having had her mother killed, hidden her body, and then hushed up the crime.

Either way, the curious fact is that in the 19th century the Banco de Castilla bought the House of the Seven Chimneys and made sweeping structural changes throughout the entire building. The floor of the basement had to be torn up to install new plumbing. One day, when the workmen were doing this, to their great surprise, buried underneath the floor, they discovered a human skeleton. Upon examination, it clearly showed that the bones were those of a woman. Even more surprising was that buried with the bones were several gold coins dating from the 16th century, the time when Felipe II reigned in Spain. But no sequels to the discovery ever materialized.

Aside from the ghost story, the mansion has another tale associated with it which is of less dubious historical authenticity, concerning the Squillace Mutiny.

SOLDIER STREET
(Calle del Soldado)

Although the Calle del Soldado no longer bears that name – it has been called the Calle de Barbieri since 1894, in honor of a local composer of *zarzuelas* – we cannot resist recounting a good tale. The story goes that a young lady of striking beauty, María de la Almudena Goutili, dwelled in a house on this street. Her pulchritude and perhaps the wealth of her family were not lost on a soldier of the guard, who made advances to her which, however, were rejected. In fact, the girl had already expressed her intention of entering a nunnery, maybe in part to put off her suitor.

Notwithstanding this, the soldier pressed his suit. Not content with just following her when she sallied out into the street, he had a picture of himself in full dress uniform painted on a pillar of the Convent of the Mercedarias Calzadas de San Fernando, which supposedly was right opposite her house and in full view whenever she looked out of her window. (In fact, this convent, built in 1698 and torn down in 1869, stood on the Calle de la Libertad, several blocks away from the Calle del Soldado, but the story is worth telling anyway!)

One afternoon when María was coming home from Mass she was again followed by the soldier and, right in front of her house, after a tiff which enraged the young man, and in which he lost all reason, was murdered by him. Such was his fury, the legend goes, that he then cut off her head, stuck it into a bag and took it to the convent she had said she was planning to enter. There he placed it in the torno (turntable) and told the nun on the other side that he had a present for the mother superior of the convent from Maria Goutili. When the mother superior opened the bag, the girl's severed head fell out and from its lips uttered the word "¡Madre!" (Mother!) The guilty soldier was soon seized, turned over to civil authorities and executed. His assassin's hand was cut off and nailed to a stick and hoisted at the scene of the crime as a warning to others whose romantic ardors were not requited when asking the hand of a beautiful damsel.

The Squillace Mutiny: the original cloaks and daggers

Of the many historical figures who at one time or another lodged in the House of the Seven Chimneys, perhaps the best remembered was Carlos III's Finance and War Minister, the Italian-born Marquis of Squillace. This nobleman has passed into the annals of Madrid history due to a riot which broke out when he forbade Madrileños to wear cloaks!

As we have earlier indicated, King Carlos III, who brought the Age of Enlightenment to Spain, introduced a sweeping agenda of badly-needed reforms. Many of these noteworthy ameliorations were carried out through the good services of his minister, Squillace, whose name was Hispanicized by the locals to Esquilache. Rather than appreciate the efforts to Europeanize the country, Spaniards

The Squillace Uprising. Moments before the uprising. To the left, sits a man converting forbidden hats into three-cornered ones, while the man beside him trims a cape. To the right, a man refuses to have his clothes altered. *19th century lithograph.*

tended to resent the reforms and improvements, preferring their own time-honored customs.

Squillace's unpopularity among the townspeople increased with every new change imposed upon them. Among the reforms decreed in 1766 was the introduction of urban sanitation, the installation of street lights and the prohibition of gambling.

In order to crack down on the rampant crime and insecurity in the streets of the capital, the carrying of weapons was outlawed. The customary garb of Madrileños in those days consisted of the traditional long cape and wide-brimmed hat. These were ideal for conspirators and criminals to conceal their faces under and hide any weapons they might be carrying.

Included in the crackdown was a decree that banned this attire. Under the supervision of inspectors, the government set up stands in the streets where on the spot the wide-brimmed hats were seized and then fashioned into the normal three-cornered ones worn in Europe. The offending capes were also modified by being cut shorter to make them more difficult to conceal weapons in.

The spark that led to what history knows as the *Motín de Esquilache* (Squillace Mutiny) came when a soldier challenged a group of passers-by wearing the prohibited garb and ordered them to remove it. The proud cape-toting offenders refused to obey, and an altercation ensued. Other becaped figures emerged from the dark recesses of the street. The soldier called for reinforcements and a tumultuous skirmish ensued; several people were killed in the encounter. Boiling over with indignation, Madrileños vowed not to kowtow to the new-fangled ordinances passed by the "Italian foreigner".

The disturbances grew far worse the following day when bands of angry becloaked Spaniards roamed the streets, demanding the resignation of Squillace. One mob headed towards the House of the Seven Chimneys, where the minister and his family lived, vowing to drag him out of his house and make him rue his decree.

The infuriated populace stormed into the mansion, and upon failing to find the despised minister, ransacked his home and flung his furniture and everything they could lay their hands on out the windows into the street. Had he been there, Heaven only knows what his fate would have been. But Squillace was lucky enough to be in the Royal Palace at that time consulting with the king. His family was also away when the house was ransacked. It was the servants in the house who bore the brunt of the ire of the infuriated mob.

In order to calm the situation, Carlos III finally had to mollify the townspeople by getting rid of Squillace and rescinding the decree. Squillace was appointed ambassador to Spain in Venice and lived out the remainder of his days peacefully in what he doubtlessly considered to be more congenial and enlightened surroundings.

Ghosts of Hemingway

Just off the Calle de Alcalá, a few steps past the Círculo de Bellas Artes (Fine Arts Circle) and the theatre and cinema of the same name on the one-block-long Calle del Marqués de Casa Riera, you come to the site of what used to be a hotel whose bar had been a popular rendez-vous for those patronizing the cultural offerings in the neighboring venues. It was called the Hotel Suecia (Swedish Hotel). Presently the building is being converted into apartments.

But for admirers of Ernest Hemingway, it was famous for another reason. For it was here that the American writer lodged during many of his later visits to the Spanish capital. A plaque to the right of the entrance, which we hope will be replaced once construction is completed, read:

"On the centenary of his birth, ERNESTO HEMINGWAY, who, seeking artistic and cultural sustenance in Madrid, chose to reside in this hotel in the 1950s, it being a retreat close to the Prado Museum, which he passionately loved, and to the Fine Arts Circle. 1999."

The use of the Spanish "Ernesto" might at first seem to

Cervecería Alemana. Located on the Plaza de Santa Ana, this old tavern used to be a hangout for Ernest Hemingway and his cohorts. It maintains much of the atmosphere of the 1950's. *Author's photo.*

be a fatuous Hispanicization of the writer's name, such as was formerly common in Spain (hence *Carlos* Marx, *Federico* Nietzsche, *Ricardo* Wagner, *Carlos* Dickens, etc.) But in the particular case of Hemingway, the reason for using the Hispanicized version of his name is that it was the one by which all his Spanish friends knew him as he caroused in the city's taverns and attended its bullfights.

Hemingway was always an enthusiastic admirer of Madrid. Though he considered the city to be modern rather than picturesque, he asserted that when one got to know it, it was the most Spanish of all cities, the best to live in, with the finest people and the finest climate. Though Ernest Hemingway lived in many other countries around the world — the United States, Italy, France, Cuba — his long love-affair with Spain was special. It not only influenced his writings but even the man himself. Starting in 1922 and until 1931,

Hemingway attended the San Fermín running of the bulls in Pamplona almost yearly; but he also saw literally thousands of other bullfights around the country at different times of the year. Some of his closest friends were bullfighters and his love and enthusiasm for Spain is palpable in every book he wrote set in the country. Later he came back as a newspaper correspondent in 1937 during the Spanish Civil War, and 15 years after that, in 1953, again returned to Spain. Thereafter he repeatedly visited the country until his suicide in 1961 in his house in Ketchum, Idaho.

Hotel Florida. This postcard from the 1920's depicts the hotel where *The Fifth Column* was written as bombs fell over Madrid. *Author's archive.*

During these sojourns, he stayed in various other hotels in the city. These ranged from a small *pensión* on the Carrera de San Jerónimo 32 (long since gone) on his first trip to the Hotel Palace when he was rich and famous. In 1937 Hemingway lodged at the old Hotel Florida on the Plaza del Callao, now the site of El Corte Inglés. It was while holing up in the Hotel Florida – not torn down until the 1960's – that, as a newspaper correspondent, and while waiting for a Republican offensive that never materialized, he wrote a play called *The Fifth Column*. In the preface, he comments that the hotel where he lived and worked was struck by more than thirty high explosive shells. When he went to the front, at its closest only 1,500 meters (less than a mile) from the hotel, the play was always slipped inside the inner fold of a rolled-up mattress to protect it from shrapnel. At that time the Nationalist forces had four columns advancing on Madrid and General Emilio Mola, leading one of these, boasted that, in fact, there was a *fifth* column: it consisted of Nationalist sympathizers living inside the city. Thereafter the term "fifth columnist" came to be synonymous with saboteurs and spies.

In the Civil War years Hemingway also stayed at the Hotel Gran Vía, still doing business, at Gran Via 25. Though the hotel was refurbished in 1999 and renamed Tryp Gran Vía, as a tribute to the American writer the hotel features a bar named in his honor. Along with the adjoining breakfast area, it is decorated with photographs of him taken all around the world, including shots snapped while he was in Spain. In fact, as a service to those of its guests who are Hemingway buffs, the hotel even provides a small lending library of his works in both English and Spanish.

During the many years Hemingway visited Madrid, he must have made the rounds of hundreds of bars and restaurants. Indeed, a Mexican restaurant called "El Cuchi", off the Plaza Mayor (now closed), even proudly announced over its doorway that Hemingway did NOT eat there.

Few of the writer's favorite hang-outs around town have survived. Gone are the "Callejón de la Ternera", an old tavern *cum* restaurant which had various photographs of him hung on its walls, as well as the Restaurante Valentín. Of the writer's former haunts Chicote continues to serve drinks though it is unrecognizable from what it was like in Hemingway's day. A better whiff of Hemingway's *time* can be gotten in Sobrinos de Botín on the Calle de los Cuchilleros 17 (see Area 3 map, Pg. 117). Don Ernesto doubtlessly dug into some of their roast suckling pig and milk-fed baby lamb in the days before the place attained its present popularity. The writer mentions Botín in *Death in the Afternoon* and also in *The Sun Also Rises* but it is unclear whether it was the *original* Botin, on the Plaza de los Herradores, long since gone, or the present Sobrinos de Botín, now known simply as "Botín".

Among the most atmospheric places where the writer hung out and which gives you an idea of the old Madrid of

Hemingway's time is the Cervecería Alemana on the Plaza de Santa Ana 6 (see Area 2 map, Pg. 85) where the writer caroused with his bibulous friends. The counter of the old tavern is often crowded, but you can usually find a table, order drinks and munch on some *croquetas* (fritters), *tortilla* (potato and onion omelet) or the more expensive *jamón serrano* (slices of cured ham). As you do so, you are immersed in a noisy atmosphere, not radically changed from Hemingway's time, although it is now a non-smoking hangout.

Perhaps you, too, will then concur with the Don Ernesto when he wrote: "To have a city with a museum like the Prado and with a bullfight season and places like El Escorial, Toledo, Ávila and Segovia nearby, makes you feel very badly to know that you will have to die and never see it again."

HEALTH STREET
(Calle de la Salud)

The origins for the name of this street date back to the time of the Catholic Monarchs, Fernando and Isabel (late 15th century). It seems that one year when the bubonic plague was decimating the city those living in this street survived the epidemic by isolating themselves from the remainder of the populace. They even went so far as to eat only home-grown vegetables and animals kept in their own yards.

After the epidemic, people started to call that section of town the *barrio de la salud* ("neighborhood of health"), and when more houses were built, the resulting street took on the present name. Moreover, one of the first drinking fountains in the city was located there, which supposedly had curative properties, and whose waters were used by those who isolated themselves from the plague.

Area 6: Cibeles

1. **Fountain and columns** (Paseo de Recoletos 7 - 9). Site where Mariblanca stood.
2. **Fundación BBVA** (Paseo de Recoletos 10). Marqués de Salamanca's mansion.
3. **Palacio de Linares** (Paseo de Recoletos 2). Raimundita's ghost tale.
4. **Palacio de Buena Vista** (Alcalá 51). Armed Forces Headquarters.
5. **Cibeles Fountain** (Plaza de la Cibeles).
6. **Palacio de Comunicaciones** a.k.a. Correos (Plaza de Cibeles).
7. **Banco de España** (Alcalá 50). Former plaques: "Plaza de Cibeles" with no "la".
8. **Naval Museum.** (Paseo del Prado 5).

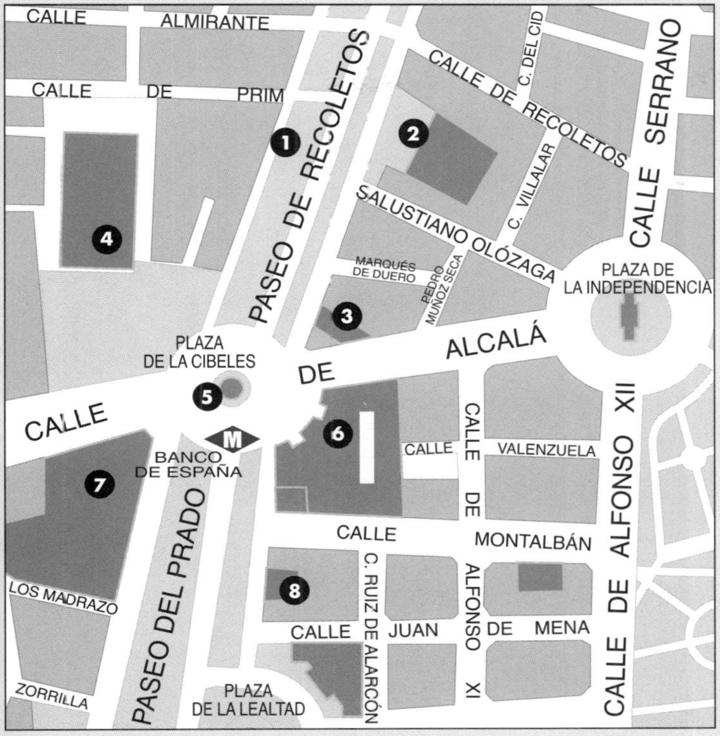
CALLE ALMIRANTE
CALLE DE PRIM
PASEO DE RECOLETOS
CALLE DE RECOLETOS
C. DEL CID
CALLE SERRANO
SALUSTIANO OLÓZAGA
C. VILLALAR
MARQUÉS DE DUERO
PEDRO MUÑOZ SECA
PLAZA DE LA INDEPENDENCIA
PLAZA DE LA CIBELES
CALLE DE ALCALÁ
BANCO DE ESPAÑA
CALLE VALENZUELA
CALLE DE VALENZUELA
CALLE MONTALBÁN
CALLE DE ALFONSO XII
C. RUIZ DE ALARCÓN
ALFONSO XI
CALLE JUAN DE MENA
LOS MADRAZO
ZORRILLA
PASEO DEL PRADO
PLAZA DE LA LEALTAD
1
2
3
4
5
6
7
8
M

Area 6 - CIBELES

La Cibeles: Icon for a city

Sooner or later anyone coming to Madrid will pass through the intersection of the Calle de Alcalá and the Paseo de Recoletos, one of the busiest and most vibrant squares in the capital. On each corner stand striking buildings: the Linares Palace, the Central Post Office (Palace of Communications as it is grandly called), most of it now taken over by the municipality, the Bank of Spain and the Buenavista Palace, the latter used as the General Headquarters of the Army.

The square is known as the Plaza de la Cibeles although a few years ago several signs were put up that read "Plaza de Cibeles", leaving out the "la". Since many Spaniards tend to be very conscientious about history and spelling, a considerable uproar ensued in the press. The result was that City Hall rectified the mistake, bowing to those taking pride in the purity of their language.

Even so, on the corner where the Bank of Spain stands, two oval plaques remained that read "Plaza de Cibeles" until 2006 when the entire building had a facelift and the two plaques were removed but the outline can still be seen. Curiously these dated back to the time the bank was constructed and no one seems to have been bothered by the misnomer.

The square gets its name from the city's best-known fountain. It depicts Cybele, the ancient Greek earth goddess and mother of Zeus. She is mounted on a chariot drawn by two

The Cibeles Fountain. Madrid's most popular icon, the Earth Goddess Cybele, which hides many a secret story. *Author's photo.*

Design for Cibeles Fountain and Amorcillos. (Left) Ventura Rodríguez's original design shows that he toyed with the idea of placing a child far in front of the chariot. (Right) Although it was not included at first, in 1895 a pair of children called *amorcillos*, were added. However, they were placed behind the chariot. *Archivo de Madrid.*

lions. Over the years, the statue has become the symbol of Madrid and every true Madrileño sings the praises of *La Cibeles*, as she is commonly called.

The fountain was built in the reign of Carlos III, designed by Ventura Rodríguez, who also designed the Apollo and Neptune fountains a little further south on the Paseo del Prado. The original design envisaged a spout of water coming out of the fountain which splashed on top of a small child sitting on a vat, about five meters (15 feet) in front of the lions. Another stream of water flowed out of the vat and into a small basin from where the water-bearers could fill their buckets. But this figure was never added.

When the fountain was installed in 1792, the king was so delighted with it that at first he wanted to move it to the gardens of the Royal Palace of La Granja, near Segovia. But the fountain had already become so popular in Madrid, that the king decided to leave it in the city. At that time it stood a little to the side of the square, in front of the Buenavista Palace, oriented southwards towards the Fountain of Neptune. In 1794, in order to supply Madrileños with water, two fountain spouts were placed on either side of the chariot. These were in the form of a bear and a dragon, honoring the city's coat-of-arms at the time. Later, in 1858, when water

supply was brought to the capital from a reservoir built near the village of Lozoya in the Guadarrama Mountains, two manual water pumps were added.

In 1895, the Cybele Fountain was moved to its present site in the center of the square and Cybele and her chariot turned to face the Puerta del Sol. The stone bear and dragon were removed and "lost" for many years. Many sources even claim that the bear was so disfigured with the passage of time that it had been discarded and destroyed. You can imagine our surprise when, upon visiting the San Isidro Museum (see Area 3 map, Pg. 117A), we discovered the original two stone statues in an inner courtyard, preserved in reasonably good condition.

After the fountain was moved to the center of the square, two *amorcillos* (cuddly toddlers) emptying out a vat were placed behind the goddess' chariot. Curiously enough these are reminiscent of the original plans drawn up by Ventura Rodríguez in which he envisaged a child sitting in front of the goddess.

Spouts added to the Cibeles Fountain. These two figures, a dragon (left) and a bear (right), both included in Madrid's former coat-of-arms, were placed on the perimeter of the Cibeles. Note the openings in the mouths from which flowed drinking water. *Author's photos.*

Lions in the Cibeles. Although mythology doesn't state clearly whether the lovers Atalanta and Hippomenes were turned into a male and a female lion or into two male ones, in the fountain there is no doubt that both lions have manes and are therefore male. *Author's photo.*

Cybele's lions in love

It is clear enough that Cybele is the Nature Goddess. But why are two *lions* hitched to her chariot? The explanation is found in Greek mythology and concerns Atalanta, a child who was abandoned by her father in the wilderness in the expectation that she would perish. However, a she-bear found the infant and nursed her as if she were a cub of her own. As Atalanta grew up, she had to fend for her own food and protect herself again predators, soon learning all the knacks and skills of survival in a hostile environment; above all, she developed a phenomenal dexterity in running.

At one point, several hunters found the wild girl and carried her back to civilization. Once grown into womanhood, Atalanta was reluctantly reconciled with her father. Upon her becoming nubile, he urged her to find a husband.

Seeking advice from an oracle, Atalanta was sternly warned that if she married she would be transformed into an animal. Dreading the prospect, Atalanta placed all sorts of obstacles in the way of her nuptials. After endless arguments with her father, they finally reached a compromise: she would

MADRID'S GODDESS IN MEXICO

A Cibeles Fountain in the center of Mexico? Yes, indeed! Just like there is a miniature of the Statue of Liberty in Paris, there is a replica of the Cibeles in Mexico City. It was inaugurated on September 5, 1980 by the president of Mexico, José López Portillo and the mayor of Madrid, Enrique Tierno Galván. Measuring approximately 12.5 x 4.7 meters (37.5 x 14 feet) and weighing 12 tons, this smaller version of the original, fully functional, was a gift from Spaniards living in Mexico as a gesture of the brotherhood between the two cities. It stands on the Avenida Oaxaca, two blocks away from the Insurgentes subway station.

only marry on the condition that her future groom could outrun her in a footrace. Moreover, if the contender lost he would have to forfeit his life.

Despite this condition, several brave suitors attempted the task, but all failed in their efforts. Atalanta's plan seemed to be working until a young man by the name of Hippomenes fell madly in love with her. He well knew he wasn't fast enough to beat her, so he travelled to Mount Olympus, the home of the gods, to seek advice from the goddess Aphrodite. The goddess agreed to help him, and plucked three golden apples from a tree in the Garden of Hesperides which he was instructed to use in the contest against Atalanta.

On the day of the race, Hippomenes secretly kept the three golden apples in readiness. As the race started, the swift young man took the lead. Whereupon Atalanta increased her own speed, but each time she was about to overtake him, he dropped one of the golden apples on the track. As he did so, Atalanta, unable to overcome her greed, stopped to pick up the golden treat. Dropping the other two apples during the race was enough to insure Hippomenes winning, much to the distress of the girl, who now had to keep her promise and wed the winner.

As it turned out, the marriage was a success and the couple loved each other dearly. Atalanta even started to think that the oracle's prophesy would never come true. However, one day while the two newlyweds were out hunting, they decided to stop to rest in a temple of Zeus. So great was their passion that they began to make love within the confines of the sacred place. Unfortunately, Zeus happened to see their sacrilegious deed and meted out punishment to them: He transformed the young lovers into lions for all eternity! Mythology has it that Cybele then came across the two lions and, taking pity on them, hitched them to her chariot so that the two lovers would always remain together, even if it was only in the form of lions.

The fountain in Cibeles, however, gives the legend a further twist. For you will notice that the sculptor has increased Zeus' cruelty by transforming them into two *male* lions, hence preventing them from making love again. You can see on the fountain that both lions have a mane, showing clearly that they are male. Was it that Zeus had a vicious streak in him, or simply that the sculptor gave the story a final nasty twist? Or was it simply that two long-maned lions are more dramatic and aesthetically pleasing than a lion and a lioness and the true myth be damned?

A mythical castration

Examining the statue of Cybele more closely reveals several other curious details on it, such as a frog and a serpent, not surprising since they relate to the watery nature of a fountain. But there are also several pine cones on the ground and pine cone motifs on the chariot which seem to be quite out of place.

The pine cones hark back to another Greek myth depicted in the fountain. At the front of the chariot, but difficult to see from the ground, you can make out a huge face that has

Face of Attis in the Cibeles Fountain. At the front of the chariot, spouting water out of his mouth, appears the head of Attis partly converted into a vegetable. *Author's photo.*

a large spurt of water coming out of its mouth. This is Cybele's grandson Attis whose story is closely linked to the pine cones.

The myth involves a series of bizarre circumstances and relationships. The Earth Goddess unknowingly had a grandson, Attis, whom she fell madly in love with. But her love was not requited, for the young man favored another woman. Furious, Cybele devised a plan to assure herself that Attis would belong to no other woman; she decided to drive him mad. Knowing this, and in total despair in view of his frustrated love affair, Attis fled into the mountains and castrated himself, eventually bleeding to death. Cybele, repentant, however resurrected him in the form of a pine tree. Attis came to be worshipped as the god of vegetation, responsible for the death and rebirth of plant life. Hence, the pine cones on the statue and the flourishing vegetation around the chariot are a reminder of his desperate deed and final resurrection.

Soccer madness imperils the goddess

It's hard to talk about *La Cibeles* without also talking about Spain's most popular sport, *fútbol* (soccer), which, as in many countries in the world, is more than just a sport: it is a national passion. In Madrid, tradition dictates that after one of the local soccer teams, El Real Madrid, wins a championship their wildly-celebrating fans head by the thousands for the Cibeles Fountain. Until recently, the celebrations and goings-on that follow a Real Madrid victory provided a local spectacle the likes of which could only be described as total hysteria. The whole center of the city became paralyzed as fans indulged in an hours-long paroxysm of *futbol*-mania.

When the Real Madrid won such important championships as the *Liga* or the *Copa del Rey* or the *Copa de Europa*, the soccer players were driven in a large bus from the Bernabéu Stadium (due north of Cibeles on the Paseo de la Castellana) to the fountain of the goddess. The wide Paseo de la Castellana was closed to traffic as thousands of Real Madrid fans clustered around the fountain waiting for the arrival of their idolized athletes. The cheering crowds included whole families, children, exuberant youths, frenzied fans and soccer-worshippers, many waving Spanish flags and all of them chanting "*¡Hála Madrid! ¡Hála Madrid!*" in what resembled a sportive frenzy. When the superstars – often more famous than politicians or movie stars – arrived, they alighted from the bus and proceeded to climb up to the Greek Earth Goddess and wrapped a long Real Madrid scarf around her neck and then jumped fully clothed into the water of the fountain. All of these shenanigans — from the moment the players stepped out of the stadium to the moment they took their dip in the fountain – were covered in detail live by the local TV stations and the avid local press corps. (Two newspapers, *Marca* and *As*, are published daily, dedicated mostly to soccer; each has far larger circulations than any of the regular Spanish papers!)

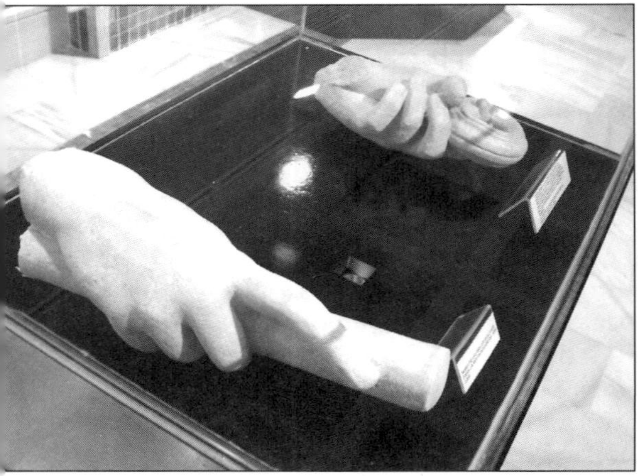

Hands of the Cibeles. These are replicas that were placed on the statue while the real ones that had been vandalized were repaired or recast. They are on display at the Museo de la Ciudad. *Author's photo.*

After the players withdrew from Cibeles and the police cordon left, many enthusiastic fans followed their heroes' example and also took the plunge into the fountain while cheering the victory of their team. These traditions and festivities would have continued for years to come if it hadn't been for the presence of the usual rotten apples and hooligans in the crowd who, after downing many cans of beer, started to get rowdy and began to vandalize the area and thus spoilt the fun for all those legitimately celebrating the victory.

In 1994, during the World Soccer Cup when Spain beat Switzerland, the vandals climbed up on the Cibeles Fountain and broke off the goddess' arm. The limb was found several days later in the rest room of a bar. This incident, and several others like it, finally obliged the authorities to put a lid on the celebrations whenever there was a key match by erecting barriers around the fountain, reinforced by a sizeable contingent of riot police. Even then, for a few years more, the players themselves were still allowed to clamber up to the statue of the goddess. Until finally the mayor asked them not to do so. But public clamor among soccer fans to maintain the tradition of hanging the scarf on the statue and jumping into the fountain was so great that City Hall gave the approval for the players to climb up on the statue, though the general public was barred from approaching the goddess.

However, vandalism didn't occur only following a soccer match. In one case it followed the celebration of a young man's birthday party in a nearby bar, at which time, on September 21, 2002, six youths broke off the left hand of the goddess and ran away with it. One of the culprits then called the newspaper *El Mundo* saying that they had dumped the hand in a recycling bin. But the hand was never found. The vandals were caught by the police and made to pay hefty fines and the cost of repairing the statue. (In the Museum of the City of Madrid, Calle del Príncipe de Vergara 140, you can see several life-sized models used for the restoration of Cybele's arm and hand.)

Finally, in 2003, on the day that the Real Madrid won the *Liga* (championship for the top Spanish team), there was the usual huge celebration and when the bus with the players arrived at Cibeles, and came to the platform constructed around the fountain for the players to celebrate on, they found that the police would not allow them to tread upon the statue or the fountain, and were restricted only to the platform.

Raúl on the Cibeles. Players of the Real Madrid soccer team used to celebrate their victories on the Cibeles fountain before it was prohibited to climb on the statue. Raúl, the team's former star, ties a scarf around the Cibeles' neck. *Author's archive.*

Raúl, the former team's star, indignantly demanded some sort of an explanation from the authorities and was told that the order barring their entry to the statue itself had come directly from the mayor. Raúl's immediate reaction was: "Fine, tell the mayor to come. I want to talk to him in person!"

Not surprisingly, the player's request was ignored by the mayor and the Real Madrid players had to celebrate their victory on the platform, therewith breaking a lifelong tradition.

Nevertheless, enthusiastic fans continue to congregate at the foot of the fountain after every important soccer victory, but always under the apprehensive vigilance of the police.

While Real Madrid is certainly the most famous of the soccer teams based in the capital, another, the Atlético de Madrid, is just as enthusiastically supported by its fans. Traditionally they whoop it up in identical fashion when their team wins an important game, except that instead of doing it at the Cibeles Fountain they celebrate at the Neptune Fountain on the Plaza de Cánovas del Castillo, a few blocks south of the Cibeles traffic circle. Sad to say, the statue of the sea god also suffered from vandalism when in 1996, after the Atlético had won the *Liga,* hooligans supporting the rival Real Madrid team in revenge ripped off his arm. Happily, skillful Spanish artisans were able to replace Neptune's arm, as they had that of Cybele.

Voices from the Beyond in the Palacio de Linares

It all began in 1990 in the dilapidated and rundown Palacio de Linares, located smack on the northeastern corner of the bustling Plaza de la Cibeles. Construction work on the building was just starting in order to restore it to its former glory and adapt the palatial house into the present Casa de América.

As work progressed, workers and night watchmen reported that strange goings-on were occurring during the middle of the night. Doors would open and close mysteriously, they claimed; the light footsteps of a child could be heard, and at times wails and even piercing shrieks would disturb the still of the night. Some of these strange phenomena centered around a wooden life-size dolls' house attached to the front of the main building, which had been constructed for the foster child of the original owner, the Marquis of Linares.

Within a month after the first reports of these untoward occurrences were published in the local press, a huge contingent of psychics, mediums, and paranormal investigators descended upon the old mansion and its worksite. In the cortège of obsessive snoopers was a certain Carmen Sánchez Castro, supposedly a doctor and para-psychologist, who claimed she had recorded strange voices called *psicofonías* in the building. In English, these are called *EVP's*, "electronic voice phenomena", and supposedly appear when background recordings throw up the voice of a dead person speaking. Curiously, it was Thomas Edison who first attempted to build a device that would record this phenomenon, which first came to public attention in 1920 when the *Scientific American* carried an article written by him on it.

In any case, apparently Sánchez had recorded the young, frail voice of a mother who had died more than a hundred years earlier accusing the owners of the palace of being murderers:

My daughter is at rest.
My daughter Raimunda,
I never heard her say mommy.
Murderers, murderers!
We are here to stay for eternity.

The news was splattered all over Madrid newspapers – always thirsting for a juicy story – and was then picked up in local magazines and on television shows and on the radio. The questions asked were: Is the Palacio de Linares haunted? Who was Raimunda? Who were the marquis and marchioness? Were they murderers?

The outcries of skeptics and historians were ignored as new lurid versions of the noble mansion's past history stoked the fires of mediatic mumbo jumbo. The tales ranged from accusations of incest to wild stories of deformed babies drowned in bathtubs.

The Palacio de Linares. Spine-chilling tales of incest, deformed children, murder and ghosts were spun around this beautiful mansion. The building is now home to La Casa de América, a center for Latin American cultural events. *Author's photo.*

However the legends smeared over the media were constantly contradicting each other; even "Doctor" Carmen Sánchez's *EVP*'s were confusing. Names were mixed up, incorrect dates given, and the entire past history of the marquis and his wife confusingly jumbled together with incongruous assertions. All, needless to say, presented as sensationally as possible.

The legend went as follows: Mateo Murga, the wealthy father of José, the future marquis, had brought up his son in a liberal environment and had told him that when he married he should do so for love, regardless of his future wife's financial condition. When the boy grew up, he fell in love with Raimunda, a young woman from a humble household. However, when the son introduced the girl to his family and expressed his desire to marry her, assuming that her low social

Dolls' house in the Palacio de Linares. Inside the courtyard of the mansion stands the wooden, life-sized dolls' house constructed by the Marquis of Linares for his adopted daughter Raimundita. It is supposedly the most haunted part of the mansion. *Author's photo.*

status would not be an impediment, his father flew into an inexplicable rage and promptly sent the young man packing to England to further his studies and hopefully forget his infatuation with the woman he was so enamored of.

It so happened that during José's long voyage to England his father passed away, prompting the son to immediately return to Spain. In due time, he married Raimunda and shortly after had a daughter who they called Raimundita. José then began the construction of the mansion and in addition, to please his daughter, decided to add a specially constructed full-size dolls' house in front of the garden. It was just at this happy juncture in time that, by accident, José came across a letter that his father had written him but hadn't been able to send due to his untimely and sudden death. The letter explained the reason for his fury when José had wanted to marry Raimunda: years earlier the father had had a secret affair with a woman that worked in the Madrid Tobacco Factory. The result of the union had been a bastard child by the name of Raimunda, the very woman who José wound up marrying. The letter had been discovered too late by José. Hence, not only was Raimunda José's half sister, but to make matters worse, their daughter, Raimundita, was the offspring of an incestuous relationship. In some versions of the story, the child was born sickly and deformed as a cause of their unholy union. In other versions, José pleads his case before Pope Leo XIII who, softened by the young man's plight, issues a Papal bull, *"Casti Convivire"*, that allowed the couple to live under the same roof but in chastity.

However, the most morbid and evidently the most

Monogram on the Palacio de Linares. Circling the entire mansion is a grille still bearing the initials of the original owner, "M" and "L", the "Marqués de Linares." *Author's photo.*

widely-circulating version went as follows: Horrified by the discovery of the letter, the couple agreed to kill their own daughter, considering her a damned child. In some versions she is drowned in one of the luxurious marble bathtubs of the mansion, while in others she is immured in the outside wall of the mansion next to the giant wooden dolls' house that can still be seen today. Legend has it that after the murder the couple was so ashamed of their deed that they decided to live in separate parts of the palace. Rumors twisted the story even further by claiming that, several years later, the marchioness passed away and José, distraught with grief, committed suicide and had his body buried in the very garden of the mansion, since in Catholic countries suicide is considered to be sacrilegious and those committing it are barred from burial in consecrated ground.

Quite an elaborate story, although most of it is easily debunked. The real story is as follows:

In the mid-19th century, a number of Spaniards succeeded in amassing great fortunes in Latin America. Such was the case with José de Murga and his father Mateo, who were involved in the construction of the first railroad in Cuba, which at that time was still a Spanish colony. After striking it rich, José married Raimunda Ossorio y Ortega on June 10, 1858. This is well documented since Raimunda came from a well-known and well-to-do family.

After their return from Cuba, the Murgas became very active in works of charity. They founded institutions and hospitals and lavished money on those in need. In 1871, Murga purchased a plot on the corner of the Plaza de la Cibeles and two years later started to build a sumptuous mansion there, using the municipal architect Carlos Colubi. Upon the building being completed, and having had no children, as once again documents of the time clearly demonstrate, the future nobleman and his wife decided to foster a girl by the name of Raimunda Avecilla who they affectionately called Raimundita.

It was at this time that José decided to construct the life-sized dolls' house for their adopted child to play in. In 1873 their humanitarian efforts were rewarded by the king when Murga was bequeathed the title of Marquis of Linares, the town in Andalucía he was originally from and where he had founded an important hospital. The first of the couple to die was the wife; several years later the marquis followed her into the grave. A large funeral was held, documented by every newspaper of the time, allowing no room for supposed secret garden burials. As of today, the bodies of the marquis and his wife rest in the chapel of the Linares Hospital in the town of Linares. As for the marquis's will, most of the estate went to several charity organizations, among them the hospital in Linares, while the mansion was inherited by Raimundita who at that time was a countess, having married Felipe Padierna, Count of Villapadierna, with whom she had two children.

The only part of the fanciful story that could be true, although there is no proof in favor of nor against it, is that José's father, Mateo, may have had an affair with a woman from a tobacco factory, and may even have fathered a child. However, this bastard child could by no means have been José's wife, for, as we mentioned earlier, the family lineage of Raimunda is well documented. Nor is there any evidence of any Papal Bull ever having been promulgated.

As for the mansion, after belonging to Raimundita, it was sold and resold a number of times, until by the mid-20th century it had fallen into a lamentable state of disrepair, its former grandeur now degraded to a dilapidated eyesore on one of the city's most important squares. The old building was even rented out at one point as a location for a popular Spanish film directed by Luis Berlanga called *Patrimonio Nacional.*

In 1988, the mansion was bought by Emiliano Revilla (owner of a well- known sausage company, still in existence) who subsequently was kidnapped and held for ransom by the Basque terrorist group ETA. After the ransom was paid and Revilla freed, he made a deal with City Hall in which he exchanged the mansion for a valuable plot of land near the M-30 highway that rings the city.

Municipal authorities then spent millions restoring the venerable mansion and upon completion of the renovations in 1992 housed in it the present Casa de América, which features Latin American film screenings, lectures, exhibits and other cultural events. Those interested in the art, history and culture of Latin America will find here a congenial venue in which to congregate, have a coffee or just chat with others. The huge dolls' house, which plays such an important part in the legend, has also been restored and is now used mainly for exhibitions.

As a final note, we may mention that during all the paranormal commotion, on June 4, 1990, the Madrid authorities allowed a great number of "parapsychologists" to descend upon the mansion, at which time over two hundred "experts" tried to record or videotape any paranormal activity they might discover. They poked about for a full 24 hours, converting the mansion into a three-ring circus. Apparently the ghosts were shy that day and the entire investigation was a bust. The hype died out, and upon closer examination of the original *EVP* recordings they proved to be bogus. "Doctor" Carmen Sánchez Castro was arrested by the police for having signed various phoney checks ten years earlier and, as had been suspected, was practicing without having ever obtained a doctor's degree. Even so, every now and then, some TV program or magazine dedicated to the occult and paranormal tries to bring up a new piece of "evidence" or recording in favor of the ghost yarn. Fortunately, by now they only cause a snicker or a lifting of the eyebrows.

The Marqués de Salamanca: flamboyant millionaire

America has had its Rockefellers, Carnegies and Vanderbilts. But Madrid, too, has had a few of its own financial moguls. Of these, certainly the most flamboyant was José Salamanca, better known as the Marquis of Salamanca.

Salamanca's life was a turbulent roller-coaster of financial ups and downs. On one occasion, after he had fled his creditors and ducked arrest warrants in Spain, he found refuge in Paris and was introduced to Alexandre Dumas. The famous

Salamanca's palace. View of the main entrance to the palace circa 1855. It still stands proudly on the Paseo de Recoletos 10. *Author's archive.*

The Marqués de Salamanca. The enterprising, picturesque and adventurous financier who lost and remade his wealth three times during his lifetime. *Photo by Martínez Hebert.*

author listened in fascination to the adventures of the millionaire, and after a few hours commented, "Had I met you earlier, instead of writing *The Count of Montecristo* I would have written *The Marquis of Salamanca.*"

If you walk a few blocks north of the Plaza de la Cibeles on the Paseo de Recoletos you can see the huge white mansion with a garden and a gate in front of it that used to be Salamanca's home. It now belongs to a foundation of one of Spain's largest financial institutions, the Banco de Bilbao Vizcaya Argentaria (BBVA). The building is one of the few remaining villas of the many that used to line the Paseo de Recoletos and its extension, the Castellana, on what in the old days was Millionaires Row.

The impressive *palacete* built by Narciso Pascual y Colomer, who also contributed to building the Congress (Las Cortes) and the swank buildings on the Plaza de Oriente, was copied from Baron Rothschild's villa in Paris. It was inaugurated in 1858 with one of the most spectacular parties seen in Isabeline times. The sumptuous building dazzled the eyes of the elegantly-clad guests with its majestic staircase, ornate columns, ceiling frescoes and splendid use of marble. Gardens and hothouses adorned its precincts and the rooms were hung with magnificent paintings culled from the best collections in Spain. This, however, was only *one* of the mansions Salamanca owned at that time; others were located in Carabanchel (the Vista Alegre palace), in Albacete (in southern Spain), which included a huge ranch, as well as others in Lisbon, Paris and Rome.

One of the most picturesque financial buccaneers of 19th century Madrid, José Salamanca made his fortune and then lost it three times during his lifetime. He made his first financial killing after arriving in the capital from his native Málaga, by managing to get permission to administer the government's monopoly on salt, for which the Ministry of Finance had not been collecting interest. Salamanca turned a losing venture into a business that in five years brought in 20 million *reales* to the crown (about $100 million by today's reckoning). Following other financial coups, including a successful mission to London to refinance Spain's debt, Queen Isabel appointed him Minister of Finance and bestowed upon him the title of Marquis of Salamanca and Count of Los Llanos.

The Marquis became instrumental in building the second railroad line in Spain, which in 1851 linked Madrid and Aranjuez. To impress Queen Isabel, Salamanca had even wanted to lay the last 100 meters (300 feet) in rails made of pure silver, but this *beau geste* never came to be. Salamanca continued to be deeply involved in the financing of Spanish railroads, the 19th century equivalent of today's telecommunication and computer technology enterprises.

Meddling in politics in those stormy times in Spain, when governments and opposing generals succeeded each other with breakneck speed, was a risky business. On one occasion, the story goes, through a spectacular twist of finance, he managed in one morning to make a clear profit of 30 million *reales* in the stock market, therewith ruining thousands of people. Many of these besieged him, imploring him for a period of grace to pay off their debts. Salamanca, in a histrionic style of which he was a master, stood in the center of the trading floor and cried out a famous line from Victor Hugo's play *Hernani*, "*Perdono a tutti!*" (All are forgiven!), and before the incredulous eyes of his debtors proceeded to tear up the stock certificates. Though his debtors went wild with joy, General Narváez, who shared in the earnings, became his lifelong enemy.

On another occasion, Narváez, whose dictatorial rule clashed with Salamanca's liberalism, began to make things hot for the marquis; the political see-saw was tilting towards the right. So much so that Salamanca countered by enlisting two generals in a plot intended to force Queen Isabel to depose Narváez. The plot was discovered, the two generals were banished from Spain and a warrant for Salamanca's arrest speedily issued on the basis of a compromising letter which he had tendered to Isabel herself.

The chief of police was given the task of making the arrest. However, when he arrived at Salamanca's villa, he found that the millionaire had already sought refuge in the Danish legation, and then in the Belgian. Narváez, furious that his prey should escape, gave orders for the Belgian legation to be searched, in violation of the usual diplomatic immunity. Soon the police were banging at the consul's door and threatening to break it down. After the door was opened, they proceeded to make a thorough search of all the rooms while the consul sat at his desk disdainfully watching the illegal proceedings. Finally, after turning the consulate upside-down, the police gave up the search. When the police were safely off the premises, Salamanca crawled out of his hiding place: throughout the search he had crouched under the consul's desk, the only place where the police hadn't looked! He then disguised himself as a sergeant in a rifle company and slipped over the border to France.

A few years later, after Narváez had been ousted, Salamanca again returned to Madrid as a new wave of liberalism, under Generals Espartero and O'Donnell, swept the corridors of power. In a few years Salamanca managed to amass another fortune, over 300 million *reales.* He now began a new enterprise, a real estate venture which involved the construction of a whole new elegant section of Madrid which was intended to rival the best of Paris. With this in mind, he bought the plots of fallow land beyond the Paseo de Recoletos that lay behind his own mansion. But, even as the first blocks of buildings were erected, ruin loomed menacingly over the project. Due to faulty materials, one of the first houses built started tottering when a rainstorm hit the city. Word spread that they were unsafe and soon no one was willing to risk his money in the venture. In his usual cunning, daredevilish fashion, Salamanca went to visit the house in question and, exclaiming, "If these houses are faulty, the best thing is to burn them!", he then set fire to his own defective building. The move saved him for the moment, and new constructions were begun, but other financial problems soon beset him.

As his debts kept mounting, the Marquis was forced to sell off most of his art treasures in auction in Paris. Even so, supposedly on the brink of bankruptcy again, he was still making grand gestures in Madrid, and invited King Alfonso XII to a junket at his Vista Alegre villa. For eight days the king and his cortège were regaled at Salamanca's expense.

Then the crash came. Salamanca had been holding on to large numbers of railway shares. When the stock market plummeted, he was forced to sell. His losses within a few days amounted to some 150 million *reales*. Despite later ventures in San Sebastián and the Philippines, he never recuperated his losses. When Salamanca died in his Vista Alegre villa in 1882, the funeral expenses had to be defrayed by the sale of furniture from the villa.

A rather unimaginative statue of him adorns the traffic circle that bears his name on the intersection of the Calle de Ortega y Gasset and the Calle del Príncipe de Vergara. As in almost all public statues, the figure is idealized and gives no clue of Salamanca's turbulent life.

In any case, it is fitting that the neighborhood where the statue stands should be named after him, since its development and initial construction was Salamanca's brainchild, using the modern grid principle of square blocks as an urban innovation in Madrid, where straight-running streets were virtually unknown. Many of the original buildings erected in the 1880's on the lower stretches of the Calle de Claudio Coello and Calle de Lagasca are little changed from the time Salamanca began his grand project. Although Salamanca didn't live to see his dream fully realized, there is no doubt that presently it is the most elegant and classy section of Madrid. The so-called Barrio de Salamanca is a quarter filled with fancy boutiques, (Loewe, Armani, Prada, Versace, Chanel, Gucci, Dior), jewelry shops (Bulgari, Pomellato, Suarez), auction houses (Durán, Sothebys), art galleries and gourmet shops making it, without a doubt, the poshest in the city.

Area 7: Retiro

1. Site of the first **Puerta de Alcalá** (Alcalá corner Alfonso XI).
2. **Puerta de Alcalá** (Plaza de la Independencia).
3. **Cañada Real** marker (Plaza de la Independencia, northeastern corner).
4. **Cañada Real** marker (Plaza de la Independencia, southeastern corner).
5. Starting point for **Retiro's Botanical Itinerary** (Puerta de Alcalá entrance).
6. **Puppet Theatre** (Glorieta de Títeres).
7. **Gazebo** (Plaza del Maestro Vilar). Concerts in summer.
8. **Casa de Vacas** (Paseo del Estanque). Exhibition hall.
9. **Francisco de Paula Monument**, stenographer.
10. Statues from **Royal Palace's** cornice (Paseo de Argentina).
11. Site of the old **Army Museum** (Calle de Méndez Núñez).
12. **Casón del Buen Retiro** (Alfonso XII, 28).
13. **Madrid's** oldest tree (Parterre).
14. **Parterre** (entrance from Alfonso XII).
15. **Dr. Benavente** bust (Parterre). **Dr. Velasco's** colleague.
16. **Dr. Pulido** bust (Parterre). **Dr. Velasco's** colleague.
17. **Estanque**, Retiro's main pond, (Paseo del Salón del Estanque).
18. **Alfonso XII Monument** (in front of Estanque).
19. Former **Casa de Fieras** (on Paseo del Duque de Fernán Núñez). Former zoo and Pizarro the elephant´s home.
20. **Paseo del Dúque de Fernán Núñez** Spring book fair and rollerblade area.
21. **Palacio de Velázquez** Exhibition hall.
22. **Palacio de Cristal** Exhibition hall.
23. **Madroño Trees** (Paseo del Dúque de Fernán Núñez).
24. **Rosaleda** (Paseo de Uruguay). Rose Garden.
25. **Fallen Angel** Fountain (Glorieta del Angel Caído).
26. **Botanical Garden** (Plaza de Murillo 2 – beside Prado Museum).
27. **Cuesta Moyano** (Calle de Claudio Moyano). Second hand booksellers.
28. **Museo de Antropología** (Alfonso XII, 68 – corner Infanta Isabel). Former home of Dr. Velasco.
29. **Calle del Dr. Velasco**.
30. **Atocha Train Station.**
31. **Basilica de Nuestra Señora de Atocha** (Avenida de Ciudad de Barcelona corner of Julián Gayarre). Virgen de Atocha.

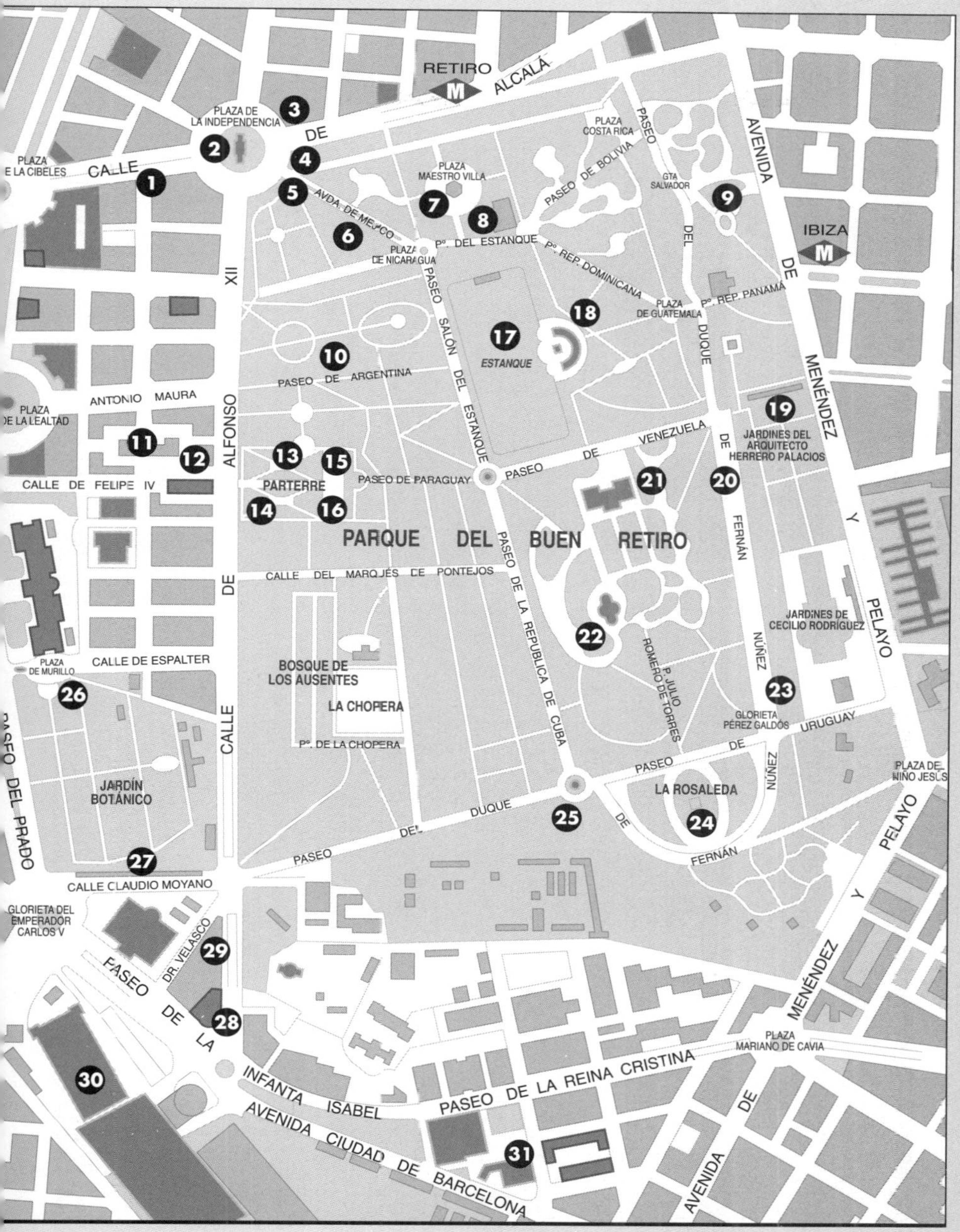
RETIRO
M
CALLE DE ALCALÁ
PLAZA DE LA INDEPENDENCIA
PLAZA DE LA CIBELES
AVDA. DE MÉJICO
PLAZA MAESTRO VILLA
PLAZA COSTA RICA
PASEO DE BOLIVIA
GTA SALVADOR
AVENIDA DE MENÉNDEZ Y PELAYO
IBIZA
M
PLAZA DE NICARAGUA
Pº. DEL ESTANQUE
Pº. REP. DOMINICANA
PLAZA DE GUATEMALA
Pº. REP. PANAMÁ
PASEO DEL DUQUE DE FERNÁN NÚÑEZ
PASEO SALÓN DEL ESTANQUE
ESTANQUE
PASEO DE ARGENTINA
ANTONIO MAURA
PLAZA DE LA LEALTAD
CALLE DE ALFONSO XII
JARDINES DEL ARQUITECTO HERRERO PALACIOS
PASEO DE VENEZUELA
PARTERRE
PASEO DE PARAGUAY
CALLE DE FELIPE IV
PARQUE DEL BUEN RETIRO
CALLE DEL MARQUÉS DE PONTEJOS
PASEO DE LA REPÚBLICA DE CUBA
JARDINES DE CECILIO RODRÍGUEZ
PLAZA DE MURILLO
CALLE DE ESPALTER
BOSQUE DE LOS AUSENTES
LA CHOPERA
P. JULIO ROMERO DE TORRES
GLORIETA PÉREZ GALDÓS
PASEO DE URUGUAY
Pº. DE LA CHOPERA
PASEO DEL PRADO
JARDÍN BOTÁNICO
PLAZA DEL NIÑO JESÚS
LA ROSALEDA
CALLE CLAUDIO MOYANO
GLORIETA DEL EMPERADOR CARLOS V
DR. VELASCO
PASEO DE LA INFANTA ISABEL
PLAZA MARIANO DE CAVIA
PASEO DE LA REINA CRISTINA
AVENIDA CIUDAD DE BARCELONA
AVENIDA DE MENÉNDEZ Y PELAYO
1
2
3
4
5
6
7
8
9
10
11
12
13
14
15
16
17
18
19
20
21
22
23
24
25
26
27
28
29
30
31

Area 7 - RETIRO

The Retiro Park

No visit to Madrid is complete without a visit to the Retiro Park. Whether it's just to get away from the city's bustle and back to nature or to watch Madrileños and their families relaxing, the Retiro provides a wonderful panorama of varied attractions ranging from the oldest tree in the city to the only commissioned public statue to Lucifer.

The Retiro offers various styles of landscaping: sometimes formally-laid-out French-style gardens, such as the Parterre and the Cecilio Rodríguez Gardens, or fairly heavily-wooded wild stretches. The park contains tennis courts, an area for playing soccer and a lake for rowing. Three large structures, the Velázquez Palace, the Palacio de Cristal (Crystal Palace) and the Casa de Vacas (The House of the Cows) are used for exhibits throughout the year. A rose garden, La Rosaleda, is always pleasant to stroll through. Numerous statues and monuments dedicated mostly to famous Spanish writers and military heroes, fountains of all sorts, occasional archeological remnants, over half a dozen outdoor cafés, a puppet theatre, cycling, an area used by skateboard and rollerblade aficionados, a gazebo where Sunday band concerts are held in season, and, of course, kilometers of paths for walking, jogging or lounging are among the park's attractions. Around Christmas the authorities even set up a temporary ice-skating rink.

As is the case with most European parks and gardens, the Retiro (meaning a place of "retirement" and repose) was

The Retiro Park. On an overcast day, lions and sirens in the monument to Alfonso XII watch over the pond in the Retiro Park. *Author's photo.*

originally an exclusive reserve for royalty and the aristocracy. On one side stood a huge palace complex, the Palacio del Buen Retiro, most of which was destroyed by a fire in the 18th century, though two notable parts of it survive: the Casón del Buen Retiro on the Calle de Alfonso XII, now is used as a venue for special exhibitions of the Prado Museum, and behind it what was until recently the Army Museum. The latter building is also earmarked to become an adjunct of the Prado.

The main entrance to the Retiro is on the Plaza de la Independencia (site of the Alcalá Gate), but nine other access points ring the perimeter. The park sprawls over 300 acres and is closed to vehicular traffic. It is extremely well patrolled by the police to insure safety.

The Fallen Angel

If you walk to the large circular intersection of the Paseo del Duque de Fernán Núñez and the Paseo de Cuba (entry through the Puerta del Angel Caído, on the Avenida de Alfonso XII), you'll come to what is thought to be the only artistic statue in the world representing Lucifer, a.k.a. the Fallen Angel. In Milton's *Paradise Lost*, Lucifer was one of the highest angels in Heaven, the "light bearer", whose pride and envy caused him to war against God and to be thrown out of Heaven into Hell.

The strikingly dramatic sculpture was fashioned by Ricardo Bellver (1845-1924) while he lived in Rome, and won for him a Medal, First Class, in the National Fine Arts Exhibit in 1878. It was then cast in bronze and presented at the Universal Exhibit in Paris that same year, causing much comment and arousing great enthusiasm from critics and admirers.

At around this time, the Duke of Fernán Núñez, who had raised financing to lay out sections of the park for horse and buggy traffic, decided to purchase the statue and provide it a place of honor in a crossroads he was constructing in the Retiro.

However, as the statue was about to be placed, a degree of controversy arose, since to many, especially religious folk, it

Fallen Angel fountain. Probably the most visited fountain in the Retiro Park is that of the Fallen Angel topped by Ricardo Bellver's winged Lucifer being pulled down into the abyss by a serpent. *Author's photo.*

was unthinkable to place a monument to Lucifer (or "Luzbell", as he is many times referred to) in a public park. But Fernán Núñez managed to convince the public and the authorities that the statue should be erected, in view of its masterful artistic workmanship and also as a reminder and metaphor of the fate that may await those showing excessive pride.

The Fallen Angel was finally mounted on a huge pedestal and surrounded by a fountain with eight jets of water issuing from gargoyle-like heads, designed by José Urioste. It was unveiled in 1885 doubtlessly for a while becoming the talk of the town due to its subject matter and striking execution. Of the public statues in Madrid, this is one that is worth making a detour for. Lucifer is depicted as a winged naked youth, crying out in agony as his right hand and both legs are entwined by a gigantic seven-headed serpent which is pulling him towards the nether world. Bellver, son of sculptor Francisco Bellver, modelled a number of other public statues in Madrid, such as a

Replica of the Fallen Angel sculpture. In the Real Academia de Bellas Artes de San Fernando there is a replica of the famous Lucifer statue. Here you can appreciate the details of his expression and discover that the serpent actually has seven heads. *Author's photo.*

Saint Andrew and a Saint Bartholomew, both in the Church of San Francisco el Grande, and one of the explorer Juan Sebastián Elcano, which stands in the Foreign Affairs Ministry building. But none is as electrifying or popular as The Fallen Angel. Curiously, the statue is believed to be 666 meters above sea level, which happens to be the "number of the beast", interpreted by some as the mark of the Anti-Christ. Thanks to a topograhical marker at its base we discovered that in fact it is 666.355 meters above sea level. Close enough!

Although it is considered to be the only statue in the world dedicated to Lucifer, (a primitive-looking modern one depicting only the face of the devil does exist in Tandapi, Ecuador) there are, in fact, others right here in Madrid. One is a life-size replica of the one Bellver sculpted in Rome in 1877 and stands at the top of the entry staircase in the Real Academia de Bellas Artes de San Fernando (Royal Fine Arts Academy) on Alcalá 13, near the Puerta del Sol (see Area 1 map, Pg. 25).

We found yet another "Fallen Angel" statue in downtown Madrid, though this one isn't official. The bronze statue weighing over 300 kilos (660 pounds) was commissioned by owners of a building and was sculpted by Miguel Angel Ruíz. It looks like a large winged angel, falling head-down into a roof balcony on the upper floor of the building at the Calle de los Milaneses and was installed in January 2006. A good view of it can be seen from the corner of the Calle Mayor.

The sculptor explained to us that it had been very difficult to secure the statue since it is exposed to the elements and the high winds. He prefers to call the statue an "aerial accident" and shies away from any association with a "fallen angel". Ruíz's explanation of its identity was as follows: "The statue is that of a Being that has been flying around the Peninsula for hundreds of centuries. Unexpectedly, in its flight,

Madrid's new "Fallen Angel" sculpture. Near the Plaza Mayor on the terrace of a house on the Calle de los Milaneses is a bizarre aqua-green "Fallen Angel" made by a private sculptor. *Author's photo.*

it encounters present-day high-rise Madrid and crashes into one of its buildings." It is a curiosity well worth seeing.

A mammoth monument to a beloved king

The most popular part of the park is that surrounding a large artificial pond called the Estanque. On one side rises a colossal monument dedicated to King Alfonso XII who reigned for ten years from 1875 to 1885, dying at the tender age of 28. The size of the monument and its wealth of sculptures make it one of the most spectacular in Madrid, reminiscent perhaps of the one in Rome dedicated to King Victor Emmanuel. Though the first stone was laid in 1902, it was not completed until 1922. The equestrian statue of the king was sculpted by one of Spain's most famous artists, Mariano Benlliure.

In the popular mind, King Alfonso XII, who ruled in the Spanish equivalent of the *belle époque,* is always associated with his romance with his cousin María de las Mercedes, whom he was passionately in love with and subsequently married. Unhappily, only six months after the wedding, Mercedes died. The short-lived, tragic romance became the subject of a famous song, *¿Donde vas Alfonso XII?* and of a celebrated film of the same title made in 1958 featuring two of Spain's matinee idols of the time, Paquita Rico and Vicente Parra which has become a Spanish film classic.

The lyrics of the song went:

¿Donde vas Alfonso XII?	Where are you going, Alfonso XII,
¿Dónde vas, triste de ti?	Where are you going, so sad?
Voy en busca de Mercedes,	I am searching for Mercedes,
Que ayer tarde no la ví.	Whom I didn't see yesterday afternoon.

For reasons of state, Alfonso soon remarried María Cristina, who became Regent when the young king followed Mercedes to the grave in 1885. But his reign was remembered as a period of relative peace and stability and Alfonso was always admired in Madrid for his simplicity, charm and for sharing interest in all the popular events of the capital.

The Alfonso XII monument in the Retiro is a favorite place for sun-worshippers to lounge, since it is usually bathed in sunlight throughout the long summer afternoons. The opposite side of the pond is lined by a promenade which in clement weather, and especially on week-ends, is always

HOW GOLD BECAME HORCHATA

Legend has it that the king of Aragón, Jaime I, unwittingly coined the term "horchata" shortly after his conquest of Valencia in the 13th century. It is said that on a hot afternoon, as he sat contemplating his new domain, a young Muslim girl offered him a typical refreshing Moorish drink. After tasting it, he liked it so much that he asked the girl, *Qué es aixo?* (What is this?) The girl answered, *Aixo es llet de chufa* (It is chufa milk). The king thereupon exclaimed, *Aixo no es llet, aixo es or, xata!* (This is not milk, it is gold, girl!) And so, the "*or xata*", literally, "gold, girl" became the term used to describe the drink, which eventually evolved into "horchata".

The tuber (*Cyperus esculentus*), commonly called chufa, originated in Egypt and it was the Arabs who introduced it to Spain. It is now grown extensively in Valencia, where the climate is most suitable for its cultivation.

crowded with amateur musicians, fortune tellers, puppeteers, rollerblade skaters, dog-walkers, tourists and idlers of all stripes. You can rent a rowboat and splash about the pond or, if you are more sedate, while away an hour at one of five outdoor cafés surrounding the pond slaking your thirst with a *limón granizado* (crushed ice and sweetened lemonade) or an *horchata*. Otherwise, there's always the standard coffee, beer, soda, wine and, in Spain, even a brandy or a whisky to slake your thirst.

One curiosity about the pond is that once a year in the summer a swimming race is held, although the schools of goldfish are not scooped out. On either end of the promenade you'll see large, handsome fountains. The so-called Fuente de la Alcachofa (Artichoke Fountain) originally stood at the former Puerta de Atocha (Atocha Gate) and the Fuente de los Galápagos (Tortoise Fountain) in the 1830's adorned the corner of what is now the Gran Vía and the Calle de la Montera, still known as the Red de San Luis.

The Oldest Tree

One of the many curiosities in the park is a huge tree reputed to be the oldest in the park, or even the city. It stands in the formal gardens called the Parterre that you enter from the Calle de Alfonso XII, opposite the Casón del Buen Retiro.

The oldest tree in the Retiro Park. Planted in 1633, the tree is considered to be the oldest in the city. During the Napoleonic wars, its thick branches are said to have been used as an embrasure for a French cannon. *Author's photo.*

Once in the gardens, bear left and about a third of the way down you'll see a Mexican conifer known in Spanish as an *ahuehuete.* In Mexico, some of these trees attain ages ranging from 2,000 to 6,000 years. One found in Santa

Botanical Itinerary in the Retiro Park. Placed around the park are signs for an itinerary that leads you through a variety of different trees and botanical curiosities. *Author's photo.*

Maria de Tula, near Oaxaca, has a trunk measuring 52 meters (about 150 feet) in circumference, and is one of the thickest known tree trunks in the world.

The specimen in the Retiro was planted around 1633 at the same time that the former Retiro Palace was being built. During the Peninsular War, the French used the Retiro as their headquarters and chopped down most of the trees then extant. However, the *ahuehuete* survived, perhaps because its thick branches were used as an embrasure to hold a piece of artillery. In 1991, the local authorities had a fence built around the tree to protect it and a year later included it in the official "catalogue of singular trees in Madrid".

Within the park, you can follow something called a "botanical itinerary" marked by signs that have been placed all around the park which highlight botanical curiosities ranging from madroños to eucalyptus to magnolias. The first sign for the itinerary starts with a *sophora japónica,* a species of acacia, located to the right of the Plaza de la Independencia entrance.

Should your botanical curiosity aspire to more exotic flora, head over to the nearby Botanical Garden (located next to the Prado Museum) which display a huge selection of trees and plants. The Garden dates back to the time of Carlos III, in 1781, when scientific interest in botany was particularly robust and when expeditions were dispatched to Spanish colonies in South America to gather specimens.

The House of the Wild Animals

Until 1972 the city's zoo, called the Casa de Fieras (House of the Wild Animals) was located in the Retiro Park. But this zoo was neither the first nor the last to be constructed in Madrid. The first on record was opened by Carlos III around 1770 beside the Botanical Garden. Its principal purpose was to

Former monkey pit in the Casa de Fieras. The old pit where monkeys used to scramble about is now dedicated to the memory of the old zoo with several signs explaining its history. *Author's photo.*

exhibit the specimens brought from the Spanish colonies in America, although it also housed animals from the Iberian Peninsula and a few from Africa and Asia.

Just before the War of Independence broke out, in 1808, Fernando VII transferred the animals to the northeastern side of the Retiro park to an area that would soon be known as the Casa de Fieras. He had cages built for felines and lodged several bears in an artificially constructed mountain known as the Montaña de los Gatos, now called the Montaña Artificial, that can still be seen beside the entrance on the corner of the Calle de O'Donnell and Calle de Menéndez y Pelayo.

During the reign of Isabel II, the small zoo was expanded and in addition began to house a selection of birds and cattle. Then, in 1868, after the queen was ousted following a revolution known in Spain as "La Gloriosa", the park was opened to the public and the Casa de Fieras leased to a lion-tamer, Luis Cavana, who transformed it and gave it a circuslike atmosphere.

Former bear grotto. This artificial stone structure, still extant, used to hold bears in the old Casa de Fieras. *Author's photo.*

Curiously, at about the same time, the director of the Botanical Garden, Mariano de la Paz Grells, decided that in order to increase the number of visitors to his Garden, he would inaugurate a menagerie. This minimal zoo was not able to compete with the Casa de Fieras and eventually failed as a business venture. After seven years it was closed down and the animals sold to the first zoo.

In the 20th century, after lengthy negotiations between City Hall and various private interests, the authorities in 1920 once more took over the administration of the Casa de Fieras. At that time, the zoo was refurbished by the park's chief gardener and architect Cecilio Rodríguez who added several avenues in the zoo and adorned it with Andalusian-style benches. King Alfonso XIII brought numerous specimens from the Spanish Sahara and Guinea, which were donated, therewith enlarging the existing collection, which already included leopards, lions, monkeys and hyenas. Later, polar bears, zebras, ostriches, two elephants and even a hippopotamus called "Pipo" were added. It was the period of the Casa de Fiera's greatest splendor.

After the Civil War broke out in July 1936 and Madrid was bombarded, most of the animals in the zoo perished, though a few, such as "Pipo" the hippo, a condor, some yaks and a polar bear somehow survived. Gradually, when the war was over, the zoo was re-stocked with animals, including a number of camels used in *Lawrence of Arabia* which were then donated to the city by the producers of the film.

As for the zoo, when a measure of prosperity started to filter into Spain in the 1960's, the old, rather rundown Casa de Fieras with its cramped cages and bedraggled animals was finally replaced by a large, spacious modern zoo in the Casa de Campo park in 1972 where most of the animals are kept outdoors. The present zoo features an aquarium with sharks, a dolphin show and hundreds of well-cared-for animals.

As for the old Casa de Fieras, a few remnants reminiscent of its past remain, such as the former entry, flanked by two lions, and installations that previously were cages, a pit where the monkeys used to clamber, and a rock cavern where a bear was formerly kept. The remainder has been turned into pretty gardens.

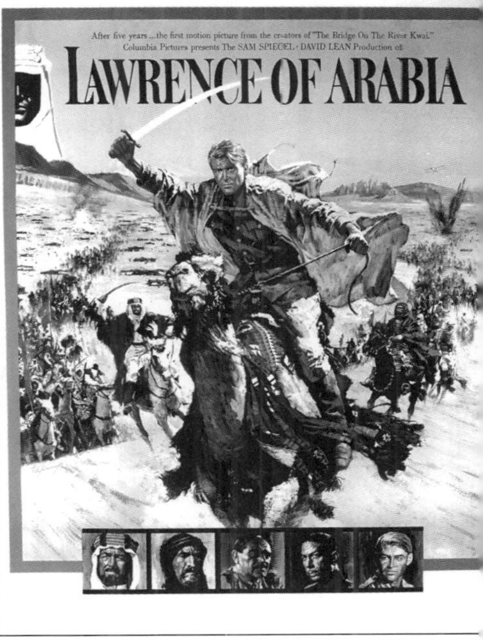

LAWRENCE OF ARABIA'S CAMELS

The late British film director, David Lean, probably never expected that some of the "props" used in *Lawrence of Arabia*, much of which was shot in Spain, would eventually wind up in the traditional Yuletide parade of the Three Wise Men held in Madrid every January 5th. The "props" were, in fact, some of the camels that Peter O'Toole cavorted with as he swept through the desert as the indomitable Lawrence.

Pizarro, the elephant

For a decade in the 19th century, the most popular animal in the Casa de Fieras was an Indian elephant called Pizarro, like the name of the conqueror of Peru. In fact, Pizarro was a female elephant and had been given her name in Latin America as a gimmick, since she toured in a circus together with another pachyderm called Cortés (Cortez). In mid-century, Pizarro was brought to Madrid. Not as a circus performer, but rather as a combatant in the arena, she was pitted against other animals such as bulls, lions and tigers.

As savage as it may sound, such contests were a common spectacle at the time. All sorts of animals were brought to bullfight rings and were set upon each other. The more exotic the animal, such as pumas and black panthers, the larger the audience drawn. The beasts would be confined in the center of the ring inside specially-built cages similar to the ones lion tamers use in the circus today. Before entering the arena, the animals would be deprived of food for days to make them more ferocious.

Posters of the time even specified the details of the spectacle. One read:

"Ferocious fight between a
five-year-old bull against a magnificent elephant.
The Bull 'Sombrerito' versus the Elephant 'Nero'.
Conditions of combat:
The elephant will be positioned in the center of the arena,
and in order to provide full protection for the spectators,
one of his legs will be tethered with an iron chain
16 meters long attached to a stake driven into the ground in
the center of the ring. The length of the combat will be
15 minutes. Thereafter a bugle call will mark the end
of the fight. In the event that neither the bull nor
the elephant remain alive at the end of the contest,
they will be removed by a team of oxen."

Other posters would trumpet such matches as,

Elephant in the Retiro's Casa de Fieras. Photograph of the old zoo shortly before it closed in 1972. In the 19th century, the famous elephant "Pizarro" was kept here. In her younger years she was forced to fight bulls and lions in the arena. *Author's archive.*

"Pandereto the bull against the lions Sabina y Nemea" or "Fight between the ferocious tiger Caesar against Regatero the bull".

It was into these gladiatorial-like spectacles, in which animals were pitted against each other, that poor Pizarro was thrown. More from instinct of self-preservation than any innate aggressiveness, the fiercer side of the elephant came out when she was attacked. Pizarro fought bulls and lions in many Spanish arenas, sometimes attacking more than one opponent set against her. On one occasion in Valladolid, the contest with a bull had become so fierce that the elephant broke off one of her tusks as she rammed it into the ground. One source even avers that once she single-handedly killed six bulls in a row.

But as Pizarro grew older it was finally decided to retire her from her gladiatorial duties and she was purchased by a certain Mr. Miller for a spectacle he had in an amusement park

Elephant in the Natural History Museum. Although the elephant displayed is not the famous "Pizarro", this one, killed by the Duke of Alba in one of his expeditions to Africa, is very impressive and well worth seeing. *Author's photo.*

called the Campos Eliseos (the Spanish translation of Champs-Elysées) located in what is now the Salamanca neighborhood. There Pizarro was trained to perform amusing tricks, among others uncorking a bottle and drinking its contents, which delighted the children.

Pizarro's fame increased tenfold when news of an episode involving her was splashed over all the local newspapers. One day, Pizarro managed to break away from the tether that held her and strolled over to one of the taverns in the fair, uncorked several bottles of wine and guzzled them down. The elephant then nimbly crossed over to the nearby Calle de Alcalá creating quite a sensation as she ambled past dumbfounded passers-by, doubtless causing not a few horses to rear in their carriages.

Presently, Pizarro caught a whiff of freshly-baked bread and made her way straight to a bakery shop. She reached for the bread with her trunk and practically cleaned out what was on the shelves of the store. After her little excursion, Pizarro was presently subdued by her keeper and peacefully led back to the amusement park. Several years later, she was taken to the Casa de Fieras where she became the major attraction in the Casa de Fieras until her death at the hands of a prankster in 1873. As a sign of affection, Madrileños in the coming years named two other elephants Pizarro. None, however, lived such an adventurous life or was as beloved to Madrileños as the original Pizarro.

Some sources say that the elephant was sent to a taxidermist and put on display in the Museum of Natural History (Calle de José Abascal 2), but this is not so. The museum does however have two other elephants on display. The one on the downstairs level, a skeleton, formed part of the Royal Cabinet of Natural History collection of Carlos III in the 18th century, which eventually became part of the present museum. The more impressive specimen upstairs, next to the gift shop, is an elephant that was hunted and killed during an expedition in Africa by the Duke of Alba and its hide donated to the museum in 1913. The pachyderm's skin weighed 600 kilograms (about 1,300 lb.) but was not displayed in the museum until October 11, 1930 when it was brought from a storage room in the Botanical Garden where it had been prepared by a taxidermist. The mounted elephant was so huge that the entranceway to the museum had to be altered in order for it to reach its present emplacement. Some quite striking photos of it being transported up the Castellana are displayed on a panel near the elephant.

The inventor of Spanish shorthand

In all likelihood, the most impressive monument ever erected to honor an inventor of *shorthand* stands in the Retiro Park, not far from the location of the former Casa de Fieras.

Monument to Francisco de Paula Martí. Tribute to Paula Marti, the inventor of a system for shorthand in Spanish. *Author's photo.*

Spain was certainly not the first country to have developed a speedy method of taking down spoken speech. Secretaries and stenographers in English-speaking countries are well familiar with the Pitman and Gregg systems, which date back to the 19th century (devised in 1837 and 1888 respectively), but different forms of "speedwriting" in fact were already in use in ancient Roman times. Thus Plutarch in 63 BC mentions that the debate on the Catilinian conspiracy, with Cicero exposing the culprits of the attempted overthrow of the Republic, was recorded in shorthand in the Roman Senate.

The earliest traces of modern European shorthand date back to Elizabethan England, when a system was invented by Timothie Bright using 500 arbitrary signs. Samuel Pepys, for example, used a system of shorthand to record his account of the Great Fire of London as well as recollections of the Plague Year.

As for the monument in the Retiro, it is dedicated to Francisco de Paula Martí (1761-1827) who in 1800 published the first study on stenography in Spain, based on the English method of Samuel Taylor which had been adapted for use in French.

Following Taylor's method, Martí at first used only the consonants in each word. However in subsequent editions of his book he refined his method, employing different signs to represent various sounds in the Spanish language.

On the headstone of the monument is inscribed a line quoted by Martí in the first edition of his work. It is by the Latin writer Martial: *Currant verba licet, manus est velocior illis. Nondum lingua suum, dextra peregit opus.* (No matter how fast the words run, the hand runs faster. The tongue has not yet completed its meaning, when the right hand has already finished its chore.)

Plaque to Francisco de Paula Martí. The site where Martí founded Spain's first school for stenography. *Author's photo.*

The first school of shorthand writing was opened under the auspices of Martí in 1802 on the Calle del Marqués de Cubas 15 (see Area 2 map, Pg. 85), near the Cortes, where a plaque now commemorates Marti's founding of the first Chair of Spanish Stenography.

Though various other Spaniards developed shorthand systems in the course of the 19th century, it is Martí who is considered to be the "father" of stenography in the Spanish language and worthy of this quite elaborate monument in the Retiro.

Puerta de Alcalá: An entry gate befitting a capital

One monument that you're almost guaranteed to drive or walk past during your sojourn in Madrid is the huge old granite entry gate to the capital, the Puerta de Alcalá, or Alcalá Gate, one of three remaining gates to what used to be, until the 19th century, a walled city. Both the Gate and the street it's on bear the name Alcalá because they lie on the old road that led to the nearby town of Alcalá de Henares, Cervantes' birthplace.

Over the centuries, the Calle de Alcalá, together with the Paseo del Prado, was the most admired street in the city due to its sweeping wide expanse and the many handsome buildings lining it. Running from the Puerta del Sol well beyond the bull ring and on to the outskirts of the city, it is the longest street in Madrid.

The 17th century Puerta de Alcalá. This gateway was the first of the arches built on the Calle de Alcalá in the 1630's. *Municipal Museum of Madrid.*

There have been three different Alcalá Gates over the centuries. The original, rather primitive-looking one, stood a bit further down the Calle de Alcalá going towards the Cibeles Fountain, at the intersection of the Calle de Alfonso XI. The second was built in the same location as the present one and featured three arches and a turret on each side. When Carlos III made his triumphal entrance to begin his reign in Madrid on December 9, 1759, he was disappointed at seeing the small and unimpressive Gate that led into the city.

Thus in 1764 he decided to tear down the old Alcalá Gate and replace it by a far larger, more sumptuous one

Details of the Puerta de Alcalá. At the top of the columns (on both sides of the Gate) can be seen angry creatures with bizarre features, possibly the ears of a bat, the whiskers of a cat and the teeth of a rabbit. *Author's photo.*

that would reflect the grandeur of the kingdom he ruled over, a regal monument that would impress all travellers arriving in Spain's capital. Work on it was completed in 1778, as can be seen in the large Latin inscription on the top of the Gate.

But there is more to the Gate than first meets the eye. Depending upon which side you approach it from, you'll see quite different architectural designs and decorations on the structure. Therein lies our story.

When Carlos decided to build the impressive Gate, he also had to determine its structural and aesthetic appearance. Various designers labored over the project, among them Ventura Rodríguez, who proposed no less than five different plans, none of which pleased the king. Finally, Carlos decided to seek the advice of the man who had been his master architect in Italy, Francesco Sabatini. Rather concerned, since his predecessor had failed miserably, Sabatini designed two alternative projects, which he then apprehensively presented to the king.

Carlos III was delighted. He loved the designs. The problem was that he liked *both* of them, and couldn't decide which of the two to use, thus again creating a dilemma for Sabatini. The architect judiciously solved the problem by using *both* designs, one on the east side and the other on the west of the Gate. Hence, if you look carefully, you'll discover numerous differences between the two sides.

East Side of the Puerta de Alcalá.
Author's photo.

Some of the differences:

EAST SIDE	WEST SIDE
Ten columns.	Two columns and pilasters.
Over the arches are three heads of a bearded man.	Three lions' heads.
On the cornice are children carrying weapons.	Formations of helmets, banners and shields.
Escutcheon of the royal coat-of-arms over the central arch.	Flags and helmets.

Most Madrileños have passed by the Puerta de Alcalá hundreds if not thousands of times but, strange as it may seem, when you ask them how many gateways (*puertas*) the monument has, most will hesitate and be uncertain what to answer. The most common replies are three and four. Try it with a real *gato*. You'll be surprised. You might even want to

West Side of the Puerta de Alcalá.
Author's photo.

place a wager. The truth is that the Gate has five entranceways: three in the center with Roman arches and two rectangular ones on the sides.

A flock of sheep on Alcalá

Once a year, all vehicular traffic is halted in one of Madrid's busiest traffic circles, the Plaza de la Independencia. No, it isn't for the usual reasons such as demonstrations, political rallies, protest marches, or sporting events. On this occasion, most of the square is filled not by cars and motorcycles but by hundreds of placid sheep! Moreover, no policeman can legally chase away the intruding animals and their shepherds.

The occasion doesn't mark some quaint local custom or holiday but rather is a reassertion of a basic right that dates

Cañada Real marker. This is one of the two "mojones" on the Plaza de la Independencia that mark the path where sheep were led down. *Author's photo.*

back to the time of King Alfonso X in 1273. At that time, livestock owners founded an organization called the Honrado Consejo de la Mesta (Honorable Council of Livestock Owners) which was empowered with keeping open livestock paths throughout the country, thus enabling sheep and cattle to be brought from the northern provinces down to the south for better grazing and to avoid the cold weather.

Sheep near the Puerta de Alcalá. As is traditionally done almost every year, a flock of more than 1000 sheep are driven down the Calle de Alcalá excercising their ancient right to use this livestock trail. *Author's archive.*

These paths were of varying width. The widest, 75.23 meters (225.69 feet), are known as the *cañadas reales* or royal livestock passageways. Nine of them still traverse Spain. Though the old Mestas were abolished in 1836, and many of the *caminos* and *cañadas* were asphalted, in 1995 a law was passed to protect those remaining and reclaim old ones. They are now used principally by hikers and cyclists for outings.

As a reminder of the rights of livestock owners, you can still see two stone *mojones* next to the Puerta de Alcalá, one on the northeast corner of the Plaza de la Independencia and the other to the left of the entrance to the Retiro Park, at opposite sides of the Calle de Alcalá. Chiselled into each one it merely says: CAÑADA DE 75,23 m. This is the stipulated width between the two markers which is ceremoniously measured by the shepherds each time they bring their flock into the center of the city thereby confirming the path established 800 years ago.

Chips off the old Gate

The pockmarked Puerta de Alcalá. Holes and chipping caused by bullets and mortar fire from various wars found on the southern end of the structure. *Author's photo.*

In the course of its long existence, many parts of the Puerta de Alcalá have been scarred and damaged by impacts from gunshots and shrapnel from explosions. Most of the damage dates from the Spanish Civil War when the city was often bombarded by Nationalist (Franco) forces. Other damage dates back to 1823 when a French force, under the Duke of Angoulême, with 100,000 troops, approached the city to help King Fernando VII put down a constitutional government that had been in power for three years. But the liberals opposed the entry and dug trenches across the Calle de Alcalá. Fierce fighting raged around the Gate and some of the stray bullets chipped out of it. The French won the skirmish and restored Fernando's absolute monarchical powers.

Over the years, the monument has been cleaned and restored, most recently in 2001. The question inevitably arises as to whether the bullet holes and shrapnel marks should be filled in. The general consensus has always remained the same: the holes, nips and chipping are part of events occurring in this historic plaza and should therefore remain as a memento of the past.

HISTORICAL HINGES

Although the Puerta de Alcalá stands isolated in a traffic circle, looking more like a monument than a functional gate, until 1868 it was part of a wall that enclosed the city. Huge iron grilles were attached to the sides of the entry gates that were closed at night and were closely guarded to control all those entering and leaving the city. If you look under the arches, you can still see the enormous hinges on which the heavy gates were hung. The trick is to dodge the circling traffic to get to the center.

The Cuesta Moyano: A bibliophile's treat

Madrid has its own *bouquinistes*, though they are not located on the banks of the Manzanares River, like the famous ones along the banks of the Seine in Paris. Originally, the ones in Madrid tended to be set up in itinerant fairs around the city, a tradition dating back hundreds of years. The last of these fairs, including rickety shacks set up by the booksellers, was camped in the region around today's Atocha railroad station.

In 1919, the booksellers' stalls were moved to in front of the Botanical Garden on the Paseo del Prado. There the booksellers continued to ply their trade until complaints were lodged by the administrators of the Garden, arguing that the booths were "improper and injurious to the public health" since some citizens used the gates of the Botanical Garden behind the stands to relieve themselves.

Feria de Libros on the Cuesta Moyano. On this steep street beside the Retiro, bibliophiles have delighted in rummaging through the 30 stalls of this second-hand bookfair. *Author's photo.*

In 1925 the booksellers were authorized to move their stands to the nearby Calle de Claudio Moyano. Locally, the street is known as the "Cuesta" Moyano, or Moyano "slope", since it runs on an incline from the side entrance to the Retiro Park (near the Puerta del Angel Caído) down to the Plaza del Emperador Carlos V, more commonly known in Madrid as the Glorieta de Atocha.

Since the bookstalls were very popular, City Hall at the end decided to build 30 permanent ones in the new location. However, booksellers renting the stalls were provided with no heating or lighting, nor were they allowed to sublet the space.

For years, booksellers, intellectuals and literati attempted to have the used-book fair moved to a more central location in the city, such as opposite the Prado Museum. But none of their petitions ever bore fruit, and the book fair remained on the Cuesta Moyano.

After the Civil War, the site of the fair had become so engrained, that there were no further efforts to move it to another part of town. Years later, in 1969, seeing that the booths were visibly deteriorating, municipal authorities came up with an ambitious project to attach the book fair to the adjoining Botanical Garden. The idea was to open three entrances to the Garden from the Cuesta Moyano, provide a landscaped strip between the book fair and the Garden and build new modern booths, 37 of them, facing both the Garden and the street. But nothing came of the project, at least as far as the book fair was concerned, though the design of the Botanical Garden was modified.

Then, in 1984 the old booths were replaced by 30 new ones with electric light, water, telephone, a communal toilet and a guard house. The traditional old wooden exterior design of the booths was preserved.

Those browsing along the 30 stalls and bargain tables on the curbside will find it most lively on weekends. Though you are not likely to find any great rarities among the selection, you might nonetheless come across an occasional oddity, maybe some old magazine from the early or mid-19th century that could be of interest, or a picture book from the Spanish Civil

War or an old museum catalogue. Usually the dealers close down their stalls around 2 p.m. when the crowds start to thin out, but open again later in the day.

Should you be in town either in May or October, you may also come across the Feria del Libro Antiguo which is really a second-hand book fair, held for 14 days on the Paseo de Recoletos (between the Cibeles Fountain and the Calle de Bárbara de Braganza). Some of the dealers in this book fair have more select volumes on sale than those you'll find on the Cuesta Moyano, and books run the gamut from new best-sellers to fairly rare 19th century tomes, some of the illustrated books attaining three-figure prices. As is also the case at the Cuesta Moyano, you can enter the booths for a look-see or just browse the display tables along the outside. It is not uncommon to bargain down the price slightly, and usually you can get a 10% discount.

If it's new books you want, the country's leading book fair (mostly Spanish) is held each year in the first week of June in the Retiro Park, usually inaugurated by a member of the royal family. You'll find literally hundreds of booths representing bookshops and dealers and publishers and official organizations from

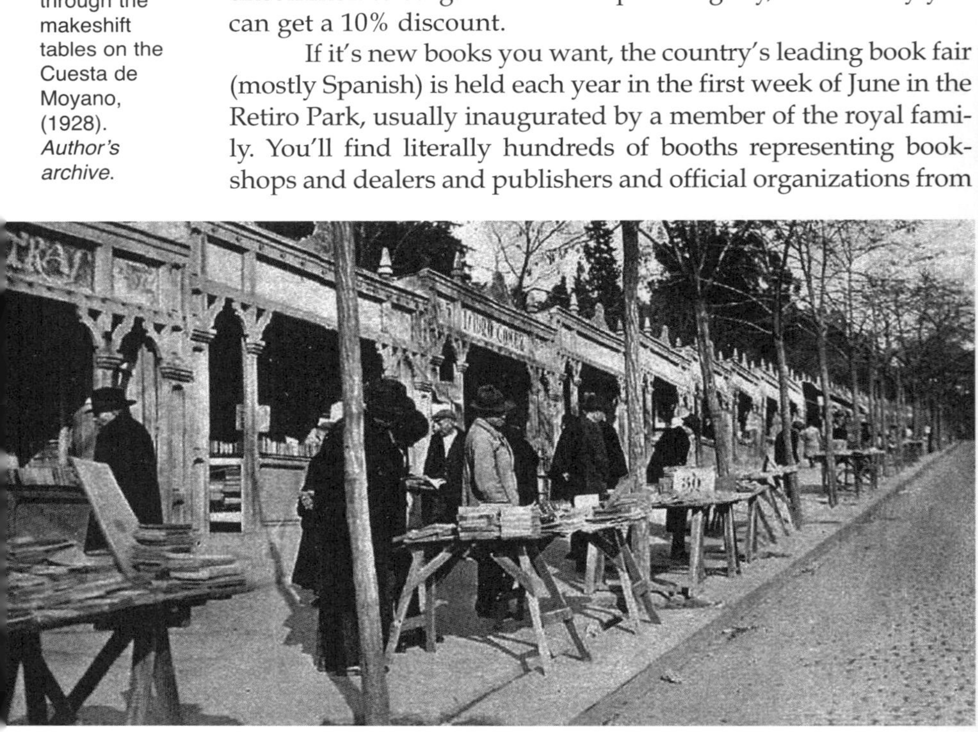

The old Feria del Libro. Book bargain seekers rummage through the makeshift tables on the Cuesta de Moyano, (1928). *Author's archive.*

Cuesta Moyano Model. This is the model for a proposed, but never executed 1970 project whereby the Feria de Libros (Book Fair) was to be joined to the adjacent Botanical Garden. *Author's archive.*

all over Spain that line the Paseo del Duque de Fernán Núñez, stretching about a kilometer in length, each displaying its wares. In addition, the fair includes presentations of new titles just published, cultural encounters, exhibits, book signing sessions by authors and, of course, ample installations for refreshments.

If you are searching for books in English, these can easily be found in the "biggies": FNAC (off the plaza de Callao) or La Casa del Libro (Gran Vía 29). However, if you are a mite more adventurous, the smaller, independent bookshops are a better bet. Try J & J Books and Coffee (Calle del Espiritu Santo, 47) opened in 2003 by American expat Jamie and her husband Javi -hence J & J- which features 25,000 new and used English-language books and a cozy ambiance to have a coffee and strike up a conversation with Anglo-speaking customers. The Bacchus bookstore is another excellent choice located in the Calle de Melendez Valdés 52, with a café upstairs, friendly staff, and a superb choice of teas. The list would not be complete without the Pasajes Librería Internacional on Calle de Génova 3 (English books are downstairs), or Petra's: The International Bookshop on Calle de Campoamanes 13, a cozy nook for second hand booklovers who like to browse in leisure.

If you're looking for antiquarian books, maps and prints, there are well over a dozen shops in town that specialize in these. Best known are Luis Bardón's Librería Para Biblíófilos (Plaza de San Martin 3), Berrocal (Calle de Cervantes 22), Guillermo Blázquez (Carrera de San Jerónimo 44) and the Librería del Prado (Calle del Prado 5).

Our Lady of Atocha: Madrid's black Virgin

As you travel through Europe and Latin America you can sometimes come across what are known as "black madonnas" or "black Virgins". These are images of the Virgin with a dark or black skin tone. Although some are actually black, most are only vaguely dark, usually due to their age, exposure to fire, or due to the color of the wood they were carved in. Frequently, they are extremely old and on some occasions are associated by some with pagan gods, such as the Egyptian Isis. Indeed, these black madonnas have been linked to everything and anything that is shrouded in mystery, from the Knights Templar to UFOs. About four hundred such images are known to exist, each associated with a legend. Among the more famous European ones are the Virgin of Guadalupe (Cáceres, Spain), the Virgin of Montserrat, a.k.a. "La Morenita" (Barcelona, Spain) and the Black Virgin of Chartres (Chartres, France).

Though not as well known as the foregoing, Madrid also has its very own black Virgin. She is the Virgen de Atocha, located in the Real Basílica de Nuestra Señora de Atocha on the Avenida Ciudad de Barcelona 1, past the Atocha train station going up the Paseo de la Reina Cristina.

As is the case with almost all madonnas, regardless of their color, it's difficult to verify their true origins or the exact date when they were discovered or carved. In the case of the Virgin of Atocha, legend has it that she was sculpted by St. Luke and that the Apostles Peter and James brought her from Antioch, and that her name is derived from that ancient city. However, it is more commonly thought that the name is derived from the Arabic *atochar,* which means a "field of esparto" (a rushlike grass), where the Christians are said to have found the image after the Muslims had invaded Spain in 710 A.D. Be that as it may, the legend of Madrid's own black Virgin is as follows:

Virgen de Atocha. Madrid's very own "black" Virgin. An Image with a bizarre legend involving miraculous lightning, battles with the Moors and the decapitation of an entire family. *Author's archive.*

After the arrival of the Apostles, the madonna had been placed in a hermitage very near the modern-day Basilica of Atocha. A certain knight, Gracián Ramírez, who lived in the village of Eldegüela near the Jarama River, was so devoted to the Virgin that he would ride every day to the hermitage to pray, regardless of the danger, for on the way he could easily be attacked by the Saracens. On one occasion he entered the sanctuary only to discover that it had been plundered and that the Virgin had been stolen. In a mad fury, he ran outside screaming and damning the Infidels for what they had done. Suddenly, as if nature had heard his desperate cries, a tremendous storm broke. Lightning struck the ground causing a small fire in the *atochar.* As Gracián ran for the reins of his frightened horse, something caught his eye. Amidst the smoke, he discovered the holy Image of the stolen Virgin.

The knight's devotion only grew stronger and he swore that he would construct a larger and safer hermitage for Her. The following day he returned with a handful of men and building material. However, the Moors, who were keeping an eye on him, believed that he was preparing to attack them. The Saracens gathered their forces and swept down upon Gracián and his unarmed workmen, mercilessly massacring the whole group. Only Gracián was able to flee and make it back to Eldegüela. There he alerted his entourage that the Moors were hot on his heel and that they must prepare to defend themselves. Bursting into his humble dwelling, he explained to his wife that an attack of the Infidels was imminent and that they were doomed, for the Christians were greatly outnumbered. Gracián's wife cried that she preferred death to outrage and dishonor for herself and her children, and pleaded with her husband to kill her rather than let her fall into the hands of the attackers.

Gracián mustered all his strength and with tears in his eyes undertook the dreaded deed: one by one, he decapitated his entire family. That very night, sneaking around the Moorish camp near the hermitage, he carried the dismembered corpses of his loved ones to the shrine. There he laid them before the image of the Virgen. All night he prayed for forgiveness and then returned to his village before daybreak.

As the first rays of the sun crept over the hilltops, the villagers started to sneak up to the Moorish camp, their swords in hand, ready for combat and disposed to die in battle for their cause. The fight was savage and no quarter was given, but contrary to what was expected, and despite being greatly outnumbered, the Christians actually came out victorious and the Moors were routed.

Bitter and remorseful, Gracián returned to the hermitage to beg pardon for his horrible mistake. As he prayed to the Virgin, he heard a voice saying: "Gracián, Gracián." The knight turned around and there stood his wife and daughters. At first he thought he had gone mad, or that they were ghosts, but when he hugged them he realized that they were real, they were alive. The only trace of their untimely death was a thin red line around each of their necks. The Virgin of Atocha had heard Gracián's prayers and had rewarded him for his devotion with a miracle.

Among those convinced of the Virgin's divine powers was King Felipe III. When he fell sick in 1580 as a cause of a widespread epidemic, he had the Image brought to his bedside in the hope that it would better his health. And, sure enough, it did! Another case was that of King Felipe IV who had a copy of the key to the door of the Basilica (at that time only a chapel) made especially for him, so that he could visit the Image at night without disturbing anyone. Yet another devotee was Queen Isabel II. On February 2, 1852, the queen went to thank the Virgin for the successful delivery of her newly-born baby. While she was entering the church, a Carlist priest, Martín Marino, suddenly jumped out of the crowd and stabbed her. But the attempted assassination failed, for the queen soon recovered and the priest was sentenced to death five days later. In a gesture of appreciation for saving her life, the queen offered the Virgin the green velvet dress that she had been wearing during the thwarted plot.

The Virgin stands (actually sits) in the Basilica of Atocha. Given her small size — she is only 64 cm. (25 inches) tall — the Image is somewhat difficult to see, especially since the statue is placed far above the main altar. She is quite dark in color, which is why she is considered to be a black Virgin. In her right hand she holds an apple while in the other she carries the Baby Jesus, quite similar to the Black Virgin of Montserrat near Barcelona. The Image used to be draped with clothes and jewelry, and at one point, to fit the clothing, part of the statue had to be sawed off. However, the Virgin was later restored and is now seen in her original form.

The Virgin still has many adepts in Madrid. She is the patron of all new-born children and Queen Sofía often pays her respects to her. Following the royal wedding of Prince Felipe and Letizia in 2004, as the cortège wound through the city, the royal couple also made a point of paying their respects to the Virgin. They did so again in 2006 after the birth of their daughter, the Infanta Leonor.

THE ROYAL BAPTISMAL FONT

When Prince Felipe and Letizia's first child, Leonor, was baptized on January 16, 2006, the much-publicized ceremony was performed in a baptismal font which has quite a history of its own. The story of the holy font dates back to 1170 AD when in the small village of Caleruega, near Burgos, it was used to baptize Domingo de Guzmán, better known as Santo Domingo (Saint Dominic), the founder of the Dominican order. After Domingo was canonized, the font came to be revered as a sacred relic. In 1605, King Felipe III had the font taken to Valladolid, where it was used to baptize his son, the future Felipe IV. In the following centuries, the font was kept by the Dominican monks in the Monastery of Santo Domingo located in the center of Madrid.

Throughout those centuries, whenever a royal birth occurred, the new successor to the throne traditionally was baptized in the font, which was carried to wherever in the kingdom the ceremony was held. Thus since the time of Felipe III, the font has been used in royal ceremonies in sites as diverse as Burgos, Valladolid, Sevilla and La Granja.

Though the font initially was made of simple white stone, it was subsequently decorated with silver and golden ornaments. Those with a penchant for monarchical tradition can view the famous font in the church of the Monasterio de Santo Domingo el Real on the Calle de Claudio Coello 112. As you enter the church, the font is located on the right, up a short staircase, behind a grille. There's a light switch on the left. The church is open every day at 8 a.m. and 8 p.m., and in addition at 1:30 p.m. on Sundays.

The strange case of Dr. Velasco's daughter

At times cars speeding down the Calle de Alfonso XII, alongside the Retiro Park, heading towards the Atocha traffic circle, will take a short cut by turning right down a small, insignificant street called the Calle del Dr. Velasco. Few drivers will know who the street was named after or that right opposite the Atocha railway station stands a handsome, white, neoclassic porticoed mansion, now the Anthropological Museum, which was the former home of one of Spain's most famous anatomists of the 19th century, Dr. Pedro González de Velasco.

Doctor Pedro Velasco. Portrait of the greatest Spanish anatomist of the 19th century. *La Ilustración Española y Americana*, Aug. 5, 1871.

Over the entrance to the building is inscribed in stone the famous Latin saying, "Nosce te ipsum" (Know Thyself). In the foyer, a large stone plaque informs us in Latin that His Majesty Alfonso XII, patron of science, literature and the arts, inaugurated here the Anatomical Museum in the year 1875. Originally the main ground level room contained a large number of wooden and glass display cabinets with anthropological and ethnographic artifacts in them; more exhibit cases were set up in a gallery that ran around the upper part of the large hall. Many of the artifacts had been collected by Dr. Velasco himself in his many travels around the world, and ranged widely over everything from African and Malayan swords and krises to a native canoe, skulls and primitive weapons.

As you enter the Sala de Orígenes, to the left of the entrance you can see a bust of the museum's founder, Dr. Velasco. It shows a heavy-set man with a wide face, large forehead, thick eyebrows and abundant hair. The eyes are left blank, in the Roman style. A beard traces the line of his chin. In a gallery of busts you would hardly notice him, but isolated as he is in the museum, the bust is striking. He has a distinguished air about him and one supposes him to have been an enlightened scion of the era of 19th century medical and scientific progress.

Dr. Velasco was, in fact, a man of great will power and energy, the archetype of the self-made man of science totally committed to his work. He arrived in Madrid alone, friendless and virtually broke and finally managed to get a job in the

Anthropological Museum. In this mansion occurred the strange goings-on with Doctor Velasco and his mummified daughter. Shown is the reconstruction of the façade undertaken around 1940. *Photo from "Un Templo a la Ciencia", Spanish Culture Ministry.*

Military Hospital as an orderly. By 1840 he had succeeded in entering the Madrid medical school and started his studies to become a surgeon, specializing in anatomy. His single-mindedness, talent and dedication paid off. Soon his fame as an anatomist and surgeon spread throughout Spain and his classes at the Faculty of San Carlos, where he was elected to the chair of First Surgeon, were crowded with students attending his lectures, demonstrations and lessons on dissection.

Though he was a great doctor of the times, he lived almost exclusively within his professional medical circles. The present museum was once his residence, and much of his medical work was done in the nearby Hospital of San Carlos, which is now the Reina Sofía Museum.

Upon entering the aforementioned Sala de orígenes, you can see death masks, a mummy, and a cabinet containing casts, such as the mold of the head of a Chinese pirate who had been decapitated in Hai-Phong. Almost unnoticed in the oddities displayed in the room is an unassuming anonymous portrait that hangs on the wall opposite the entrance to the room next to that of Dr. Velasco. It shows a young girl in the bloom of her youth. She is identified as Dr. Velasco's daughter, Concha.

A strange story is associated with the good doctor's daughter...

Having attained fame and fortune, Dr. Velasco decided to have a mansion built for himself, which was to serve not only as a private home but also as a museum to house the large ethnological collection he had painstakingly gathered during his many years of travel abroad at his own expense, as well as a lecture hall and an amphitheatre. The mansion was to provide a meeting place for all those interested in the study of medicine and, in the best liberal tradition of the late 19th century, for those encouraging the dissemination of science. The doctor sank every *peseta* he owned into the construction of the building and its collections.

The original museum contained a huge array of fossils, sea shells, minerals, tropical plants, skeletons of animals, birds in full plumage, polished ax-heads and Greek ceramics. But the main part of the exhibit was dedicated to man (hence the aforementioned inscription on the front of the building) in which the modern theories of the time were illustrated, with special emphasis on the relation between man and the macro- and microcosmos that surrounds him.

But Dr. Velasco was not besieged by ambitious students, as might have been expected. Instead, fewer and fewer people attended his lectures. What was to have been the crowning achievement of his life was tainted by quite unexpected and bizarre events. These concerned his only daughter, Concha.

Eleven years earlier, in 1864, Dr. Velasco's 15-year-old daughter came down with a serious case of typhus. After the girl's condition seemed not to be responding to treatment by a colleague of Velasco's, Dr. Benavente (father of the playwright), and not heeding his advice, the father decided to administer a purgative to the daughter to bring the illness to a head. The results that Benavente had warned of came to pass, and the child hemorrhaged. Benavente was urgently summoned. When he arrived, Concha was already dead. The father, frantic with grief, reproached him, saying: "Why didn't you kill me first? I've killed my own daughter!"

Velasco never got over his loss. But before Concha was buried, he carefully embalmed his daughter, working at the task on his own.

In the ensuing years the memory of Concha haunted Velasco. He placed pictures and photographs of her in his workroom, in his wallet, in his bedroom and even in his carriage. A bust of her occupied a place of honor in his house, and another one in marble in the house he owned in Zarauz in northern Spain.

He even built a small chapel for her inside his new mansion/museum, which he moved into upon completion in 1875. Once settled in his new home, he decided he wanted to have Concha's remains moved to the very same house in which he lived. To an anatomist who in his lifetime had dissected 8,000 cadavers, the idea of a corpse in his house obviously had no particular onus of morbidity, though his wife frowned upon the idea. But her objection was overruled.

Hence one morning, in May of 1875, a few days after the royal inauguration of the museum, Concha was exhumed from the Cemetery of San Isidro. With great care the body was transported to the doctor's house and deposited in one of the private studies. An account of that memorable day has been left us by Dr. Angel Pulido, one of the most famous Spanish doctors of his time, author of dozens of books on medicine, travel in Spain, a great champion of Sephardic Jews and an associate and student of Velasco's, who donated the bust of him that presently stands in the foyer of the museum. (Busts of Dr. Pulido and Dr. Benavente can be seen in the Parterre of the Retiro Park.)

In his account, Dr. Pulido writes that he and Velasco pried open the lid of the coffin and beheld… not the decomposed body of a corpse long since putrefied, but the body of Concha perfectly preserved! She lay there in her burial dress, as pure and beautiful as she had been during life. Dr. Velasco could not contain himself and fell upon the corpse and embraced the long-lost daughter whom he so adored. There

Busts of Dr. Benavente and Dr. Pulido. In the Parterre of the Retiro Park is the bust of Dr. Benavente (left), who was called in to counsel Dr. Velasco when his daughter reached a critical point in her illness. On the opposite side of the Parterre you can find the bust of Dr. Pulido (right) who reputedly helped Velasco exhume his deceased daughter from the San Isidro Cemetery. *Author's photos.*

was Concha wondrously intact! The embalming of the body had been a miracle of perfection. With all the tenderness of a father, he lifted the body carefully out of the coffin, and to his enormous amazement and unspeakable delight, saw that the embalming had been done so well that he could even bend the joints of her body, which had retained an extraordinary degree of elasticity. He stared at her as though demented, and a strange thought surged to his mind, a thought which gained momentum with each minute that passed, which took such a hold on the venerable doctor that his decision was soon as steadfast as the love he bore his daughter. The thought of her slipping out of his paternal hands again, of seeing her buried underground and being forever removed from his sight, seemed unbearable. No, there was a better solution. His mind was made up. He would refuse to let her go as he had in the past: he would keep her with him forever! And she would participate in his daily life, just as though she were still alive!

Thus the unclothed corpse of Concha was placed in one of the rooms, with the window left wide open so that the preservative fluids would evaporate. In the autumn, when the body had completed the process of mummification, he paid a visit to a dressmaker to have Concha fitted out in the most elaborate of wedding gowns, for at the time of her death she had already been betrothed to a certain Doctor Teodoro Núñez Sedeño. In addition to the dress, Velasco is said to have bought the choicest jewels for the corpse, had her hair properly done, her nails manicured, her face made up and every possible attention paid to her personal appearance so that she should truly appear the loveliest creature in all of Madrid.

As was to be expected, there were protests, not only from his wife, but from friends as well. Moreover, news of these bizarre proceedings began to leak out, for though fellow doctors may have taken a more or less indulgent view of the matter, certainly neighbors, servants and casual visitors must have looked upon the goings-on with alarm and repugnance. Soon the news of Concha was all over town, properly embellished, like a sailor's yarn, with grotesque details, which doubtless were further fueled by conservative members of the medical profession, the Catholic Church, and even politicians who would not be sorry to see a leading proponent of modern liberal views fall into disgrace.

Dr. Velasco had meanwhile placed Concha near the family chapel in the house. It was gossiped that not only did the pallid daughter stare out of her glass cabinet, but that the doctor took her out once a week and sat her at the family table. There she would remain while the bread was broken and the soup spooned. After the meal, the doctor would ceremoniously arise from his chair and escort Concha back to her glass cabinet. Malicious stories spread that she was seen accompanying him in his carriage during the late evening hours. Neighbors reported that they saw three figures emerging from the side entrance of the building. Supposedly these were the famous doctor himself, the former fiancé, Núñez Sedeño, and a figure clad in wedding white, who was propped up between the two. The sinister threesome would then get into the doctor's carriage and go rumbling off into the dark umbrage of the Paseo de la Reina Cristina.

Whether any of these lurid details have an element of truth to them is hard to tell. Dr. Pulido denies most of them, such as the carriage rides and the participation of Dr. Núñez

Sedeño, but substantiates all the rest. A publication put out by the Museum in 1992 categorically denies that *any* of the stories are true, though it doesn't enter into details, since they understandably underscore Velasco's medical achievements, his championing of progress and education, and his lifelong dedication to science.

In any case, pressure on Dr. Velasco finally became so strong that he agreed to bury the daughter under the floor of his mansion, as had been his original intention. There, in the center of what is now the main floor of the museum, Concha was laid to rest.

Dr. Velasco died in 1882, and was in turn embalmed by his students and his body also laid under the floor of the main hall of the museum. However, upon his death his wife ordered Concha's restless corpse to be exhumed and given proper Christian burial in the Cemetery of San Isidro. But Dr. Velasco's remains rested for sixty-one years under the floor of the museum. Finally, on November 12, 1943, when work on the building's first renovation was begun, in a ceremony of great solemnity, his remains were also transferred to the Cemetery of San Isidro, where his wife and daughter were buried as well.

Even so, contradictory versions are still put forth today by local writers about whether or not Concha's body was buried in the cemetery or whether instead it was stored in the Anatomical Department of the Faculty of Medicine in the University of Madrid. The latter conjecture seems to arise due to a glass cabinet with an embalmed body found in one of the university's halls. This female mummy is somewhat over a meter (three feet) in height. A small handwritten label states that it is Concha Velasco. Though there are no official documents proving that the label is true, an attending professor says that it's always been assumed, in fact, to be the body of Dr. Velasco's daughter.

In the 1980's, the building, at that time known as the Ethnological Museum, which had fallen into bad disrepair, was refurbished for the second time. More recently, the Ministry of Education, Culture and Sports carried out further modernization. Now called the Anthropological Museum, restoration

THE GIANT OF ALCOCER

While you are in the Anthropological Museum, don't miss the impressive skeleton of the *gigante extremeño* (the giant from Extremadura.) The bones are those of Agustín Luengo Capilla, born in 1849 who, 2.35 meters (7 feet 4 $^{1}/_{2}$ inches) tall, towered spectacularly over his diminutive compatriots.

The museum's founder, Dr. Velasco, obtained the body of the giant in the following manner: During one of the many trips that the celebrated doctor took around the country, and while travelling through the northern province of Asturias, Velasco was introduced to Luengo and was intrigued by him as being a clinical case of acromelagy, a hormonal disorder that causes excessive growth of the extremities. With an eye to embellishing the museum, which he already had in mind, he made a deal with the giant, a sort of Faustian pact, as it were, in which Velasco agreed to cover Luengo's expenses during the giant's lifetime in exchange for which he would leave his body to the Anatomical Museum after his death. The giant, apparently had no scruples in the matter and at once accepted the offer.

Shortly afterwards, the giant came to Madrid and plunged into a carefree profligate life. This dissipation naturally aroused public comment and on one occasion Velasco advised him to be less reckless with his health. "But why should you be concerned about that, doctor?" said the giant. "The sooner I kick off, the quicker you can have me in one of your exhibit cases." Luengo's words were prophetical and before long Madrid's fast-living ways and a case of bone tuberculosis did him in. Agustín died on New Years Eve in 1875 at age 26.

Velasco claimed the body and immediately went to work on the corpse making a plaster mold of it and saving the bones, which were soon displayed in his Museo Anatómico y Universal de Curiosidades, as it was then called.

Should you want to further follow the trail of the giant, in the Ethnographic Museum in the village of Puebla de Alcocer, Extremadura, where he was born, they still exhibit a pair of huge boots that were presented to the giant by King Alfonso XII, a large felt hat he owned and a big hand-painted poster with his likeness on it that was used to advertise him as the main attraction in a circus he worked in.

on it was completed in 2004. The new museum features a large ground floor atrium, with two upper floors running around it, and includes a library in which are stored important collections of documents, engravings, lithographs and photographs from the 19th and 20th centuries. And, as previously mentioned, the room set aside for Dr. Velasco, which includes a letter from Darwin, an 18th century human mummy, scientific paraphernalia and the portrait of Concha, can still be visited.

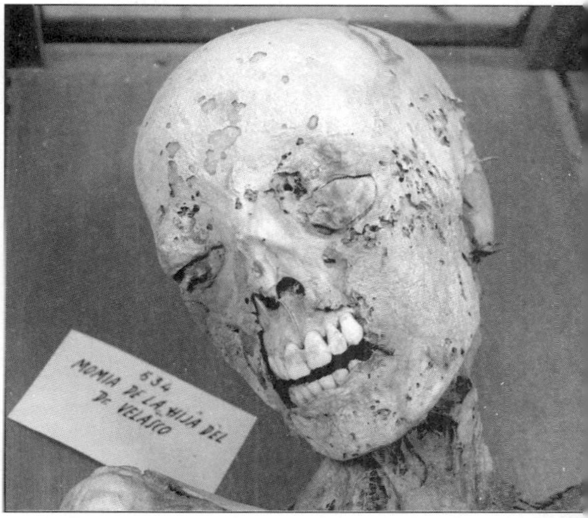

Carmen's mummy. Detail of the head and the note claiming it was Concha's body. The mistery, now resolved. *Revista de la Escuela de Medicina Legal.*

If Conchita's body remained in the San Isidro Cemetery starting March 8, 1886 when her mother ordered her remains to be removed from the museum, then whose is the mummified body in the Faculty of Medicine and what relation does it have to Dr. Velasco?

Thanks to research carried out in 2009 by Dr. Enrique Dorado and several of his aides, all indications are that the body is that of Carmen Tarin y Perdiguero, daughter of a respected 19th century doctor. The girl had died of pneumonia in 1867 aged only 12. Due to the poor condition of the niche in the cemetery where the body was laid to rest, caused by seepage from a nearby stream, the natural conditions were such that the body mummified. Dr. Velasco's interest was aroused by this curious development, and the girl's body was ceded to the doctor by Carmen's father and the mummified body taken to his house in 1873. Given the similarities between Concha and Carmen, both being young mummified girls which were kept in the same building, it is easy to see how subsequently Carmen was mistaken for Concha when years later her body was deposited in the Faculty of Medicine.

TICKET - TOROS
BULL - FIGHT
闘牛のチケット
BILLETES - TOROS - FUTBOL
LA CENTRAL
闘牛のチケット - BULL - FIGHT
3
TOROS
DE LAS VENTAS
MADRID
Feria de San Isidro 2006
Del 10 de Mayo al 2 de Junio
LA CENTRAL
BOROX
13
PABLO HERMOSO DE MENDOZA
JOSE MARIA MANZANARES
PALOMO LINARES
La vida, más vida

TOROS

Love 'em or hate 'em, it's hard to avoid 'em

No subject on Spain provokes so much controversy among foreigners as that of bullfighting. Discussions of politics and religion can certainly raise hackles, but the mention of bullfighting tends to trigger an instant emotional reaction which is usually a strange amalgam of revulsion, fascination, curiosity and, to some, admiration.

For better or worse, a visit to Spain during the bullfight season (March to October) inevitably raises the question for visitors whether or not to attend a *corrida*. The highlight of the Madrid season is mid-May, during the festivities of San Isidro, when *corridas* (literally, "running of the bulls") are held daily, with the top *toreros* performing. (The word *"toreador"* does not exist in Spanish; it is a word used only in the French opera *Carmen*).

It's certainly not the purpose of the authors to take sides on this centuries-old bone of contention, since hundreds of books have been written about the subject, both in Spain and abroad, and just about every travel writer has added his or her own short or long comments on what is still called the *fiesta nacional* (National Fiesta). The most famous of the non-Spaniards was Ernest Hemingway, whose *Death in the Afternoon* can still be recommended for those who are open-minded enough to want to know a little about bullfighting before entering the Plaza de Toros for the first time. Indeed, if you're going to see a bullfight, it behooves visitors to at least try to understand something of the spectacle they will see in the

Bullfight tickets. One of the various ticket offices on the Calle de la Victoria where you can purchase bullfight tickets for an added 20% commission. *Author's photo.*

arena and the reasons why the crowds cheer and boo certain parts of the bullfight. In fact, we strongly urge anyone attending a bullfight for the first time to go accompanied by someone who knows something about it, otherwise the experience may be unpleasant and meaningless.

It is never referred to locally as a "sport" since it is not meant to be a competition between bull and matador. A *corrida* is defined as "a fiesta of fighting and deceiving a bull in an enclosure, avoiding his attacks, and finally killing him".

Since Madrid is the undisputed capital of bullfighting, it naturally has a number of sites associated with the *fiesta*. The most striking is the bullfight ring itself, the Plaza de Toros Monumental, on the upper stretches of the Calle de Alcalá. The building was completed in 1929 and cost four and a half times more than it had been budgeted for. It was inaugurated on June 17, 1931 with a charity fight and was officially known as the Plaza de Toros de Ventas del Espiritu Santo, the name of the neighborhood it is located in, though most people refer to it simply as "Las Ventas". Among the *toreros* in the ring on that "monumental" day, were Diego Fortuna, who had several years earlier dispatched a bull on the Gran Vía (see Pg. 217) and other glories of the day such as Manuel Mejías Bienvenida and Fausto Barajas.

However, it was determined that the area surrounding the plaza wasn't properly suited for spectacles of this magnitude. At that time it was a slum crisscrossed by shantytowns, on the road to undertakers catering to a nearby cemetery and was near a stream, the Abroñigal, making the terrain muddy and impassable. Hence it was decided to clean up the whole area around it and the ring was re-inaugurated on May 24, 1939, ten years after its initial construction.

The structure is impressive, built in the *mudéjar* (Moorish) style, seating over 23,000 people, which makes it the second biggest in the world after the one in Mexico City, which holds over 40,000. On occasions the arena is also used for rock concerts – such as ones with Whitney Houston, Prince, Sting, B.B. King – or motorcycle spectacles, or even opera. When The Beatles came to Madrid in 1965, it was in the Plaza de Toros that they held their first concert in Spain. In fact, on occasion travelling circuses set up their big top tents in the back parking lot.

The arena stands in the center of an extensive square which provides ample space for the thousands of spectators that mill about in front of it when bullfights take place (usually on Sundays, but sometimes also on weekdays).

Traditionally, bullfighting has always been one of the very few activities in Spain that *always* starts on time, so don't get to it late. Once in your seat you'll see a clock which, exactly when the hands touch 6 p.m. (or 7 p.m. as the days grow longer), marks the beginning of the spectacle.

Upon arriving outside the Plaza de Toros you'll observe many stands selling all sorts of food, drinks, cigars and cigarettes, including the ever-popular *pipas,* or sunflower seeds, potato chips, water and beer. The name *fiesta* is here lived up to since it's customary to take the food and drinks with you to your seat and consume them during the afternoon. The most "typical" thing these days to do is drink a glass of whisky on the rocks and smoke a cigar as you watch the *corrida,* both on sale by the vendors in the hallways. If you're too lazy to get up, you can catch the attention of one of the itinerant vendors who come around between the killing of a bull and the entry of a new one. Instead of hot dogs and roasted peanuts as in the States, the vendor will dispatch beer, whisky and soft drinks.

Some people bring along the more traditional wineskins, called *botas*. These are made of goatskin with the hairy part inside. The hairs are left about a centimeter in length, so that a resinlike substance called *pez* can accrue to it, making the *bota* impermeable. Should you want to buy one, we recommend the brand Tres Zetas, but be sure to read the instructions since they require special conditioning before being used.

The bullring is broken up into ten sections, or *tendidos,* like a pizza pie. The real hardcore *aficionados* sit in *tendido* (section) 7, which is in the sun. These are always the most critical and finicky spectators in the audience, prone to insult the president of the bullring for allowing lame bulls into the arena or to shouting at the *matador* for sloppy bullfighting or at the *picador* for poking the *vara* (pole) in the wrong place in the bull. It is best for non-*aficionados* not to sit in this section.

However, bullfighting is a spectacle geared to all audiences, regardless of economic status, sex, age or nationality. In the old days, before cinema and television, it was even common to see women who were breastfeeding their infants as well as small children attending. Although the best front seats (*barrera*) are very expensive, about €134, the ones in the upper balcony go for as little as €4.70. The higher up the seat, the more inexpensive it is. Another price distinction depends on whether the seat is in the shade (*sombra*), where it is more expensive, partial shade (*sol y sombra*) or in the sun (*sol*) where it is cheapest. A good place to sit on your first visit is between rows (*filas*) 13 - 18 in the shade (*sombra*) costing between €37 - €42.

When the bulls in the arena are younger and hence smaller (about four years of age instead of five) and are considered less dangerous the event is called a *novillada*. The prices for these are lower, ranging from €2.40 in the highest parts of the balcony to about €67 in the *barrera*. In front of the ring you'll see several wooden stands that also sell tickets for all events held in the bullring, charging you a 20% commission.

Rather than buy your tickets at Las Ventas, you can also purchase them on the Calle de la Victoria (so named for an old Convent of the same name that once stood there), right off the Puerta del Sol, where they have traditionally been sold for a half century. Four ticket offices continue to ply the trade, also charging you a 20% commission over the official price.

An alternative to the usual *corrida* on foot is a variation called "*rejoneos*" or equestrian bullfights in which the bull is baited on horseback, and the rider, mounted on pureblood Arabian steeds, places the *banderillas* and kills the bull from his saddle. Such *corridas*, preferred by many tourists, provide beautiful and graceful spectacles, but are not frequently held. Prices are the same as a regular *corrida*.

Once you are seated in the bullring, you'll see and *feel* that the seats are very narrow and uncomfortable, since basically they are just stone steps with numbers painted on them. To alleviate the pain on your backside, you can rent a

cushion in the hallways of the plaza for €1.50 before entering the ring, well worth it for even those with the stoutest bottoms. The custom is to give your tickets and the cushions to the usher, who will then place them on the proper seats. A small tip is appreciated. When the *corrida* ends, you just leave the cushion on the step where you sat.

***El Yiyo* statue in front of Ventas.** Beside the main entrance to Madrid's impressive bullring stands a statue in memory of the bullfighter *Yiyo* who was mortally gored in 1985 *Author's photo.*

When settled in, look for the *palco*, or balcony, from which a purple-colored tapestry with the coat-of-arms of Madrid is hung (over *tendido* 10) which shows where the "president" of the bullring sits. It is he who is in charge of initiating the three different parts of the *corrida* (called *tercios*) by briefly hanging a white handkerchief over the railing. In the event that during the *corrida* the bull is deemed to be unworthy (perhaps he limps, or has some other physical defect), the president will hang a green handkerchief over his railing, whereupon the fight is stopped and the bull is led away. This is done by letting a number of *cabestros* (cows) into the ring; the bull is then herded back with them, sometimes aided by a herder with a long pole. A new bull is then admitted into the arena. However, the cost of the new bull must be defrayed by the owners of the bullring, an expensive proposition, since each fighting bull costs in the range of €3,000 – €9,000. Hence the president tends to be reluctant to send back a bull to the stalls and usually does so only when the hooting from the audience rises to such a pitch of indignation as to oblige him to do so.

After the killing of each bull, the president determines how well the *matador* performed and if he is to receive an award, if any. It is at this time that you may find that the spectators are waving white handkerchiefs. This means that the public is asking the *matador* to be rewarded. The usual award consists of letting the bullfighter walk around the ring to receive the applause of the spectators. He may also be awarded an ear of the bull he has killed, or in exceptional cases, *both* ears. The greatest honor of all for a *torero* is to be carried out the *puerta grande* (main gate) on the shoulders of the crowd. This occurs at the end of the *corrida* if he has cut a minimum of two ears after killing his two bulls. In less important bullrings, the president may even award him the bull's tail.

Almost all bulls will in any case be eventually killed, whether in the arena or immediately after the fight. Once dead, the bull is taken to a small slaughterhouse (the *desholladero*) in the back of the ring (*tendido* 2 exit), dismembered and distributed to commercial outlets.

Only on rare exceptions does the president of the plaza give the bull an *indulto* (pardon) because he considers that the bravery, caste and physique of the bull is so extraordinary that it is best to spare him and use him for breeding purposes.

Those seeking a souvenir of the day's fight can buy posters sold in front of the bullring, with the name of the *toreros* in the arena that day; for an additional sum you can even have your own name added to the day's roster on the poster.

After you come out of the arena, you might want to have a look at the various statues placed around the entrance. In front of the building are two bullfight statues. One is dedicated to Antonio Bienvenida, unveiled in 1977, one of the best-loved *toreros* of the period; another is dedicated to José Cubero *El Yiyo*, who died after being gored in Colmenar Viejo (near Madrid) in 1985. There is also a monument of a *torero* saluting a bust of Dr. Alexander Fleming (1881-1955), the discoverer of penicillin, the antibiotic that saved the lives of many bullfighters who were gored. It was unveiled in 1964. An important Madrid street is also named after the Scottish doctor, north of the Bernabéu soccer stadium.

Doctor Fleming statue beside Ventas. Thanks to Fleming's discovery of penicillin hundreds of gored bullfighters' lives were saved. Hence this statue was erected beside the bullring as a sign of appreciation. *Author's photo.*

The Taurine Museum: The art of tauromachy showcased

Most of those watching a bullfight are not aware that a taurine museum, which opened in 1951, is located at a back entrance to the arena. However, the museum is only open in the mornings, even on bullfight days. Though not very large, it does display some curious exhibits. There are six main sections dedicated to the history of bullfighting, the clothing worn in the ring, sculptures and busts of famous taurine personalities and an area on bulls and their breeding.

Of particular interest is a section dedicated to *Manolete*, one of the most revered *toreros* of his day, who died in 1947 after being gored by a bull in the village of Linares in Andalucía. You can see his *traje de luces* ("suit of lights") worn on that fateful occasion. The blood stains from the mortal wounds are still visible. Also on display are medical instruments employed to try to save his life. These include one specially made for him at the time for "arm to arm" blood transfusions, consisting of a pump and two intravenous tubes. In the days when these types of transfusions were not common, loss of blood was one of the most common causes of death for those gored in the ring. Another memento displayed is *Manolete*'s small, almost symbolic pony-tail, such as all *matadores* wear when they are in the ring and which, when they retire, in a ritualistic gesture, are cut off.

Further curiosities in the museum include a framed copy of a Papal Bull (no pun intended) promulgated by Pope Pius V in 1567 stating that bullfight spectacles are worthy "not of man, but of the Devil" and excommunicating those participating in bullfighting and denying Christian burial to anyone dying as a result of it. Also on display is a royal decree from 1790 prohibiting bulls from running through the streets, whether by day or night.

In a showcase are displayed a number of bullfighting costumes, along with a model dressed in a long loose skirt rather than the usual tight-fitting trousers. This was worn by Juanita Cruz, the "goddess of bullfighting", popular in the 1930's and 1940's, who was forced to leave Spain due to her political convictions. Other highlights are the scissors with which *Joselito*'s pony-tail was cut off; diagrams and models of the bullring; and the *estoque* (sword) that belonged to *Frascuelo,* the famous 19th century bullfighter. Busts of famous bulls of the past have been included in the collection, including one of *Burlero,* the bull that killed *El Yiyo* in 1985.

SERVICE LTD

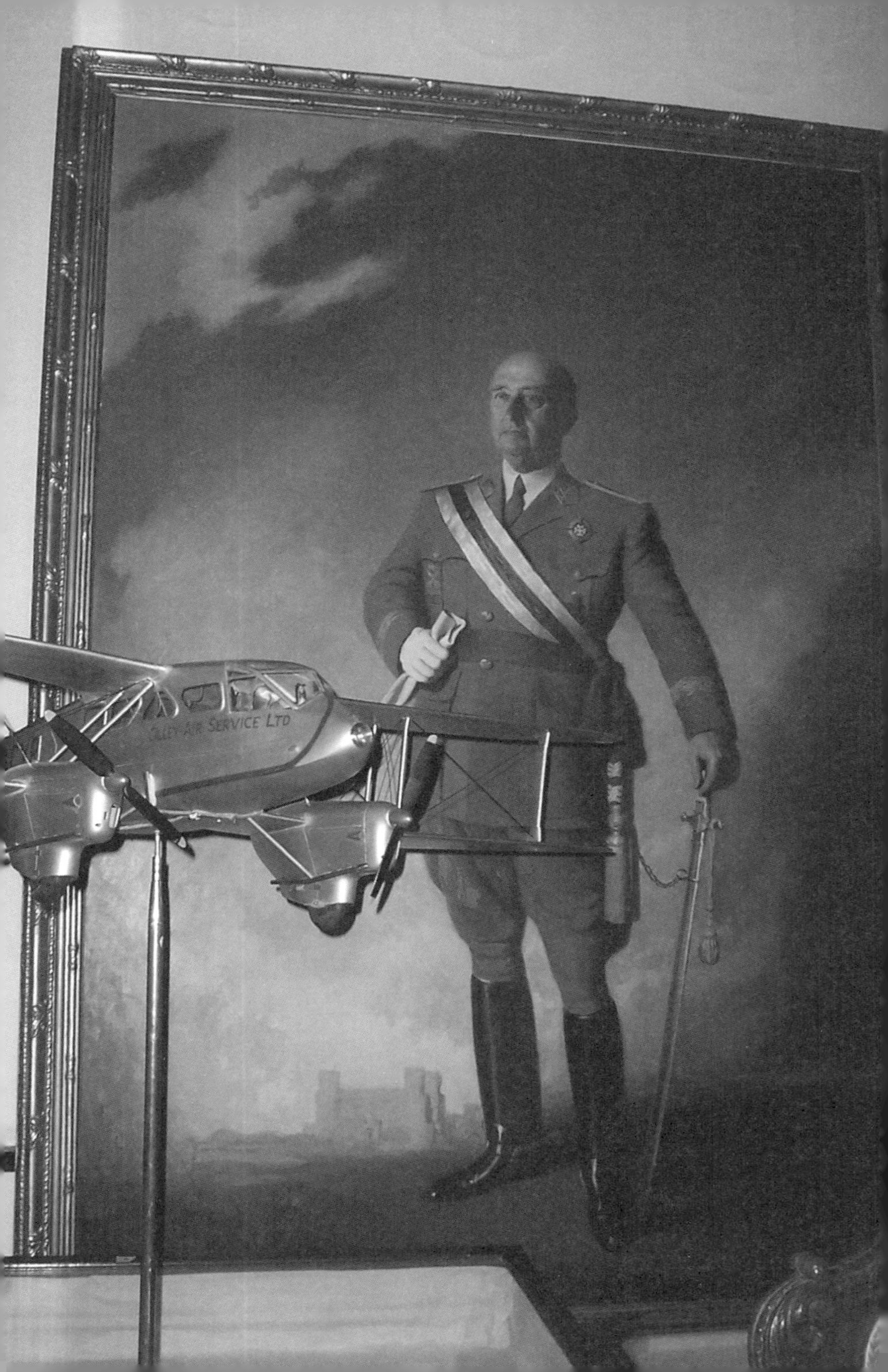
AIR SERVICE LTD

FRANCO
The lingering vestiges of a dictatorship

The subject of Generalísimo Francisco Franco, Spain's dictator for over 35 years, is one which is for the most part studiously soft-pedaled in Spain by both the government and the media. Unlike Hitler in Germany or Mussolini in Italy, there is no law on the books that actually in any way prevents the open expression of sympathy or praise for "El Caudillo" (the Leader) and his years as Head of State. In fact, in December 1994 an independent poll found that 28% of Spaniards had good things to say about the former dictator. And in August 2006 another poll published in the liberal daily *El País* showed that 43.1% of Spaniards felt that statues and the names of streets relating to Franco's uprising should be kept, compared to 40.9% who said they should be removed. Moreover, Franco continues to be honorary mayor of the city of Salamanca. A motion to eliminate this honor was rejected by the city in January, 2007.

However, after long debates among Spain's political parties, a new "Historical memory" law was passed on Dec. 27, 2007. Among other stipulations, it prohibits the presence of "coats-of-arms, insignias, plaques etc. gloriflying the military uprising that led to the Civil War and the repressions during the dictatorship", and orders them to be removed from *public* buildings and sites. Nevertheless such removals do not apply when "artistic, architectural or religious considerations protected by the law" are involved.

The somewhat nebulous anomaly between those still

Former Army Museum. Portrait of Franco and a model of the airplane "Dragón Rapide". *Author's photo.*

Official Housing Plaque. These plaques, with the symbols of the Falange, were affixed to buildings obtaining subsidies from the National Housing Institute. This particular one can be seen on the Calle del General Pardiñas 118. *Author's photo.*

defending and those condemning Franco is the result of a peaceful political transition after the dictator's death in November of 1975. This saw a gradual succession of politicians and parties moving the country away from its former autocratic regime to one of full democracy, regional rights, free elections, elimination of censorship, a new constitution under the monarchy of King Juan Carlos, and an ongoing shift towards increased rights for women, homosexuals, immigrants, and so on.

Since it *was* a transition and not a rupture, and since the old Left vs. Right incriminations were sought to be avoided by most of those concerned, no sort of witchhunting ever took place, though the fact of some politicians (such as Sr. Fraga Iribarne, head of the regional government in Galicia for 15 years until 2005 and now a senator) having once been a Franco minister was used against them in political campaigns. For a while there did exist a legal extreme-rightwing neo-Fascist party called Fuerza Nueva which obtained one or two seats in

Imperial eagle emblem from Franco's regime. Until 2010 you could see the coat-of-arms shown in the left-hand photo on the façade of a Civil Guard building on the Calle de San Nicolás, one of numerous vestiges of "Franco Spain" still visible in the city. It has since been covered over, as shown in the right-hand photo. *Author's photos.*

Parliament. But its adherents dropped off until they could not muster enough votes to maintain parliamentary representation. However the Falange Española, as a private organization, continues to exist and occasionally tries to flex its muscles in the form of rallies.

A plaque dedicated to José Antonio Primo de Rivera, who after a visit to Mussolini in Rome founded the Falange in Madrid in 1934, is still visible on the corner of the Calle de García Gutiérrez, at Calle de Génova 26, a block down from the headquarters of the conservative Partido Popular. Displaying the Falangist emblem of the yoke and arrows, the plaque identifies the building as the birthplace of José Antonio on April 24, 1903. After the outbreak of the Civil War, the political leader was put in front of a firing squad on November 20, 1936 in a prison in Alicante. (Franco died 39 years later exactly on this same day!)

Over the intervening years since Franco's death there has been a determined effort by some political parties to try to "forget" Spain's Fascist past as the country became an integral

José Antonio Primo de Rivera plaque. This plaque on the Calle de Génova marks the birthplace of the founder of the Falange. *Author's photo.*

part of the European Union. The moves to expurgate all traces of the Franco period from public places were especially noticeable during the 12 years that the Socialist Party, under Felipe González, ruled the country (1982-1996). The names of major streets that the Franco regime had changed to honor its heroes and generals were changed back to what they had originally been prior to the outbreak of the Civil War. Thus, the Avenida de José Antonio Primo de Rivera again became simply the Gran Vía, (it was called the Avenida de Rusia from 1936-1939), the Calle del General Mola reverted to being the Calle del Príncipe de Vergara, and the large Avenida del Generalísimo became the Paseo de la Castellana, though the modern stretch north of the Plaza de Emilio Castelar had not been built before the Civil War and some argued that since it was built under Franco, its name should remain the Avenida del Generalísimo.

The Spanish national flag reverted to the one used before the Republic, the same one that Franco had used, but under the dictator it had included a large emblematic eagle - a throwback to that used in the coat-of-arms of the Catholic Monarchs — and the motto *"una, grande, libre"* ("united, great, free"). The Marcha Real (Royal March) (a.k.a. the Grenadier March), which dated back to the 18th century, was kept as the official national anthem, but without the lyrics that had been added to the music by a Franco-sympathizing poet, which had never really caught on. Hence, curiously enough, on official occasions when the anthem is played, there are no words to go with it.

Most of the names of buildings, hospitals, foundations etc. built under the Franco regime and bearing political allusions have been renamed or reverted to their former names. Thus, for example, the Hospital Francisco Franco is now called the Hospital Gregorio Marañón and the Franco era Labor

Union building is now the Ministry of Health and Consumption. However, a hospital on the Calle de Joaquín María López 6 at the time of writing is still called the Hospital Militar de Madrid Generalísimo Franco.

Interestingly, coins from the Franco period continued to freely circulate as legal tender until the introduction of the Euro in 2001, though of course each time new coins were minted in that period they bore the head of the king. You can buy the Franco coins in the Sunday morning coin- and stamp-collectors' market held in the Plaza Mayor. The last ones minted show an effigy of him encircled by the words, "Francisco Franco Caudillo de España por la G.[racia] de Diós." (Francisco Franco, Leader of Spain, by the Grace of God).

Thus, despite the concerted efforts of the past years by some political parties to obliterate all traces of Franco's presence in Madrid, some visible remnants survive in and around the city.

A controversial equestrian statue

After decades of protests, especially from leftwing groups, a huge equestrian statue of General Franco which stood on one side of what are still referred to as the "New Ministries" buildings on the Plaza de San Juan de la Cruz (they were "new" when erected in the 1950's), was finally removed from its pedestal on March 18, 2005, *under cover of the night*. The removal was done by the Public Works Ministry, using as a pretext a construction license issued to repair part of the façade of the building. The next day a group of 700 Franco supporters hung a large painting of the dictator at the base of where the statue had stood to protest its removal and saluted the painting. Hundreds of flowers and wreaths were laid at the site. A few days later, as a further sign of rightwing protest, a statue of Francisco Largo Caballero, Socialist leader and one-time president of the Republic, was splattered with paint and "Franco" written on the base of the monument, also located outside the New Ministries building.

Removal of the statue of Franco. Under cover of the night, the last of the statues of Franco remaining in Madrid was whisked away on March 18, 2005. *Author's archive.*

A week after the incidents, another large statue of Franco and one of José Antonio Primo de Rivera were withdrawn, also during the night, from central squares in the city of Guadalajara. Another, still standing at press time in the northern city of Santander, is also due to be removed. Nonetheless, it was reported in the local press that in Madrid alone there still remain 167 visible public references linked to the period of the dictatorship. Among these are street names such the Calle de los Caídos de la División Azul, Calle del General Moscardó and the Pasaje del General Mola.

Since legally the nomenclature of streets falls entirely within the jurisdiction of municipal authorities, streets named for Franco's supporters during his rule remain in place in many conservative cities, towns and villages around the country. The largest number of monuments evocative of Franco can probably be found in the city of Burgos, 240 kilometers (150 miles) north of Madrid, which was Franco's headquarters throughout the Civil War.

The equestrian statue of Franco, sculpted by José Capuz, which was removed from in front of the New Ministries building, was unveiled on July 18, 1959, the 23rd anniversary of the outbreak of the Civil War. It was originally supposed to have been placed under the Arch of Victory (see next entry), but Franco then decided he didn't want it there. Whereupon the Ministry of Housing took charge of placing it in the inner courtyard of the ministry building. Later it was moved to its recent location in front of what is now the Ministry of Air Pollution Control (Medio Ambiente). A fence and a small but deep moat around the statue were intended to prevent anyone from defacing it. Nonetheless, in 2001 the statue was one day drenched with red paint by protesters.

Each November 20th, the anniversary of the dictator's death in 1975, pro-Franco sympathizers still place wreaths where the statue stood before undertaking their trek to the Valley of the Fallen, near El Escorial, where he is buried. In August 2006 even the pedestal where the statue formerly stood was removed.

The Victory Arch

One of the largest surviving monuments that glorified General Franco in Madrid is the Arco de la Victoria, or Victory Arch, a huge structure erected on the main northern highway entrance to the capital, in a neighborhood called La Moncloa.

Those looking at the arch today will find no trace of General Franco's name on it anywhere, though it was he who had the arch built in commemoration of his victory in the Civil War. Since the arch is situated on a plot with non-stop

Victory Arch. One of the largest monuments constructed by Franco, built to commemorate his victory in the Spanish Civil War. *Author's photo.*

traffic flowing around it on two sides, it is difficult to walk up close to it. However, you can still read the Latin inscription on both sides of the upper part of the arch: From the front (west side, coming into the city): *Armis hic victricibus mens igitur victura monumentum hoc. DDD. Anno 1936 alpha, Anno 1939, omega.* A loose translation might read: This monument is

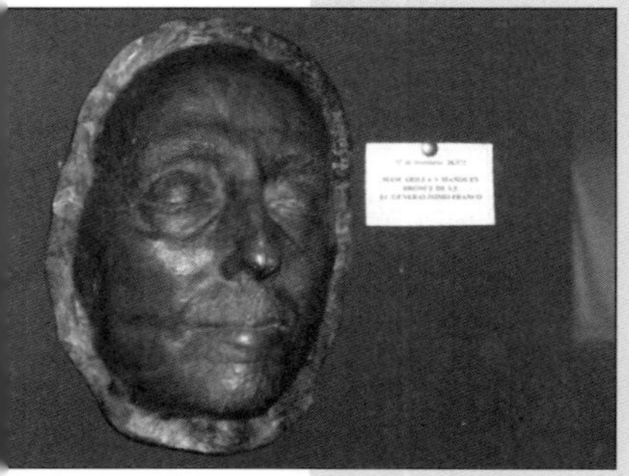

THE DEFUNCT ARMY MUSEUM

Until June 2005 the Army Museum, spectacular in size and contents, exhibited a superb collection of military paraphernalia, paintings, weapons, models, statues, armor and banners from Spain's past to present times.

Of all the wealth of displays, one good-sized room had been set aside for the Spanish Civil War. In it were three large portraits of the Generalísimo, a huge canvas of the executions of Nationalists by the Republicans at Paracuellos de Jarama, personal mementoes of General Queipo de Llano, portraits of many of Franco's generals, models of besieged strongholds taken by Franco during the war, and a small model of the Dragon Rapide, the plane that took Franco (top) from the Canary Islands to Morocco, from where he initiated the rebellion on July 18, 1936. The room even contained a bronze death mask of Franco (top) and a cast of his hands.

Other curiosities in the Army Museum included a painting of the night of July 17 in Tetuán (Spanish Morocco), the day after the Nationalist uprising, with an inspirational madonna and child in the sky overseeing the start of the insurrection. A small room was dedicated to Spain's "Blue Division", which had enlisted volunteers who fought side by side with German troops in Russia during the Second World War.

Some of the contents of the Army Museum were moved into a new museum in the Alcázar of Toledo which opened in September 2010. Considerable criticism was voiced about the installation and the government was accused of "trying to equivocate history" and censor the history of the resistance offered by Gereral Moscardó and his followers during the Republican siege of the Alcázar. See pg. 331 "The Siege of the Alcázar". The huge building of the former Army Museum in Madrid is slated to become an annex of the Prado Museum.

dedicated to the here victorious armies and to its superior ideology. Begun in 1936, concluded 1939. *Dat, donat, dicat,* i.e. Gives, offers, dedicates. On the other side of the arch: *Munificentia Regia Condita ab Hispanorum Duce Restaurata aedes studiorum matritensis florescit in conspectu dei*. Founded in regal munificence and restored by the Leader of the Spaniards, so that, under God, Madrid may flourish.

The arch was completed in 1956, designed by Modesto López Otero and Pascual Bravo. It is 39 meters (120 feet) high and is built of concrete covered by granite. The sculptures on the frieze depict allegorical figures, and on top of the arch is a huge sculpture of a bronze chariot drawn by four horses carrying Minerva. Two elevators on either side of the arch lead to the upper part of the structure, but are no longer usable since there is now no electricity in the monument. Near the top is a large 80 square meter ghostly windowless chamber. This was to have been used as a museum and contains a huge 25-square-meter model of the University City and the original designs for the arch. But the museum never opened and the arch is now closed to the public.

The Aeronautical Museum and Franco's plane

The original plane, the Dragon Rapide, which transported Franco from the Canary Islands to Spanish Morocco where he started his insurrection is one of many noteworthy displays in the huge Museo del Aire (Aeronautical Museum) outside town at Cuatro Vientos (Four Winds), located at Paseo de Extremadura, N-V, Kilometer 10.5. Among the hundreds of other full-sized airplanes from all eras of aviation is a replica of the Plus Ultra, the plane piloted by Franco's brother in his record-breaking non-stop almost 60-hour-long solo flight across the South Atlantic from Spain to Argentina in 1926.

The museum, which sprawls over seven hangars and a huge lawn, features a vast collection of aeronautical displays

Aeronautical Museum. The actual plane, named the "Dragon Rapide", that carried Franco from the Canary Islands to Spanish Morocco just before the outbreak of the Civil War. *Author's photo.*

Aeronautical Museum. Loaves of bread were dropped from airplanes as a propagandistic tactic by the Nationals. *Author's photo.*

including 150 full-sized aircraft, among them fighter jets, hydroplanes, bombers (many from the time of the Second World War), vintage Spanish airplanes, and even the first autogyros, the precursor to today's helicopter, invented by Ricardo de la Cierva in the 1920's. (His C-6 made the first autonomous autogyro flight from this very airport to Getafe, 11 kilometers (7 miles) away.

Not surprisingly, in the vast array of displays, a few hark back to the Civil War and the Franco era. Thus you can see a Junker 52 that flew in the Condor Legion and a Heinkel 111 used in the war. In a few of the display cabinets, medals, decorations and mementoes from the Second World War can be seen, and even a propaganda gimmick used by the Nationalists consisting of a piece of bread dropped behind enemy lines with a little note attached saying: *En la España nacional, una, grande y libre, no hay un lugar sin lumbre ni una familia sin pan* (In Nationalist Spain, no house is without a fire nor a family without bread).

But these Franco-related curiosities only make up a tiny part of a museum which deserves to be seen by a far greater number of visitors due to its spectacular and well-ordered exhibits.

Sala XVI of the Naval Museum

The Naval Museum, on the Paseo del Prado 5, (see Area 6 map, Pg. 235) between the General Post Office and the Prado Museum contains an impressive collection of naval artifacts tracing the glorious history of Spain's maritime ventures over the centuries. Here you'll find models of ships, entire boats, paintings of famous naval battles, portraits of admirals and captains, and a wealth of displays ranging from shipbuilding to ancient navigational instruments, cannon, weapons and its most important display, Juan de la Cosa's map of the New World in 1500, drafted while he accompanied Columbus on one of his voyages, the first known map to show the coastline of America.

Naval Museum. A metal model of a galleon marks the entrance to the museum. *Author's photo.*

Among the curiosities is a tree trunk beside which Hernán Cortés is said to have wept on June 30,1520 when he was defeated in Mexico and had to flee from the Aztecs on the night known as *La Noche Triste* (The Sad Night). You'll also see a model of a submarine built by

Isaac Peral. This was the first to use an electric propulsion system and the first to be fitted with tubes from which torpedoes could be fired.

In its over 20 exhibition rooms, one, conveniently tucked out of the way, *Sala XVI*, is set aside for the more recent history of Spain. It is dedicated to the Jefatura de Francisco Franco y Reinado de Juan Carlos I (Franco's term as Head of State and the reign of King Juan Carlos). Here you can see a large portrait of

THE LAST OF THE MEMORABILIA HAWKERS

Anyone seeking memorabilia harking back to the Franco dictatorship can easily find them right in the center of town in the small "Galería Comercial" on the Calle de Goya 43, corner Núñez de Balboa. There during weekdays "Paco", now aged 82, keeps

open a stand featuring a wide selection of flags, pins, pennants, lighters, key-chains, bracelets and CD's all glorifying Franco and José Antonio Primo de Rivera. Paco originally hails from near Bilbao, but has lived in Madrid for most of his life.

Once a legionnaire, Paco originally started out with a small stand in the Rastro, but has been in his present location since 1976. "If we're living in a democracy, then everyone should be able to express his political opinions openly," he argues. Though on occasion he has been harassed by leftwingers, he now shrugs off any criticism of his activities. "They can say and publish what they like. It's all the same to me."

Asked where the modern artifacts that he sells come from, he told us that they are made in small factories in Barcelona which also manufacture pins and accessories for many other purposes, such as sporting events. Paco says he has no steady outlets, though on occasion organizations such as the Falange will purchase a whole batch of his items. "Most of my customers tend to be teen-agers," he explained, "not old nostalgia seekers. These days, my best-selling items are bracelets and dog leashes and collars with the national colors on them. They are quite decorative."

Admiral Carrero Blanco, Franco's righthand man during the last years of the dictatorship. Under the painting stands a bust of General Franco.

The Valle de los Caídos

The Valle de los Caídos (Valley of the Fallen) remains to this day the largest monument harking back to Franco and has and continues to be a controversial reminder of his rule. On November 20, the dwindling group of hard-core supporters traditionally make the 57 kilometer (34 mile) trek out to it to pay homage to the ex-dictator, though the new Historical Memory las now outlaws "acts of political nature" in the Valle de los Caídos.

The gigantic cross topping the monument which towers above the surrounding hills can be seen from a great distance as you approach it on the La Coruña highway (N-VI). In fact, it rises 150 meters (450 feet), more than three times the height of the Statue of Liberty, and measures 46 meters (150 feet) across. It holds the record as the world's largest standing cross.

Some visitors may wonder what exactly is the significance of this huge cross.

Is it a monument? a church? a mausoleum? an homage to those who perished in the Civil War? Or is it perhaps merely no more than the capricious and megalomaniacal whim of a dictator? Actually, it is *all* of these.

Purportedly, the structure was built as an homage to those who died on both sides in the Spanish Civil War, Nationals as well as Republicans. Indeed, the remains of about 40,000 civilians and soldiers are buried beneath the huge crypt that lies under the cross. However, the number of dead from each side is not equally balanced, for there are far more who fought for Franco than against him. Though the site of where the remains were buried is not accessible, what is in plain sight are the tombs of Franco, behind the main altar, and José Antonio Primo de Rivera's, in front of it.

Just past the entrance to the crypt, you come to a plaque on the wall which reads in Spanish, "Francisco Franco, Leader

Early sketch for El Valle de los Caídos. Various designs were submitted in a national competition. The one shown here was the winner. However, Franco rejected it. *Author's archive.*

of Spain, patron and founder, inaugurated this monument on April 1, 1959. His Holiness (Pope) John XXIII raised the church to the status of a basilica by brevet on April 7, 1960 and it was consecrated on June 4th of the same year by Cardinal Gaitano Cicognani." Behind the monument, as part of the monumental complex, there is a reformed Benedictine abbey with living quarters for the monks. Hence, the Valley of the Fallen is, in fact, equally a mausoleum, a church, an abbey and a monument to those who died in the Civil War.

Aside from the plaque at the entrance and Franco's tomb there is virtually no other mention of the dictator found anywhere else inside or outside the structure. Even the guide books sold at the gift shop studiously avoid mentioning any link to the monument's Franco-related past nor are there any illustrations or postcards of him or of his tomb. Clearly, a determined effort to blot out all references to the former dictator has been made, perhaps to allow the artistic and architectural merits of the structure to stand out rather than the deep-rooted political controversies the monument has always aroused.

The Valle de los Caídos was Franco's dream child, and he personally overlooked each and every detail of its construction, including the selection of the precise site where it was to be built. He carefully monitored the design of the huge cross. Even the wood of the cross on the altar on which Christ is crucified came from a tree which Franco personally chose.

As early as April 1, 1940 (the first anniversary of the end of the Civil War) he passed a decree ordering the construction of a monument to honor combatants who died in the conflict. At that time the Falangist magazine *Vértice* published an article mentioning several proposals made by the architect Luis Moya, the sculptor Manuel Laviada and the Viscount of Uzqueta. One design was a triumphal arch (totally different from the one now standing in Moncloa) and the other was intended as a funerary monument. Surprisingly, it consisted of a huge 150 meter (450 foot) hollow pyramid, larger than the Cheops one in Egypt. The suggestion was rejected early on.

Franco's sketch for El Valle de los Caídos. This is a drawing that Franco made for the monument's cross. Muguruza, the chief architect, redesigned the project, but Franco still wasn't content. It took another ten years before the dictator finally approved a project for the cross. *Author's archive.*

The first to put forth an acceptable design for the magnum project was the Director General of Architecture, Pedro Muguruza. While work was already in progress on the crypt, which consisted of boring a mammoth tunnel into the living rock, heated debate still raged concerning the design of the huge cross that would crown the structure. The leading Spanish architects of the time submitted their projects in a public contest.

In 1943 the winner was announced and his work published. The winning design envisaged a tall slender cross with two smaller ones flanking it. But the design failed to please the Caudillo. Believing that if you want things done properly you have to do them yourself, Franco started to draw up his own plans. He then called in Muguruza to take his design and use it as the basis of a more detailed blueprint of how the cross should look. But when Muguruza handed in the finished design, it still failed to gain Franco's acceptance. Three other architects were called upon to draw up designs for the cross. Finally, that submitted by the architect Diego Méndez was accepted by the Caudillo in January 1950. By the end of that year, he was officially given the title of Architect of the National Monument of the Fallen, putting an end to the decade-long "battle of the crosses."

Nine years later, on April 1, 1959, on the occasion of the 20th anniversary of the end of the Civil War, the Valle de los Caídos was finally opened publicly with much pomp and fanfare. It had taken a labor force of around 20,000 men working in eight-hour shifts, night and day, for 20 years to complete the structure. Many of these were political prisoners who were given the option of working there instead of serving out their prison terms. They were paid a daily wage and many even continued working on the project after they had been freed. In all, doctors interviewed after Franco had died, say that only about 18 of the workers died as a result of labor accidents, though some may later have succumbed to silicosis.

You can reach the platform on which the cross was erected above the entrance to the crypt by climbing up a long staircase or by taking a funicular. There is an elevator inside the cross and an extremely narrow spiral staircase leads to the top, but this is closed to the public. One of the early designs had even envisaged placing a restaurant in the horizontal section of the cross, but this was rejected and denounced as being sacrilegious. It would have considerably increased the size of the cross.

As for the crypt/basilica, it is shaped like a long tunnel and runs 262 meters (close to 800 feet) in length. In the early stages of its construction, its width was 11 meters (33 feet). But when Franco saw it on an early inspection tour, he expressed his displeasure with its size. "It looks like a tunnel in a Metro station!" he exclaimed. Whereupon he ordered the diameter of the tunnel to be doubled. It now measures 22 meters (66 feet) in width.

As you enter the long crypt, going past a gift shop, you come to a series of religious and allegorical figures, the first being two eight-meter-tall (24 foot) winged, guardian angels cast from cannon. Two swords clutched in their hands give them the semblance of being the custodians of the sacred precincts.

Originally, eight magnificent tapestries depicting scenes from the Apocalypse that had been brought from Belgium by Felipe II in 1553, and which had hung in the La Granja de San Idelfonso palace, were hung in the crypt. However, due to the humidity there they began to deteriorate. Franco ordered to have copies made, a process that took over 12 years. The new ones now hang in the place of the originals.

As you continue down the corridor, you'll then pass four

pairs of allegorical figures representing the branches of the armed forces. Those resting on a sword are the army, on an anchor the navy, on a propeller the air force and the ones with a quiver and arrows are the militia.

Finally, you come to the main altar, the deepest part of the tunnel. Before you, on the floor, is the tomb of José Antonio Primero de Rivera. Above it is a cupola with a mosaic transept which supports the huge exterior cross weighing more than 180,000 tons. On the ground, behind the altar, is Franco's tomb. Four archangels, Michael, Raphael, Gabriel and the sinister-looking Uriel (also known as Jazrael or Azrael), his face partially hidden by a hood, watch over the site. It is the Archangel Uriel that in the Christian faith is the one who drives the souls of the dead to God so they can be judged.

El Pardo: El Caudillo's residence

The Palace of El Pardo (occasionally confused by tourists and foreign writers with the Prado) lies just outside Madrid, on the highway that passes by the Victory Arch. Following the signs to El Pardo, you turn off on a small side road which, after driving a few kilometers, takes you to the palace. El Pardo was already a royal residence as far back as 1405. Over the centuries it was enlarged and embellished, and eventually became one of the favorite royal haunts that kings and the nobility passed leisure hours in. King Alfonso XII died in the El Pardo palace in 1884.

The village of the same name is a popular place for Madrileños in the summer, since a dozen outdoor restaurants specializing in roast baby-fed lamb, game, and other regional goodies cater to both locals and tourists and provide an ideal venue for leisure dining, far removed from the bustle of the big city.

The palace was chosen by General Franco as his official residence and he lived there until the time of his death. Upon his passing, the building and its grounds reverted to the National Patrimony, which presently administers it. You can take a tour of the palace and see some of the rooms that Franco used, including his rather austere bedroom with twin beds and a small commode on which stood a reliquary with the incorrupt arm of Santa Teresa. Most interesting perhaps is a room used by Franco for screening films, often in the company of his family or with some of his most intimate hangers-on.

In the village of El Pardo, the main square is still called the Plaza del Caudillo, and a kilometer away, in the Mingorrubio Cemetery, are buried Franco's wife, Doña Carmen Polo, and one of Franco's staunchest supporters, Admiral Luis Carrero Blanco.

Franco and films

Of the many films made in Spain during the Franco years glorifying the regime, none was as famous, or notorious, as one the Caudillo personally became involved in called *Raza* ("Race", as in "racial"). This idealized semi-autobiographical picture was directed in 1941 by José Luis Sáenz de Heredia and concerned a struggle between two brothers, one a staunch paragon of all the traditional Spanish values that Franco admired, the other a model of all that was meretricious and worldly. Some say that Franco himself wrote or suggested the prevalent themes for the screenplay, which is signed by a certain Jaime de Andrade, believed to be Franco's pseudonym.

"Raza" Film Poster. This is the original poster used to promote the film supposedly written by Franco. *Author's archive.*

More overtly propagandistic was another film called *Franco, ese hombre* (Franco, That Man) made in 1964, to celebrate "25 years of peace", also directed by Sáenz de Heredia, which cloyingly traces Franco's background. The film avoids delving into the Civil War itself but instead emphasizes Franco's skill in rejecting Hitler's efforts at embroiling Spain in the Second World War and shows massive rallies of his supporters in the Plaza de Oriente as well as the economic and industrial progress made under his rule.

In addition to these old films, a book and video were put out by the Filmoteca Española (Spanish Cinemathèque) in 2001 called *"No-Do, El tiempo y la memoria"* (Noticiarios y Documentales Cinematográficos, Time and Memory). The two-hour video, containing a selection of newsreels shown each week in cinemas in Spain, quickly ran into three editions. Though the newsreels cover many other subjects, not surprisingly the footage glorifying Franco and his regime is disproportionally large. With a little scouting, all three films can be obtained on video or DVD.

The siege of Toledo's Alcázar

Should you take the half-day excursion to nearby Toledo, one of the Franco-related spots you can visit is the huge Alcázar fortress. Much of this great pile standing on the highest point in the city was originally built by Alfonso VI "the Brave" after conquering Toledo from the Moors in the 11th century. It has since burned down and been rebuilt numerous times by successive kings.

Its last reconstruction dates from after the Civil War following its partial destruction during a two-month-long siege which became one of the great heroic events boasted of by the Franco regime throughout its rule. Shortly after the outbreak of the Civil War in July 1936, Toledo fell to the Republican government forces. But 1,300 people, of which 1,000 were rightwing militants, barricaded themselves in the old fortress and held out there for over 70 days against tremendous odds. They endured all manner of privations, until the Nationalist forces finally liberated them.

Until recently you could wander through the underground tunnels, passageways and basements where the defenders lived and where they set up a makeshift infirmary. Chapels and commemorative plaques dedicated to the defenders by successive army units lined the walls, and display cases exhibited artifacts dating from the siege. Among them was a newspaper that was printed there at the time, appropriately enough called

El Alcázar (for many decades after the war this became a Madrid daily, the mouthpiece for the Falange), a motorcycle which was used to generate electricity and various autograph documents and diaries. In 2010 a new National Army Museum was opened in the Alcázar building which incorporated some of the former Madrid Army Museum exhibits. As we went to press (April 2011) work was underway to build a replica of one of the most evocative of the Alcazar's old rooms, the office containing the telephone from which the commanding colonel, José Moscardó, military governor of the city, spoke to the Republican general besieging the Alcázar. The Republicans had seized Moscardó's son on July 23, five days after the outbreak of the war, and vowed to shoot him if Moscardó did not surrender the fortress. Father and son then had a brief conversation, in which Moscardó told his son to commend his soul to God, shout *¡Viva España!* and die like a hero. The 24-year-old son was shot a month later, in reprisal for an air raid, though the father assumed he had been summarily executed after the conversation.

The admiral whose car went to heaven

Across the street from the U.S. Embassy on the Calle de Serrano stands a fashionable modern church called the Iglesia de los Padres Jesuitas. To the rear of this church, on the Calle de Claudio Coello, you can see a large stone plaque commemorating Admiral Luis Carrero Blanco, former President of the Spanish Government. If you look up at the cornice of the church, high above the plaque, you'll see that a piece of it has been torn off and repaired. The reason for the damage is a most unlikely one, but true.

During the final years of the dictatorship, Carrero Blanco had become Franco's right-hand man and at that time was strongly favored to succeed the dictator when he died. Carrero Blanco's views were staunchly reactionary and it was feared that if he were ever to come to power his rule would be far harsher than that of the last years of Franco's regime, which were marked

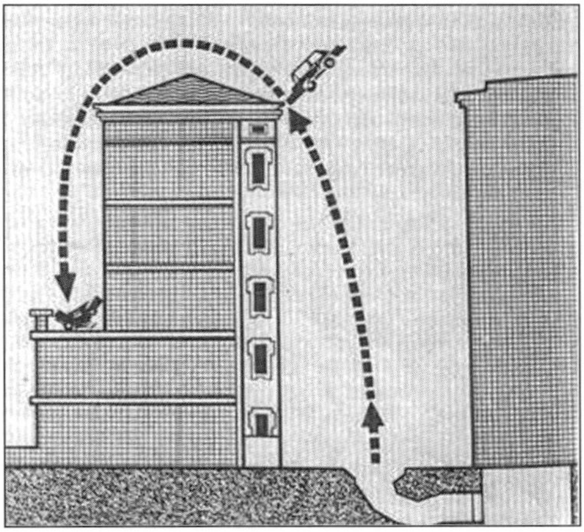

Trajectory of Carrero Blanco's car. This graphic shows the path of Admiral Carrero Blanco's armored car after the terrorist group ETA blew it high into the air. *Author's archive.*

by a progressive softening of repressive policies.

On December 20, 1973 (less than two years before Franco's death), the admiral at-tended Mass at the church and then climbed into his heavily-armored car and drove off towards his home, followed by a police escort. His car turned into Calle de Claudio Coello, in back of the church, and a loud explosion was heard. The police escort turned the corner into the street and saw a huge crater in the center of the block. But Carrero's limousine was nowhere in sight. Where had it gone? The escort's first thought was that some sort of gas main underneath the asphalt had exploded causing the roadway to cave in, but that it had happened right

Cornice on the Calle de Claudio Coello. Even today, almost 40 years after Carrero Blanco's assassination, you can still see where the car hit the ledge as it blasted over the roof. *Author's photo.*

after Carrero's car had passed the spot and that the admiral had meanwhile turned the next corner and proceeded on his way home.

However upon checking by radio, the escort failed to make contact with Carrero's car. As the puzzled men stood around the huge hole in the ground, peering down into it, but not seeing the admiral's car in it, and quite at a loss to figure out where the large bulletproof car had gone to, nor what to do next, a priest came hurrying over to them.

"There's a car on the ledge of our courtyard," the priest excitedly exclaimed.

"What do you mean 'your courtyard'?"

"Yes, on the top of the roof in the inner courtyard of the church!"

The police escort looked up at the top of the church, and to their amazement saw that a piece of the cornice had been knocked off. The huge, heavy limo that Carrero Blanco was travelling in had been blown five stories high, knocked off a piece of the cornice and landed on a second story ledge in the inner courtyard of the church, mortally wounding its occupants!

What had caused the explosion? It hadn't been a gas main, but a huge charge of explosives planted in a tunnel

Aftermath of Carrero's assassination. The blast was so powerful that it left a huge crater in the street. Many water pipes burst and within a few minutes the hole filled with water. *Author's archive.*

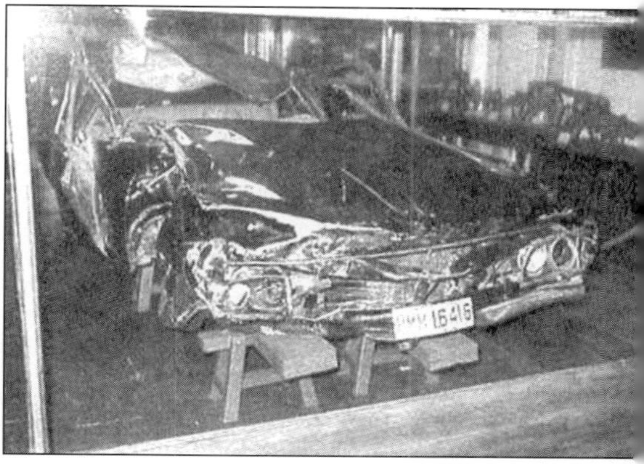

underneath the street which had painstakingly been dug over several months. The perpetrators were the Basque terrorist group ETA who had rented a basement in Calle de Claudio Coello 104 and excavated the tunnel, knowing that the admiral always took this route back to his home after attending church services. On the day of the assassination, one of the terrorists had been placed as a look-out at the end of the street, and when the admiral's car was over the tunnel, he connected the two wires that set off the explosion.

Carrero Blanco's car. Carrero Blanco's car was recovered and its twisted and bent frame for many years was showcased in Madrid's Army Museum. *Author's archive.*

The assassination was spectacular enough for a film about it to be made by the Italian director Gillo Pontecorvo in 1979, called *Operación Ogro,* dramatizing the events leading up to the terrorist attack, including the blast that vaulted Carrero's car over the top of the church. "*Ogro*" or "ogre" referred to the terrorists' nickname for the admiral and was the code name of the secret operation.

Later, a large plaque was affixed to the side of the church, which can still be seen. It reads in Spanish: "Here Admiral Luis Carrero Blanco, President of the Spanish Government, who rendered his last service to his country, sacrificing his life, victim of a vile attack. The people of Madrid dedicate this plaque to honor his heroic death and perpetuate his memory. 20-XII-1974."

The murder that ignited the Civil War

Only two blocks away, on one side of the entrance to a building on the Calle de Velázquez 89, you come to another plaque. This one is dedicated to José Calvo Sotelo, a fiery monarchist Member of Parliament, an eloquent and able orator, and a staunch opponent of the Republic.

At about 3 a.m. on July 13, 1936 a group of Republican assault guards went up to Calvo Sotelo's apartment, roused him from his bed, and "took him for a ride", during which they put two bullets through his head. It was one of the "last straws" before Franco and three other generals launched their military insurrection against the government five days later. Throughout the Franco era, Calvo Sotelo was honored by having major streets and squares named after him in Spain. In Madrid, the Paseo de Recoletos, between Cibeles and Colón, was known as the Avenida de Calvo Sotelo.

Calvo Sotelo's former house. For years before the building was demolished, a photograph of Calvo Sotelo was placed in the corner window, keeping his memory alive. *Author's archive.*

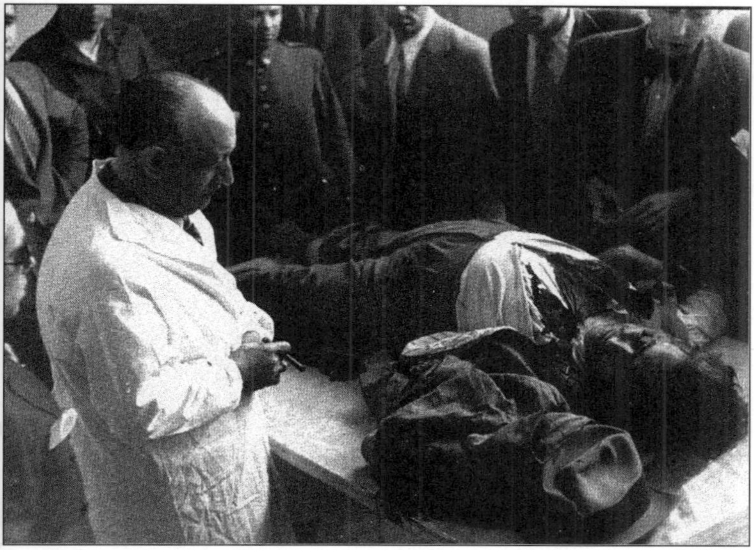

Calvo Sotelo dead.
The cadaver of Sotelo is inspected by the forensics at the Cementerio de la Almudena.
ABC.

The simple plaque reads: "On this spot stood the building from which José Calvo Sotelo was taken the morning of July 13, 1936 to generously sacrifice his life. The City Hall of Madrid commemorates this date in the history of Spain."

SILVER SCREEN MAGIC

Madrid's first film screening

Only 20 weeks after the official public presentation by the Lumière Brothers of their cinematographic machine in Paris' Grand Café on December 28, 1895, and a mere three weeks after the historical first public performance of moving pictures in Koster & Bial's music hall in New York, the first cinematographic spectacle was shown in Madrid. The site chosen was in a locale on the ground floor of the Hotel Rusia near Lhardy's which had been rented by a representative of the Lumière Brothers, Sr. Promio. He had transformed a former jewelry shop and with minimal alterations converted it into a modest screening salon. The room had a low ceiling and Promio placed 20 rows of rented chairs. In the rear he placed a rudimentary projection cabin, which was carefully shielded so that no one could see how the mechanism worked, and set up a small white screen in the back of the room.

Indeed, five days earlier, in an installation known as the Parish Circus, an American by the name of Rousby had displayed a marvellous "cinetoscope" invented by Thomas Alva Edison which was viewed like a Nickelodeon and hence could only be viewed by one person at a time.

Lumière Brothers' film projector. This revolutionary device was used to project the first film screenings in Madrid. *Author's archive.*

Promio's projections, of course, promised to be far more spectacular. The press eagerly sought information on the newfangled invention, and the coming projection became the talk of the town. On May 13, 1896 Promio organized a press screening for his films. The result was that news of the moving pictures was splashed over all the local papers as the "wonder

Monsieur Promio. Representative of the Lumière Brothers, this was the man credited for the first film screenings in Madrid in 1896. *Historia del cine español.*

of the century". Two days later, the official public screening of the Lumière films was held. Promio ran six hours of 20-minute sessions, projecting a selection of eight to ten films, among them the well-known *The Waterer Hosed, The Champs-Élysées* and *Workers Coming Out of the Lumière Factory*. The spectacle was a rousing success and Promio doubtless was delighted to see how Spanish audiences too cringed and oh'd and ah'd upon seeing an omnibus or a buggy heading right towards them on the screen. The exhibition effectively triggered the opening of dozens of projection salles around Spain.

Although the Hotel Rusia has long since been closed, the building in which it was housed is still in existence. As a reminder of the historic filmic event, a plaque has been affixed to the side of the building on the Carrera de San Jerónimo 34 (see Area 2 map, Pg. 85) commemorating the site of that first public screening of cinema in Spain.

The Roman Forum, the Russian Revolution and Peking all filmed in Madrid

It is the actor Omar Sharif, playing the part of the anguished Dr. Zhivago in the famous film by David Lean. The scene is an old train station in Moscow in 1917. Billows of steam are rising from the locomotive as it prepares to leave, while Julie Christie longingly kisses her ill-fated lover on the station platform as crowds of Bolshevik soldiers push by on the way to the front.

Around that same time-frame, also in the railroad station

in Moscow, American revolutionary John Reed, played by Warren Beatty, after a long, harrowing separation, dramatically rushes into the arms of his beloved, played by Diane Keaton, in the film *Reds*.

Both scenes were shot not in Moscow but in the Estación de Delicias, a railroad terminal that opened in 1880 to service railway traffic between Madrid and Cáceres, with a connecting link to Lisbon. The charming old metal-and-glass *belle époque* station was taken out of service in 1971 but happily it was not torn down, as occurred with the much-lamented Penn Station in New York and the Euston Station in London, but was preserved and eventually turned into an excellent but relatively seldom-visited Railroad Museum. The site is now an attraction for train *aficionados*, and displays a sizeable number of old locomotives which stand on the tracks of the station. In addition to various large rooms filled with railroad paraphernalia, you can peer into a luxurious carriage used by the director of the railroad company, which gives an idea of how posh rail travel could be in the 1920's.

Present-day *Time* correspondent, Jane Walker, recalled visiting the set of *Dr. Zhivago*: "There was one place where they had the street where Zhivago lived. It was fascinating. We went there two or three times, on the outskirts of Madrid. There were all these façades. They had actually built several Moscow streets. All the shop windows and the newspapers were in Russian. And they had what was presumed to be a railway line, but you couldn't see it. The wall was there, and they had something going along pumping smoke. It was meant to be winter, but it hadn't snowed in Madrid. So they had tons and tons of crushed marble covering the street. To walk along it was just like walking on snow, and it crunched like snow does.

"We then went to the Delicias station and they had the old train and the Russian flags. At one point, the regular modern train from Lisbon, the Lusitania Express, pulled into the station. It was quite a shock to the arriving passengers, in Franco Spain, to see all these red Communist flags in the station."

Though Madrid never became the backdrop of filmic masterpieces such as Paris in *An American in Paris*, Vienna in *The*

Bronston's city.
The producer had contracted so many workers, over 3000, that a small city was constructed to lodge them - and all were on payroll. *Author's archive.*

Third Man or Rome in *Roman Holiday*, the capital was for many years a popular shooting site for many non-Spanish films. These were made on locations in and around the city, partly because Spain could provide not only inexpensive facilities, but also because there was a large community of film technicians and crews as well as skilled artists available to foreign filmmakers. In fact, two Oscar-winners, Yvonne Blake (costume designer for *Nicholas and Alexandre*) and set designer Gil Parrondo (*Nicholas and Alexandre* and *Patton*) both reside in Madrid.

While Almería on the Mediterranean coast became a favorite site for everything from "spaghetti westerns" toplining Clint Eastwood, such as *The Good, the Bad and the Ugly,* to the desert scenes for David Lean's *Lawrence of Arabia* and sequences from Steven Spielberg's *Indiana Jones and the Last Crusade*. Madrid doubled as 19th century France or England in horror films, some based on Edgar Allan Poe stories, and the palaces around the city were perfect sites for period films dealing with past royalty. Ken Annakin's *The Battle of the Bulge* was shot in and around Madrid as were other war films. *Conan the*

Barbarian was partly lensed near the city of Cuenca, while the main square in nearby Chinchón was used by Mike Todd for the delightful bullfight scene with Cantinflas in the 1956 version of *Around the World in 80 Days* featuring David Niven and Shirley MacLaine.

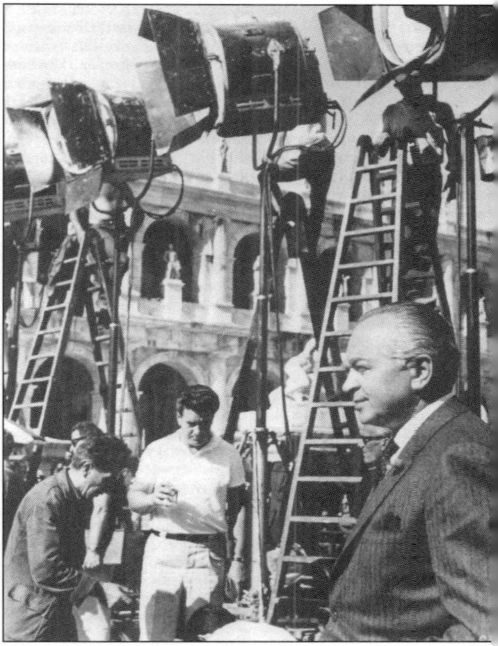

Samuel Bronston. On the set of *The Fall of the Roman Empire.* This American film producer constructed lavish sets representing Rome and Peking. He created Madrid's very own Hollywood and kept more than 3000 workers on his payroll. *Filmoteca Nacional.*

In addition to the many locations apt for filming, Madrid boasted half a dozen large film studios where many of the country's major Spanish pictures were shot in the post-war era, a time when Spanish cinema made high-budgeted folkloric and historical movies which, in the days before television came to Spain (1956), proved hugely profitable both on local turf and in Latin America. By the 1970's, studios such as Chamartín, Moro, Roma and CEA were hurting and were occasionally rented out to American producers such as Alexander Salkind (*The Three Musketeers* and *Robin and Marian*, both directed by British filmmaker Richard Lester). But eventually they had to shutter. Most of the studios have been torn down and some converted into supermarkets, such as the Alcampo on the Avenida de Pío XII (formerly the Sevilla Studios), though two of the studios, the Chamartín and the Roma, are still used for TV and movie filming.

The most ambitious filmic undertakings were those financed by American producer Samuel Bronston in the late 1950's and early 1960's. Bronston rented the huge Chamartín studios, containing three or four sound stages, changed their name to the Bronston Studios (now called the Luis Buñuel Studios, used by Spanish Television), and started rolling some of his blockbusters, the most famous, perhaps, being *El Cid* with Charlton Heston and Sofia Loren. But even these large studios were too small for Bronston, and he rented a huge stretch of land

Still from *Circus World*. For the grand finale in this expensive American film, a large platform was constructed over the pond in the Retiro Park. In the background, the enormous monument to Alfonso XII can clearly be seen. The cast of the film included Claudia Cardinale, Rita Hayworth and John Wayne. *Author's archive.*

just outside Madrid, near Las Matas, and proceeded to build gigantic sets for films such as *55 Days in Peking*, *Circus World* and *The Fall of the Roman Empire*. For the latter, he actually rebuilt an exact replica of the Roman Forum, refusing to use just two-dimensional façades for the buildings. For *55 Days in Peking* he constructed a sprawling set consisting of a walled city, complete with Chinese palaces, parapets, a bridge, gardens, military defenses – the whole works! The Spanish government was delighted, as were all those getting jobs as extras, carpenters, painters and drivers at a time when work possibilities were scarce.

Those were the days, in the early 1960's, when Madrid's Castellana Hilton hotel (now called the Intercontinental Castellana) was the meeting place for dozens of famous American and European movie stars. These ran the gamut from James Mason, Ava Gardner, Oliver Reed, Tyrone Power, Yul Brynner to Claudia Cardinale, Rita Hayworth and Gina Lollobrigida.

One of Bronston's most spectacular and foolhardy feats involved some scenes in *Circus World*, a stinker of a film which gave the *coup de grace* to his decline and ruin, when he managed to get permission to cover part of the pond in the Retiro Park and converted it into a Big Top to shoot some of the spectacular trapeze sequences at the end of the film.

One of our friends and readers, Chisca Leroy Muñoz, recalling the golden era of American cinema in Madrid, told us the following anecdote concerning *King of Kings* (1961) directed by Nicholas Ray, which is still often screened during Easter. She commented: "I must have been about six years old when the

King of Kings. The actor Jeffrey Hunter feared not the Romans, but rather the freezing cold in the outskirts of Madrid. *Author's archive.*

film was shot. My father, who was working as a photographer, took me along one day when they were filming the crucifixion of Christ. The actor Jeffrey Hunter played the part of The Messiah. It was very cold up in the mountains where they were filming, and there was Hunter, crucified, wearing only a loincloth, looking up at the sky, speaking to his "Father". Suddenly he shot a glance at Nick Ray and shouted, 'Goddam it! May ass is going to freeze; get me down from here!', thereafter adding a very Spanish curse word, *coño*. I couldn't believe that Christ on the Cross was spewing forth those lines!

Though the heyday of foreign production shooting in Madrid is pretty well over, big films do still come to Spain in search of locations. The most recent were Ridley Scott's *Gladiator* and one on the Crusades, *Kingdom of Heaven*, which shot on sites around Spain for weeks in the early part of 2004. Such films as King Vidor's *Solomon and the Queen of Sheba*, Stanley Kubrick's *Spartacus*, Steven Spielberg's *Empire of the Sun*, Paul Verhoeven's *Flesh and Blood* and Roman Polanski's *The Ninth Gate* were all partially shot on Spanish locations. The productions were received with open arms by the government and by locals. The old castles, palaces and Moorish remains are still here, as are the professional film crews and new international productions are already slated to arrive in Spain.

BIBLIOGRAPHY

Books Consulted

ABC "El diestro *Fortuna* lidia y mata un toro en la Gran Vía". Jan. 24, 1928.

ALONSO LUENGO, Luis. "El reloj de la Puerta del Sol. Vida y genio de su constructor Losada". Madid: Comunidad de Madrid, 1990.

ALTABELLA, José. "Lhardy" Madrid: 1985.

ALVAREZ, Miguel. "Memoria Monumental de Madrid". Madrid: Ed. La Librería, 2003.

ALVAREZ, Miguel. "Personajes Ilustres de la Historia de Madrid". Madrid: La Librería, 2000.

ANDERSEN, Hans Christian. "In Spain and A Visit to Portugal". Boston: Houghton, Osgood & Co., 1879.

APARISI LAPORTA, Luis Miguel. "Madrid en sus animales". Madrid: Rubiños-1860, S.A., 1999.

ARANDILLAS, Antonio & IÑIGO, José María. "Vírgenes de Madrid". Madrid: La Librería, 1999.

AZORÍN, Francisco. "Leyendas y anécdotas del viejo Madrid". Madrid: La Librería, 2005.

BENITO RUANO, Eloy. "Losada, el relojero de la Puerta del Sol". Madrid: Instituto de Estudios Madrileños, 1993.

BESAS, Peter. "Strange Vignettes of Old Madrid". Madrid, 1969.

BESAS, Peter. "Behind the Spanish Lens". Denver: Arden Press, Inc., 1985.

BESAS, Peter. "The Written Road to Spain". Madrid, 1988.

BRAVO MORATA, Federico. "Los Nombres de las Calles de Madrid". Madrid: Colección de Bolsillo Fenicia. Vols. 5 & 6, 1970.

CABEZAS, Juan Antonio. "Madrid". Barcelona: Editorial Destino, 1971 (3rd ed.)

CALLEJO, Jesús. "Un Madrid Insólito". Madrid: Ed. Complutense, 1997.

CANEYRO, Rosario Mariblanca. "El Retiro: sus orígenes, 1460-1988". Madrid: Ayuntamiento de Madrid, 1991.

CAPMANI Y MONTPALAU, Antonio. "Orígen histórico y etimológico de las calles de Madrid". Madrid: Manuel B. De Quirós, 1863.

CARR, Raymond. "Spain. 1808-1939". Oxford: At the Clarendon Press, 1966.

CASTILLO PUCHE, José Luis. "Hemingway in Spain". London: New English Library, 1975.

CLARK, William George. "Gazpacho: or, Summer Months in Spain". London: John W. Parker and Son, 1851.

COLOMO, Luis. "Ratoncito Pérez y otros cuentos para niños.". Bilbao: Ediciones Mensajero, 2003.

CORRAL, José del. "Curiosidades de Madrid". Madrid: El Pais/Aguilar, 1990.

CORRAL RAYA, José del and SANZ GARCÍA, José María. "Madrid es así". Madrid: 1955.

DE AMICIS, Edmondo. "Spain and the Spaniards". New York: G.P. Putnam's Sons, 1881.

DORADO FERNÁNDEZ, Enrique *et al.* "La momia de la hija del Doctor Velasco. Disección de una leyenda". *Revista de la Escuela de Medicina Legal.* Febrero 2010.

DURÁN CERMEÑO, Consuelo. "Jardines del Buen Retiro". Madrid: Ed. Doce Calles, S.L., 2002.

EL PAÍS. "La resurreccion de Max Estrella", Apr. 24, 2004.

EL PAÍS. "Rajoy acusa al PSOE de romper el espíritu de la transición al retirar la estátua de Franco". Mar. 19, 2005.

EL PAÍS. "Un recuerdo constante de las dos Españas". Mar. 19, 2005.

EL PAÍS. "8,000 personas conmemoran en el Valle de los Caídos la muerte de Franco". Oct. 21, 2004.

EL PAÍS. "Fomento aprovecha una confusa licencia de obras de reforma para desmontar la estátua de Franco". March 18, 2005.

EL PAÍS. "Pintadas e insultos contra Largo Caballero". Mar. 20, 2005.

EL PAÍS. "Franco vuelve a las calles de Melilla". Nov. 16, 2005.

EL PAÍS. "El régimen franquista sigue vivo 30 años después en 167 calles de la capital". Nov. 20, 2005.

EL PAÍS. "¿De quién es esta Franco?" Nov. 5, 2005.

EL PAÍS. "¿Adiós al callejero franquista?" Aug. 9, 2006.

EL PAÍS. "El Gobierno quitó de la ley de la memoria el consejo de suprimir símbolos franquistas" Aug. 25, 2006.

EL PAÍS. "Claustros adentro" Jan. 29, 2006.

EL PAÍS. "Franco continuará como alcalde honorario 'a perpetuidad' de Salamanca" Aug. 26, 2007.

ESDAILE, Charles. "The Peninsular War". London: Penguin Books, 2003.
FERNÁNDEZ ALMAGRO, Melchor. "Vida y literatura de Valle-Inclán". Madrid: Taurus, 1966.
FERNÁNDEZ DE LOS RÍOS, A. "Guía de Madrid". Madrid: Oficinas de La Ilustración Española y Americana, 1876.
FIGUEROA Y TORRES, Conde de Romanones. "Salamanca, conquistador de riqueza". Madrid: Espasa-Calpe, 1931.
FORD, Richard. "A Hand-Book for Travellers in Spain". London: John Murray, 1845.
GARCÍA DEL CANTO, Antonio "Candelas y los bandidos de Madrid". Madrid: Librería Americana, 1866.
GARCÍA SANZ, Ana and SANCHEZ HERNANDEZ, María Leticia. "Monasterios de Las Descalzas Reales y de la Encarnación". Madrid: Patrimonio Nacional, 2003.
GEA, María Isabel. "El Madrid desaparecido". Madrid: La Librería, 2003.
GEA ORTIGAS, María Isabel. "Curiosidades y anécdotas de Madrid". Madrid: La Librería, 2001/2002.
GÓMEZ DE LA SERNA, Ramón. "Elucidario de Madrid". Madrid: Sección de Cultura, 1957.
GUERRA DE LA VEGA, Ramón. "Guía de Madrid. Siglo XIX". Madrid, 1993.
HEMINGWAY, Ernest. "The Fifth Column". London: Penguin Books, Ltd., 1966.
HEMINGWAY, Ernest. "Death in the Afternoon". London: Penguin Books, Ltd., 1966.
HERNÁNDEZ GIRBAL, F. "José de Salamanca". Madrid: Ed. Lira, 1963.
HERNÁNDEZ GIRBAL, F. "Bandidos célebres españoles". Madrid: Ed. Lira, 1968.
HOLT, Edgar. "The Carlist Wars in Spain". London: Putnam, 1967.
JÁUREGUI, Fernando and MENÉNDEZ, Manuel Angel. "Los Que Nos Queda de Franco". Madrid: Ed. Temas de Hoy, 1995.
LESTA, José & PEDRERO, Miguel. "Franco Top Secret". Madrid: Ed. Temas de Hoy, 2005.
LÓPEZ, Mercedes. "Puerta de Atocha". Barcelona/Madrid: Lunwerg Editores, 1992.
MACKENZIE, Alexander Slidell. "A Year in Spain". Boston: Hilliard, Gray, Little and Wilkins, 1829.
MARTÍN EZTALA, Federico. "Francisco de Paula Martí". Madrid: *Figuras de la Raza*, 1927.
MENA, José María de. "Historias notables de Madrid". Barcelona: Plaza y Janés, 1997.

MÉNDEZ-LEITE, Fernando. "Historia del cine español". Madrid: Ediciones Rialp, 1965.
MESONERO ROMANOS, Ramón de. "Manual histórico-topográfico, administrativo y artístico de Madrid". Facsimile of Madrid: Antonio Yenes, 1844 ed. Madrid: Abaco Ediciones, 1977.
MESONERO ROMANOS, Ramón de. "Manual de Madrid. Descripción de la Corte y de la Villa". Facsimile of Madrid, 1833 ed. Madrid: Fernando Plaza del Amo, 1990.
MIGUEL, Andrés de and MÁRQUEZ, José Ramón. "Adiós, Madrid". Madrid: Ed. La Librería, 1998.
MONLAU, Pedro Felipe. "Madrid en la Mano". Madrid: Trigo Ediciones, S.L., 1996.
MONTERO ALONSO, José et al. "Diccionario de Madrid". Madrid: Rubiños-1860, S.A., 1997.
MORENO BURGOS, Maria Dolores. "Madrid-Delicias. Historia de Una Estación." Madrid: Fundación de los Ferrocarriles Españoles, 1986.
MOTA, Francisco & FERNÁNDEZ-RÚA, José Luis. "Biografía de la Puerta del Sol". Madrid: Editorial Colenda, 1951.
NASH, Elizabeth. "Madrid". Oxford: Signal Books, 2001.
PARDO CANALÍS, Enrique. "Eloy Gonzalo, heroe de Cascorro". Madrid: Instituto de Estudios Madrileños, Nº 22, 1983.
PARDO CANALÍS, Enrique. "El Palacio en las Cortes". Madrid: Instituto de Estudios Madrileños, Nº 13, 1971.
PÉREZ BARRADAS, José. "Guia del Museo Etnológico". Madrid: 1947.
PINTO CRESPO, Virgilio. "Madrid en 1898". Madrid: La Librería, 1998.
POTELLANO PÉREZ, Pedro. "Los relojes de la Plaza de la Puerta del Sol". Madrid: Instituto de Estudios Madrileños, 2000.
PULIDO FERNÁNDEZ, Dr. Angel. "Pedro González Velasco". Madrid: Ed. E. Teodoro, 1894.
RÉPIDE, Pedro de. "Las Calles de Madrid". Madrid: Afrodisio Aguado, S.A., 1985.
RAMOS, Rosalía & REVILLA, Fidel. "Historia de Madrid". Madrid: La Librería, 2005.
RINCÓN LAZCANO, José. "Historia de los Monumentos de la Villa de Madrid". Madrid: Imprenta Municipal, 1909. Facsimile edition: Madrid: Asociación de Libreros de Lance de Madrid, 2001.
RÍO LÓPEZ, Angel. "Los Viejos Cafés de Madrid". Madrid: Ed. La Librería, 2003.
ROMERO, Federico. "Por la calle de Alcalá". Madrid, n/p, 1953.
ROMERO DE TEJADA, Pilar. "Un Templo a la Ciencia. Historia del Museo Nacional de Etnología". Madrid. Ministerio de Cultura, 1992.

SAINZ DE ROBLES, Federico Carlos. "Madrid, Crónica y Guía de una Ciudad Impar". Madrid: Espasa-Calpe S.A., 1962.

SUEIRO, Daniel. "La verdadera historia del Valle de los Caídos". Madrid: Ediciones Sedmay, 1976.

TAHOCES, Clara. "Guía de Madrid mágico". Barcelona: Ed. Martínez Roca, 1998.

TORNERO, José Manuel. "Santa Cruz del Valle de los Caídos". León: Ed. Everest, 1990.

VALLE-INCLÁN, Ramón del. "Luces de Bohemia". Edición Alonso Zamora Vicente. Madrid: Colección Austral, 1961.

VARIOUS. "Los Toros. Bullfighting". Madrid: Indice, 1964.

VILLARS, Madame. "Lettres de Madame de Villars à Madame de Coulanges". Paris: A. de Courtois, 1868.

ZURDO, David & GUTIÉRREZ, Ángel. "La vida secreta de Franco". Madrid: EDAF, 2005.

Index

C

G

H

N

O

P

T